P9-CCM-028

Using Assessment Results in Career Counseling

Using Assessment Results in Career Counseling

Vernon G. Zunker

Southwest Texas State University

Brooks/Cole Publishing Company
Monterey, California

Brooks/Cole Publishing Company
A Division of Wadsworth, Inc.

© 1982 by Wadsworth, Inc., Belmont, California 94002. All rights
reserved. No part of this book may be reproduced, stored in a
retrieval system, or transcribed, in any form or by any means—
electronic, mechanical, photocopying, recording, or otherwise—
without the prior written permission of the publisher, Brooks/Cole
Publishing Company, Monterey, California 93940, a division of
Wadsworth, Inc.

Printed in the United States of America
10 9 8 7 6 5 4 3 2 1

Library of Congress Cataloging in Publication Data

Zunker, Vernon G., date
    Using assessment results in career
counseling.

    Bibliography: p.
    Includes index.
    1. Vocational guidance. 2. Occupational
aptitude tests. 3. Vocational interests.
I. Title.
HF5381.Z87   371.4'25   81-18008
ISBN 0-8185-0512-5   AACR2

Subject Editor: Claire Verduin
Manuscript Editor: Pamela Fischer
Production Editor: Suzanne Ewing
Interior Design: Katherine Minerva
Cover Design: Ryan Cooper
Typist: Betty Ritter

Preface

"What do you want to be when you grow up?" is a question frequently asked of children. One suspects that many of their responses are based on the fantasy role models supplied by television, children's books, or comic strips. These naive conceptions of the world of work do not necessarily end in childhood; they are often carried into adulthood depending, for the most part, on the experiences of the individual. Thus, romantic notions as well as realistic experiences enter into the career decisions of almost everyone. However, unlike the young child, the adult cannot afford to be unaware of the un-realistic aspects of his or her choice.

I have written this book to illustrate how assessment results can be used in career counseling to increase self-awareness and thus to lead to rational career choices. To accomplish this goal it has been necessary to look beyond the typical subject matter covered in mea-surement and evaluation textbooks and to think of practical applica-tions. It is not my intent to completely deemphasize measurement theory. However, I have left theoretical foundations to others while I pursue the practical.

The motivation for writing this book has come primarily from two sources. First, practicing counselors and school psychologists have expressed a need for a textbook oriented toward the use of assessment results in a wide variety of counseling situations. Second, counseling interns and practicum students have expressed a need for ideas about how to apply their knowledge of tests and measurements in counseling encounters.

This book may be used as a supplement in test and measurements courses and in counseling courses typically offered in counselor training programs. Other professional groups such as school psycholo-gists, rehabilitation counselors, and industrial psychologists, may find this book useful. I also hope that practicing professionals will find the material in these pages helpful in their attempts to effec-tively meet the needs of their clients.

In Chapter 1 a frame of reference for using assessment results in career counseling is established. A conceptual model for using assess-ment results is discussed in Chapter 2. Chapter 3 provides an overview of interpretive procedures; this chapter is designed to be a reference.

Chapters 4-9 illustrate the use of results of ability tests, achievement tests, career maturity inventories, interest inventories, personality inventories, and value inventories. In Chapter 10 examples of how to use combinations of assessment results in career counseling are given. Chapter 11 covers the use of assessment instruments especially designed for the handicapped and academically disadvantaged. Chapter 12 covers the use of nonstandardized self-assessment devices in career exploration.

The pages that follow are an expression of my appreciation to all those who influenced my values and enabled me to assess my own strengths and weaknesses in an ever-changing world. Many influenced my development through precept and example. Others revealed the stark realities of life directly. From all, I have learned something about myself. I hope that the systematic methods of enhancing individual development illustrated in this book will aid others in becoming self-aware.

I am grateful to many students and a number of my colleagues who offered words of encouragement and wisdom while I was putting these pages together. I am especially grateful to Gregory Snodgrass, who read every page of this manuscript and offered constructive criticism that greatly improved the final version. Other colleagues to whom I am indebted are Dean Geuras, Thomas McGee, Mary Grant, and Victor Garcia. Students who provided valuable assistance are Constance Barr and Cecil Moore.

I am also most grateful to my typist, Jennifer Helmcamp, who somehow found her way through the maze of notes, inserts, and corrections to produce a readable manuscript.

I also acknowledge the assistance of the manuscript reviewers: Dr. Barbara Benton, Ohio State University; Dr. Ronald D. Bingham, Brigham Young University; Dr. Clarke G. Carney, Ohio State University; and Dr. Robert C. Reardon, Florida State University. Also, I thank Claire Verduin who helped prepare the manuscript for publication.

I would like also to recognize individuals outside my work environment who helped me immeasurably: Nelda Zunker, Irma and Sig Fritschel, and Rollie Hamilton. Above all I am most grateful to my wife, Rosalie, who encouraged, prodded, and kept her vivacious sense of humor throughout the entire writing of this text. Without her encouragement, the entire project would have been less meaningful.

Vernon G. Zunker

Contents

1
Interpreting Assessment Results

This book begins where courses in assessment usually end. Instead
of emphasizing the procedures used for standardizing tests and inventories and the methods used to develop them, this book illustrates
the use of assessment results. The material is presented with the assumption that the reader has a substantial foundation in tests and
measurements. In each chapter representative examples of tests, inventories, and self-assessment measures are reviewed with an explanation
of how results are used. Fictitious cases further illustrate the use
of many of these instruments. These cases resemble actual counseling
encounters that I have had or that counselors I have supervised have
had. The cases do not include descriptions of the entire information-
gathering process and all counseling encounters. In each case only
material relevant for illustrating the use of assessment results is
presented. All standardized assessment instruments mentioned in this
book are listed in the Appendix along with the names of the authors
of the instruments and the names and addresses of the publishers.

Various approaches to assessment interpretation have been reported
in the literature since Parsons's (1909) seminal work. The trait-and-
factor approach advocated by Parsons and later by Williamson (1939,
1949) was straightforward—it matched individual abilities and aptitudes with the requirements of a job. This approach has been drasti-
cally modified over the years toward considering, for example, many
different individual characteristics and traits. In other words,
individuals are being encouraged to consider many aspects of themselves in the career decision-making process, including their abilities, interests, personalities, values, past work and leisure
experiences, and total lifestyles.

This broad approach has been accompanied by computer scoring, new
assessment instruments, and economic and societal changes, which have
all complicated the issues of measurement and certainly the interpretation and use of assessment results. Computerized reports provide
an almost unlimited amount of assessment information. The introduction
of new measuring instruments and the refinement and revitalization of
established tests and inventories provide further information to the
career counselor. In addition, new technology has created a variety of
new occupations, and the changing values of society have motivated
many to change careers. (Sarason, Sarason, & Cowden, 1977). The

stereotype of the breadwinner father and the homemaker mother, for example, has undergone significant modification. A greater proportion of
women are entering the work force than before with the prediction that
six out of ten women will work for 30 years or more in the future
(U.S. Department of Labor, 1978). The increasing number of workers in
transition (Arbeiter, Aslanian, Schmerbeck, & Brickell, 1978) has led
to the development of assessment instruments to meet their special
needs. Special instruments have also been developed for the disadvantaged and handicapped. All these factors have made it necessary for
counselors to reevaluate how they can most effectively use assessment
results.

This chapter provides a general background for the interpretation of
assessment results. First, it discusses assessment as a diagnostic and
predictive tool and as a means of comparing an individual with criterion groups. Second, this chapter discusses norms: when to use them,
what kinds to use, and what weight to give them. Third, it describes
the interpretation of the score profile. Fourth, it reviews the limitations of one-shot counseling. Finally, it provides a preview of the
following chapters, which illustrate the use of assessment results in
specific situations.

USE OF ASSESSMENT RESULTS

Assessment results are counseling tools for fostering career exploration. They provide the information an individual needs in making
career decisions. Career development is a continuous process involving
many decisions during one's life. In making these decisions, an individual combines assessment results with other relevant data. Another
important use of assessment results is in evaluating the effectiveness
of career education programs. For that reason examples of program
evaluations are included in the chapters that follow.

How, when, and whether to use assessment results are decisions
shared by the counselor and the counselee. These decisions are based
primarily on evaluation of the purpose for using measuring instruments. Can assessment results provide the information sought and is
that information relevant for the decisions that are to be made? This
principle is followed when using assessment results for individuals as
well as for groups. Tests are not to be given indiscriminately, and
the same tests are not to be given routinely to everyone. Individuals
in different phases of career development have different needs, which
must be considered when determining whether to use assessment procedures. One individual may need assistance in developing an awareness
of her interests. Another may need to clarify his values in order to
establish priorities. Personality conflicts may be a deterrent for another individual who is considering a job change. Yet another may need
assistance in clarifying her expectations about work in general.

A careful analysis of the purpose for using measurement devices
would answer these questions: When is the most strategic time in the
career decision-making process to introduce assessment? What are the
alternatives the individual is considering? Does the information provided by the test correspond to the requirements of the particular
jobs or training programs under consideration? Or, if a group is

being counseled, will the results from the inventory introduce pertinent information for group discussion?

Because career exploration follows paths determined by individual needs, the use of assessment results in career counseling will vary and should be geared toward meeting specific objectives. Later chapters show how the use of assessment results in counseling can be designed to meet individual objectives. This chapter discusses assessment in a general way as a diagnostic and predictive tool and as a means of comparing an individual to criterion groups.

Some overlap in the use of measuring instruments may occur. For example, a diagnostic test may be used to predict performance. However, a diagnostic test used to determine treatment for deficiencies may not be useful in predicting how well an individual will perform on a specific job. Likewise, a test used to predict performance may not be useful for determining treatment or for comparing an individual with criterion groups. For each client, a counselor must decide what kind of test or inventory to use.

Diagnostic Uses of Assessment. Achievement and aptitude assessment results in particular are often used to evaluate individual strengths and weaknesses in order to determine preparedness and potential for training and for beginning work. The identification of skills and aptitudes may broaden the individual's options for careers and education. In the same sense, the assessment of academic and skill deficiencies may help in the identification of the need for treatment, remedial training, or skill development.

Jake, a high school senior, was among a group of students participating in career exploration with his high school counselor. During the initial interview Jake told the counselor that he wanted to go to college but that he had a lot of interests and was not sure which one to pursue. Also, he expressed concern about his ability to succeed academically in college. After further discussion, the counselor and Jake agreed that he would complete an aptitude battery. The assessment results identified several academic strengths and a few specific deficiencies. Next, Jake and the counselor spent several sessions relating Jake's strengths to career fields and college majors that might be explored. Finally, they reviewed the curriculums of nearby colleges and decided, in light of Jake's academic deficiencies, which remedial courses he might take during his freshman year. By the end of counseling, Jake, though still not decided, had narrowed his ideas about a career choice. Moreover, he indicated that he felt positive about his initial academic plan.

Interest, value, personality, and career inventories may also be used diagnostically. Typically, these measures are used to raise an individual's level of self-awareness and to indicate to counselors when clients are lacking in self-awareness or have views of themselves that are inconsistent with assessment results.

Predictive Uses of Assessment. Assessment results may also be used to predict future academic and job performance. The probability of performing well on a job, in a training program, or in an educational program is relevant information on which to base further exploration.

Herb wanted to know whether he could qualify for a machine operator's job in a local industrial plant. Fortunately, Herb's counselor had worked closely with the personnel division at the plant and, in fact, had assisted in gathering data for selection and placement. As a result, the counselor administered the test that had been used to develop cutoff scores for a variety of jobs in the plant. Herb's score was sufficiently high for him to qualify for a machine operator's job. In this case, Herb was provided with information that helped him evaluate his chances of meeting the requirements of a specific job.

Noel decided that she would like to attend the local community college. However, she was concerned about her chances of being a successful student in that college. Her counselor had developed an expectancy table (see Chapter 3) based on test scores and grades earned at the college by students who had attended the high school from which Noel was graduating. Noel agreed to take the test used in the study, and the counselor was able to assess her chances of making a "C" or better at the college. The prediction of success based on local data was of vital importance in Noel's career exploration.

When assessment results are used to predict subsequent performance, the counselor should ensure that relevant predictive validity has been established for the tests that are used. For example, a test used to predict job performance should have a previously established high correlation with performance criteria for that job. Likewise, tests for predicting academic performance should be used only when relevant expectancy tables have already been established. Predictive validity is discussed further in Chapters 4, 10, and 11.

Comparative Uses of Assessment. Comparing one's personal characteristics (abilities, interests, values) with those of criterion groups is a stimulating part of career exploration. For example, it can be enlightening for individuals to compare their interests with the interests of individuals in certain occupational groups. The similarities and differences found can encourage discussion of the relevance of interests in career exploration.

The Strong-Campbell Interest Inventory is an example of an interpretive report that compares an individual's interests with those of people in a wide range of occupations. Although an individual may be pleased to find that her interests are similar to those of social science teachers, she should also be encouraged to pay attention to interests that are dissimilar to those of other occupational groups.

NORMS

The usefulness of assessment results in career counseling is determined by the types of norms available. In using norms, the counselor should keep the following questions in mind. When should norms be used? What kind of norms should be used? How much weight should be given to norms?

Norms represent the level of performance obtained by the individuals (normative sample) used in developing score standards. They may thus be thought of as typical or normal scores. Norms for some tests and inventories are based on the general population. Others have norms for specified groups such as all 12th-grade students, 12th-grade students who plan to attend college, left-handed individuals, former drug abusers, former alcoholics, and the physically handicapped.

The organization of norm tables varies somewhat from test to test. For example, the manual for the Differential Aptitude Test (Form S and T) lists separate norms for boys and girls by semester from fall of grade 8 to fall of grade 12. The Adult Basic Learning Examination (Level III) provides norms for adults by sex, age, race, last grade completed, and median Stanford Achievement Test score.

The description of the normative sample is of primary concern. In some manuals only a brief description is given, leaving counselors to assume that their counselees resemble the normative population. Others, such as the Kuder Occupational Interest Survey, provide specific definitions of normative groups. Such detailed descriptions of persons sampled in standardizing an inventory provide good data for comparing the norm samples with counselee groups. In many instances more information would be useful such as score differences between age and ethnic groups and between individuals in different geographical locations. The more descriptive the norms the greater utility and flexibility they have.

When using norms, counselors must carefully evaluate the population from which the norms have been derived to determine whether that population resembles the counselees in background and individual characteristics. We would not want to use norms derived from a sample of Puerto Ricans in the Northeast to advise a group of Chinese students on the West Coast. However, norms derived from Puerto Ricans in the Northeast are more appropriate for use with Puerto Ricans living elsewhere in the country than are general-population norms.

National norms, sometimes referred to as general-population norms or people-in-general norms, are generally controlled in the sampling process to be balanced in regard to geographical area, ethnicity, educational level, sex, age, and other factors. National norms may be helpful in determining underlying individual characteristics and patterns. For example, an individual whose measured values suggest only an average need for achievement compared with that of business executives and entrepreneurs may exhibit a moderately high need for achievement when compared with people in general. This information suggests an underlying or secondary need for achievement that may not have otherwise been clarified. The identification of lower order yet important personal traits affords greater depth for career exploration.

In many instances national norms should not be used. National norms based on a sample of 12th graders are of little value in predicting success in a particular university. Appropriate norms would be those derived from students who have attended the university under consideration. Likewise, norms based on a general population are not useful in predicting success in a certain job at a local factory. Selection and placement in an industry are usually based on norms derived from workers in a specific occupation or work setting.

Because occupational and educational requirements vary from one location to another, the use of local norms is recommended. For example, you will recall that, for predicting Noel's chances of being successful in a particular college, the counselor had collected data from former students from Noel's high school to develop the norms. Local norms are also useful for job placement. Although more weight can be given to local norms than to general norms and local norms should be developed whenever possible, counselors usually do not have the necessary time and resources to devote to such projects. Most counselors must rely on the published norms furnished in test and inventory manuals. Most of the counseling cases discussed in later chapters illustrate the use of assessment results with published norms.

SCORE PROFILES

In early counseling approaches the profile served as the primary tool for making one-shot predictions of vocational choice (Goldman, 1972; Prediger, 1980). Choices once made were considered definite and irreversible (Cronbach, 1970). Currently, the score profile is considered as only one source of information on individual characteristics.

To make assessment results as meaningful as possible, computer-generated narrative reports are increasingly being used as supplements to the profile. The computer interprets the score results in narrative form according to a planned program. These narrative reports are often sent directly to students and parents. Because score profiles alone do not always stimulate individuals to explore careers, such supplementary materials and follow-up exercises are needed to complement the interpretation process (Prediger, 1980). Although supplements to profiles may prove to be helpful in stimulating career exploration, the counselor should not completely abandon the role of interpreting the profile. In fact, the potential for increasing the number and variety of computer-generated score interpretations in the future is almost a mandate for counselors to sharpen their skills in this respect.

Regardless of the format of the score profile, three important principles of interpretation must be retained: Differences between scores should be interpreted with caution. Profiles should be interpreted with concern for the influence of norms. Scores should be expressed in ranges rather than points.

Differences between Scores. Caution must always be used when interpreting differences between scores on a profile. Small score differences are meaningless and should be attributed to chance effects. Counselees may be tempted to make much more of small score differences between subtests than is plausible. But one would not want to eliminate second-, third-, or fourth-order measured interests and consider only highest measured interests in career exploration. Likewise, when interpreting the score profile from a general abilities test, one would not want to consider only a career in mathematics because the score in mathematics was a few percentile points higher than the other scores. To point a person narrowly to a slightly higher measured characteristic is counterproductive in developmental counseling. (Score differences are discussed further in Chapters 3 and 4.)

Relation of Norms to the Shape of a Profile. An individual's profile must be carefully interpreted in light of the norm reference group. The position of scores on a profile (its shape) is determined by the norms used. For example, Everett, who is interested in architecture, has taken the Differential Aptitude Test. His score profile compared with that of men in general suggests that his general abilities are high enough for him to consider college. To obtain a reliable estimate of his chances of success in a school of architecture, his scores were

compared to norms derived from architectural students. The shapes of
the profiles were quite different. When Everett's scores were plotted
against those for men in general, all were considerably above average.
When compared with scores of architectural students, most of his
scores were in the average range. This profile gives a much more valid
estimate of his chances for success in a school of architecture than
does the general profile. Whenever possible, score profiles used for
predicting performance should be compared with those of competitors
(Cronbach, 1970).

Scores as a Range. On some score profiles results are reported as
points on a scale; on others scores are reported as a range that includes the error of measurement of each test. The range may be represented on a percentile graph by a bar, line, or row of xs, with the
obtained percentile at the center. This method reflects the individual's true score more accurately than does the single-point method.

Because career development is a continuous process, the score profile provides information from which only tentative decisions need be
made. These decisions, not being binding or irreversible, provide information on which to base a further study of individual characteristics. Therefore, the range is more appropriate as a reference for
individual decisions than is a single point. Because we are usually
not able to obtain precise measures in career exploration, the error
of measurement should be considered for all scores recorded as a single
point on a scale.

ONE-SHOT COUNSELING

People have different expectations for career counseling. Some take a
realistic approach and expect to spend considerable time in individual
study and in counseling encounters. Others expect counselors to analyze their assessment results and prescribe a career in one counseling
session (Cronbach, 1970; Prediger, 1980). To illustrate this second
kind of expectation, imagine yourself as a counselor in the following
two cases.

Ed, a high school senior, drops by the counseling office one week
before graduation and tells the counselor that he would like to know
what major he should select for his first summer session in college.
"I would like to take the test that will tell me what to major in."
As Ed sees it, the test holds the key to his future.

Ann, a second-semester college sophomore, makes an appointment in
the college counseling center during mid-semester break. She explains
"I would like to take those tests that will tell me what career I
should choose so I can register for the courses next semester." She
has an entire half day to make this decision!

Often, in more subtle ways than these, parents and students expect
one-shot assessment interpretations to resolve the issue of career
choice. They feel that tests have a mystical power to foretell the
future. As Thompson (1976, p. 31) puts it, "Psychological tests are
supposed to unravel this mystery, and client expectations are usually
high." Within this frame of reference a counselor's major responsibility is to test clients and place them in the right job.

The limitations of one-shot counseling are apparent. First, in career exploration, many decisions are tentative. One-shot counseling approaches give just the opposite impression. Second, there is little opportunity to confirm the decisions based on assessment results. One-shot counseling does not provide for follow-up through observation, continuous discussion of assessment results, or retesting. Third, a one-shot counseling approach affirms the individual's desire to make decisions without devoting time to gathering information and considering alternatives. There is little opportunity to develop a systematic method of decision making. In effect, the counselee is seeking the counselor's approval to approach career decision making from a single throw of the dice without considering alternative information.

Ideally, the use of assessment results should be only one phase of career exploration. Individual characteristics measured by tests and inventories should be only one facet considered in the career decision process. Assessment results should be combined with background information for making career decisions over the life span. Counselors and counselees can then periodically verify or reevaluate assessment results along with other material and experiences in the continuous process of career development. In the next chapter, I develop models other than one-shot counseling for using assessment results in career counseling.

PREVIEW OF BOOK

In Chapters 4-12 I review a variety of tests and inventories selected because they are widely used or provide innovative methods of presenting score results or both. They are representative of the tests and inventories available. One should consult *Tests in Print* (Buros, 1972) or the *Mental Measurement Yearbooks* (Buros) for a complete evaluation and listing of published tests and inventories.

Each review in this book follows approximately the same format, providing the following information: purpose of instrument, description of subtests, description of reliability and validity studies when appropriate, description of profile and score results, and method for interpreting the results. Case studies are provided for a number of instruments illustrating how they may be used in career counseling. The cases demonstrate the use of assessment in career counseling with those ranging in age from high school youths to middle-aged adults.

SUMMARY

Computerized narrative reports, the refinement and revitalization of tests and inventories, societal changes, and the development of new technology have caused counselors to reevaluate the use of assessment results in career counseling. As a diagnostic tool, assessment results identify individual strengths and weaknesses. As a predictive tool, assessment results forecast the probability of performing well on a job or in a training/educational program. By comparing an individual to criterion groups, assessment results are used to stimulate career exploration.

Norms should be carefully evaluated to determine whether the population sample resembles the counselee in background and individual characteristics. Whenever possible local norms should be developed. More weight can be given to norms that are established on the basis of successful performance in a particular educational/training program or an occupation than to general norms.

The profile is the primary tool used to interpret assessment results. When using the score profile, the counselor must be cautious in interpreting differences between scores, must carefully evaluate the norms used, and must consider scores as ranges rather than as points on a scale.

Expectations of career counseling differ. Some counselees expect a one-shot counseling encounter to answer the questions of career choice. One-shot counseling provides little opportunity for developing methods of decision-making.

QUESTIONS AND EXERCISES

1. What kind of norms should be used to predict an individual's chances of making a "C" or better at a certain community college? Explain your answer.

2. How can national norms be most effectively used in career counseling? What are the limitations? *To determine underlying individual characteristics + patterns. Limited in determining specifics ie. success in a particular university.*

3. What kinds of tests are most often used for diagnostic purposes? Explain. *score profiles.*

4. Describe one circumstance where assessment may be used as (a) a diagnostic tool, (b) a predictive tool, (c) a means of comparing an individual with a criterion group.

5. How would you answer the request of Ed, the high school senior used as an example of one-shot counseling?

2

A Conceptual Model
for Using Assessment Results

The increasing number of sophisticated assessment instruments requires career counselors to continually upgrade their skills in using assessment results to meet the demands of a wide range of individuals. More than ever, career counselors are challenged to convert the statistics associated with test data into meaningful information.

As an integral component of the career counseling process, assessment is also changing and growing in complexity. Crites's (1977) evaluation of five major career counseling approaches indicates that the use of assessment results in the counseling process has evolved from an analytical, diagnostic, counselor-dominated task to a developmental, client-centered task. This change has paralleled a general transition in career counseling from an emphasis on trait-and-factor identification and matching to an emphasis on life stages and developmental tasks. Super, Starishevsky, Matlin, and Jordaan (1963), among others, have had tremendous impact through their focus on the use of self-concept in the career decision process. Moreover, the relatively recent translation of Super's (1974) career maturity concept into career counseling and education objectives has focused attention on career decision making as a developmental process. The developmental approach, like the previous trait-and-factor approaches, sees assessment as essential in enhancing self-awareness. However, added emphasis is placed on client involvement in the selection and interpretation of assessment measures. More important, within the developmental framework assessment results are considered as a tool to promote career exploration rather than as the primary or sole basis for decisions.

The increasing complexity and diversity of assessment results suggest the need for a systematic model that will permit counselors to make an effective analysis of the assessment procedures and results appropriate for specific counseling needs. This chapter discusses a conceptual model for using assessment results in career counseling. I first provide the rationale for using assessment results. Then I present a model for use in individual counseling. Finally, I illustrate how the model can be used to stimulate career exploration among groups of individuals.

RATIONALE

In this model, the use of assessment results is conceptualized as a learning process emphasizing the development of self-knowledge (Bradley, 1977). Identification and verification of individual characteristics are the main information provided by assessment results. This information is used with other information in career decision-making. Although assessment results are used in a variety of ways (as discussed in Chapter 1), career counselors are encouraged to look beyond the score report in order to facilitate meaningful learning experiences that will enhance self-awareness and lead to effective career exploration.

Thus, assessment results should be only one kind of information used in career counseling. Testing and interpretation of score reports should not dominate the counseling process. Other factors such as work experiences, grades, leisure activities, skills, and attitudes toward work should receive equal attention. Assessment results are best used when they can contribute information that is relevant within this overall context.

The process is complex in that individuals must consider their own values, interests, aptitudes, and other unique qualities in making decisions. Although the method of career decision-making is a relatively easily learned skill, one's application of the scheme involves consideration of one's complex and unique characteristics. For example, in the Gelatt (1962) model of decision-making, the process begins when an individual recognizes a need to make a decision and subsequently establishes an objective or purpose. Then the individual collects data and surveys possible courses of action. Next the individual utilizes the data in determining possible courses of action and the probability of certain outcomes. Estimating the desirability of outcomes centers attention on the individual's value system. The final step involves making and evaluating the decision—either a terminal decision or an investigatory decision. If a terminal decision is reached, the individual once again evaluates the possible outcomes. Individuals with the same objectives will undoubtedly reach decisions by different paths based primarily on personal values and knowledge.

Other examples of decision models have been suggested by Krumboltz and Sorenson (1974), and Krumboltz, Mitchell, and Gelatt (1975), among others. These models specifically use assessment results to identify and clarify individual characteristics in order to enhance the decision process. For example, Sandra, a high school senior, is attempting to decide which college to attend. She collects information concerning entry requirements, costs, faculty/student ratios, academic programs, and other data from five colleges. Using assessments of her skills and abilities, she weighs her chances of being accepted by the colleges under consideration and the probability that she will be able to meet academic requirements at these institutions.

In determining a major at the college chosen, Sandra considers results of value inventories. These are among the questions she asks herself: "How much do I value a high salary? And if I do value a high salary, which college major would most likely lead to a high-paying job?" Value assessment is essential for making satisfactory decisions here. After Sandra selects an institution and major, she once again evaluates the possible outcomes of the decision.

In sum, decision-making requires the counselee's self-knowledge of abilities, interests, values, and relevant past experiences, and the application of this knowledge to the consideration of alternatives. The more informed an individual the greater probability of a desirable outcome (Pietrofesa & Splete, 1975). In the case of Sandra, tests that measure scholastic aptitude and achievement were used with other data such as earned grades to make adequate predictions. These assessment results provided support information that is not easily attained through other means such as by interviews or from biographical data. Assessment data have the distinct advantage of stimulating discussion of specific individual characteristics that can be linked to educational and occupational requirements.

A MODEL FOR INDIVIDUAL COUNSELING

The effective selection and implementation of assessment devices in career counseling can best be attained through the use of a conceptual model. Such a model provides a systematic method for establishing the purpose of testing and the subsequent use of assessment results. To be operationally effective, a model must be flexible enough to meet the needs of a wide variety of individuals in different stages of their lives. In essence, a model should provide guidelines that are applicable to individuals at all educational levels, in all population groups, of both sexes, and of all ages.

Drawing from the works of Cronbach (1970), Anastasi (1976), and Prediger (1974), I conceptualize a model for using assessment results in developmental career counseling as having four major steps. As shown in Figure 2-1 (page 13), these steps are analyzing needs, establishing the purpose of testing, determining the instruments, and utilizing the results. The process is cyclical and continuous. One may return to the first step during career exploration, after a period of being employed, or after completing an educational/training program. For example, an individual who is exploring careers has discussed general interests with a counselor and, after reviewing occupational requirements, has identified a need for an assessment of abilities. An individual who is dissatisfied with his current career wishes to begin the process anew and to select a different career based on his increased understanding of needs that are not being met. After completing a training program for licensed vocational nurses, another individual has decided that this occupation is not what she wants; she wishes to meet with a counselor to analyze why she is dissatisfied and to reassess her career decision. Because career development is a continuous process, assessment may prove to be useful at any point in the life span.

Analyzing Needs. To assure that we are on the correct course for meeting individual needs, a needs analysis may be accomplished by using interviews, a biographical data form, educational and work records, or a combination of these. The underlying goal is to encourage counselee participation. Counselees who recognize their needs are likely to participate actively and enthusiastically in all phases of preparing for and using assessment results. For example, when Beth recognizes that she needs a structured approach for career exploration, she can

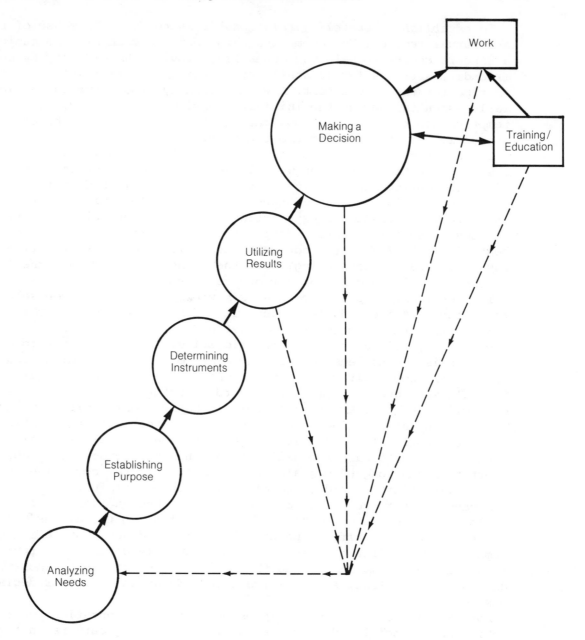

FIGURE 2-1. Cyclical and continuous model for using assessment results in career counseling.

be shown how assessment results can assist her. Likewise, when Ron recognizes the need for help in predicting his chances of success in an educational program, he should be motivated to do his best. Thus, the first key to effective use of assessment results is the counselor's skill in aiding the counselee in identifying needs and in relating needs to the purpose of testing.

The following four objectives are designed to assist the counselor in identifying needs: establish the counseling relationship, accept and adopt the counselee's views, establish lifestyle dimensions, and specify the needs. The accomplishment of these objectives may extend beyond the initial interview.

To *establish a counseling relationship* is to foster a sense of trust and mutual respect. To accomplish this goal the counselor communicates a sincere desire to help the counselee, provides hospitality by being friendly, arranges for personal introductions of staff members, and is on time for the appointment. A warm, friendly atmosphere is particularly essential during the initial interview (Tyler, 1969). Every attempt should be made to communicate to the counselee that he or she has the undivided attention of the counselor.

To launch the initial counseling session the counselor may start with a simple question: "How can we help you?" The counselor listens for clues to continue the session. Although individual needs vary, the counselor should attempt to answer some of the following questions: What are the counselee's expectations of career counseling? Where is the counselee in the career decision process? Are tests indicated or contraindicated? Will the counselee be willing to invest the time necessary for career counseling? Does the counselee understand the role of the counselor and his or her own role as a counselee?

To *accept and adopt the counselee's views* requires the counselor to recognize that individuals are unique and have the right to their own viewpoints. The counselor should listen carefully for expressions of commitments, self-awareness, and priorities. The counselor's role here is to assist counselees in becoming aware of their viewpoints and in recognizing how their viewpoints may affect career decision-making. The following questions may be used to structure this part of the counseling session: Are the counselee's aspirations limited by lack of exposure to careers? Does the counselee have realistic expectations about the world of work? What is the counselee's level of sophistication in regard to career considerations? Has the counselee established short-term and long-term goals? How committed is the counselee to his or her viewpoints? Would value clarification be helpful?

Because career decisions can greatly influence an individual's style of life, the counselor should attempt to *establish the dimensions of lifestyle* when identifying needs. Place of residence, work climate, family responsibilities, use of leisure time, leadership opportunities, financial needs, mobility, and the desire to contribute to society are dimensions of lifestyle that warrant consideration in career decision-making.

For example, an individual expresses a strong orientation toward achieving financial independence but is considering careers that may not be suitable for meeting this objective. The counselor can encourage this individual to clarify priorities for lifestyle, and through this process realistic alternatives and options can be developed.

Questions such as these help establish lifestyle dimensions: Does the counselee recognize that career choice will affect lifestyle? Has the counselee set lifestyle priorities? Would an interest, value, or personality inventory help this individual clarify needs? Are there significant discrepancies between lifestyle dimensions and the needs most likely to be met by the careers under consideration?

Finally, to *specify needs*, the counselor can maximize the counselee's participation by using statements and questions such as these: "Tell me more about your desire to explore interests." "You mentioned earlier that you are interested in knowing more about your aptitudes." "Can you explain how you could meet your personal goals by selecting this

career?" "Why do you think you would like this kind of job?"
"How would you describe an individual who chooses jobs that help
others?" "Would you like to know more about your interests?" As the
counselee states needs the counselor summarizes and records the statements for later use in reinforcing the purpose of testing.

After doing a needs analysis counselor and counselee may decide that
assessment is not needed. Individuals seek career counseling for a
variety of reasons. For example, an individual who has decided on a
job may come to a career counselor for educational/training information, not for testing. Individuals who have given considerable thought
to selecting a career and have narrowed their choices to a particular
field are probably best served by providing them with an opportunity
to discuss that field and with sources of information about it.

Establishing the Purpose. Following the needs analysis, the counselor
and counselee decide on the purpose of testing. Both should recognize
that testing cannot be expected to meet all identified needs. As
stated in Chapter 1, testing can be used for diagnosis, prediction,
and comparison of individuals with criterion groups. The results can
be used to stimulate further study of individual characteristics in
relation to potential career choices. In some instances, the purpose
of testing is to answer a specific question, as in predicting chances
of success in a training program or an occupation. In other instances,
the purpose of testing may be less specific, as in establishing a direction for career exploration for an individual who is floundering.
In cases such as this, where the purpose of testing is less tangible,
the counselor may be tempted to prescribe a battery of tests without
obtaining agreement on the purpose of the tests from the counselee.
To avoid this pitfall, the counselor should establish the policy of
explaining the purpose of each measuring instrument selected.

The purpose of each test and inventory should be explained in terms
that the counselee can comprehend. For example, the purpose of an interest inventory may be explained to a high school student as follows:
"This inventory will help us identify your interests. We can then compare your interests to the interests of groups of individuals in certain jobs." A high school student who is in the process of determining
which college to apply to and who has inquired about an aptitude test
will find the following explanation appropriate: "These test scores
will give us some idea of your chances of making a "C" or better at
the college you are considering." The purpose of a test may have to
be explained in simple terms to an individual who has a limited educational background: "This achievement test will show us how well you
can read, spell, and do arithmetic problems. We can use the scores to
help us choose a job or a training program for you."

In all instances, in order to make assessment results meaningful,
we should attempt to relate the purpose of testing to the needs the
counselee has identified (Cronbach, 1970). The counselee should also
be made aware of how assessment results are used with other data in
the career decision process. The following dialogue illustrates how a
counselor can accomplish these objectives.

   Counselor: As you will recall, we agreed to record your needs for
     information, materials, programs, and tests. Let's review our com-
     ments on testing possibilities. Do you remember any of the testing
     needs agreed on?

Counselee: Yes, I want to take an interest inventory.

Counselor: Do you remember why?

Counselee: I am not sure about what I want to do. I believe knowing more about my interests would help in choosing a career.

Counselor: Do you recall specifically how the results of an interest inventory would help the career decision process?

Counselee: Yes, I believe that I will be able to compare the interests of people in different occupations with my own interests.

Counselor: Go on.

Counselee: This will give me information about personal traits that I can use with other things I've learned about myself.

Determining the Instrument. A considerable amount of literature has accumulated concerning the selection of measuring instruments. The central consideration is meeting the standards for educational and psychological tests established by the American Psychological Association (1974). As you will recall, this book is to be used following or in conjunction with courses in tests and measurements. Therefore, technical methods of evaluating measuring instruments for selection will not be covered. Practitioners must be thoroughly familiar with the basic standards of test reliability and test validity before an effective evaluation of tests can be made. The types of reliability and validity that should be established for a test are determined by the purpose and use of the test. A review of the procedures for determining and comparing different types of reliability and validity may be found in several texts including Anastasi (1976), Cronbach (1970), and Allen and Yen (1979).

In this book I concentrate on tests of ability and achievement and on inventories that measure career maturity, interests, personality, and values. Ability tests are used primarily to identify the probability of successful performance on the job or in educational or training programs. Ability tests can also be used to determine assignment to appropriate remediation levels.

Achievement tests aid the counselor in the evaluation of educational strengths and weaknesses. These tests may also be used for selection and classification in the same way that ability tests are used.

Career maturity inventories are used to assess vocational development in terms of self-awareness, planning skills, decision-making skills, and other equally important variables. Parts of career maturity inventories are self-report measures, on which individuals describe their characteristics and traits (Cronbach, 1970).

Interest measures, long associated with career counseling, provide a means of comparing an individual's interest patterns with those of reference groups. Personality inventories provide clues to individual traits that influence behavior. Value inventories also reflect individual traits; they identify value constructs that influence behavior. Results from interest, personality, and value inventories promote discussion of the counselee's relation to the working world and the satisfaction the counselee may derive from a career.

In the chapters that follow, each of the test categories mentioned here is discussed in detail.

Utilizing the Results. Because individual choice patterns are unique and can be influenced in part by economic conditions and experiences over the life span, the utilization of assessment varies greatly. More than likely individuals will find that assessment results can assist them at various stages of their lives particularly in clarifying needs and in developing self-awareness. Contemporary thought places considerable importance on the individual's responsibility for finding satisfaction in the ever changing world of work. This concept was succinctly stated by Shakespeare in *Julius Caesar*: "The fault, dear Brutus, is not in our stars, but in ourselves, that we are underlings."

The use of assessment results in career counseling is to be carefully calculated and systematically accomplished through established operational procedures. In general, assessment results identify individual characteristics and traits, which in turn point to possible avenues for career exploration. The counselor and the counselee discuss potential career fields using assessment results to facilitate the dialogue.

Beyond this pragmatic and operational procedure for using assessment results are considerations that place testing and the use of test results in perspective—that help counselees use test results to view themselves as total persons. So far I have dealt with some specific uses of assessment, and in the chapters that follow I illustrate these uses in detail. In all this reporting and confirming of assessment data, counselors are in effect helping counselees build and generate a broad concept of themselves. Counselors segregate and clarify individual differences in order to formulate plans for the present and lay the foundations for planning in the future. Counselees integrate their individual traits and characteristics to stabilize their sense of direction in an ever-changing society.

The concept of career development as being continuous over the life span suggests that individuals change. There is, therefore, a tentativeness to many career decisions. One consistency in career decision-making is a conceptual framework that provides for in-depth and effective use of assessment results because clarification of an individual's traits will always involve, at least to some extent, the measuring instruments available at the time.

STIMULATING CAREER EXPLORATION IN GROUPS

In the early 1970s a new concept of education emerged that emphasized career development, attitudes, and values as well as traditional outcomes of career choices (Hoyt, 1972). The career education concept is a comprehensive one that focuses on relationships between traditional education programs and the world of work. The major objective of career education is to prepare individuals for living and working in our society (Zunker, 1981). The impact of career education programs on career counseling has not been fully determined. But there is little doubt that career education programs will increase the need for counselors to turn to group procedures when using assessment results to stimulate career exploration because of demands on their time and the ratio of students to counselors.

The model proposed for utilizing assessment results in the previous section can easily be adapted to groups. The same steps apply. However, methods used in applying the model may have to be altered. For example, a needs analysis can be accomplished through group discus-

sion, with each individual noting his or her own needs. Some will find
that testing is not necessary at this point in their career development. Those who decide that testing is appropriate will move to the next
step of establishing the purposes of testing. After purposes are identified, different types of tests and inventories can be selected. Small
groups may be formed for administering the tests and sharing results.
Individuals or entire groups may then go back to the first step, to re-
establish needs, at any time in career exploration.

A modification of the model for groups could include the following
procedures: Introduce the concepts of career development. Explain the
use of assessment. Introduce the types of measuring instruments. Interpret the results. Introduce support material. Interest inventories are
especially effective in promoting group discussions and are usually
less threatening than aptitude or achievement tests. However, other
types of measuring instruments may also be effectively used to generate
activities for groups. The following example illustrates the use of an
interest inventory in a classroom setting.

Ms. Smith, a high school counselor, was invited to a high school
class in the process of working through a career education program. She
was asked to present the types of measuring instruments available and
to explain how the students could use the career resource center. Before the presentation Ms. Smith asked the teacher's permission to introduce the steps in career decision-making and to make some comments
on the basic elements of career development. As she presented this material she emphasized the purpose and use of assessment results.

The students requested that an interest inventory be administered.
Afterward, the counselor explained how to interpret the score profile.
Considerable time was given to individual questions concerning the results. The counselor emphasized that interests are one of the important
considerations in career decision-making.

Following the interpretation of results, the counselor introduced
the next step in the career decision process. Some of the students decided to take additional tests and inventories. Others took different
courses of action. Several decided to collect information about selected careers in the career resource center, and some members of the
group chose to visit work sites.

In this case interest inventory results stimulated students to generate further activities within the framework of a decision model. This
example illustrates the importance of clarifying the role of assessment
within a career decision-making model. The counselor emphasized that
career decision-making involves a sequence of steps and the use of support materials. By placing assessment in proper perspective, the counselor was able to enhance the group's utilization of assessment results.

SUMMARY

Assessment results may be effectively used to enhance the development
of self-knowledge. Within a career decision-making model, assessment
results are used to clarify individual characteristics and to generate
further activities. A model for using assessment results has the following steps: analyzing needs, establishing the purpose of testing,
determining the instruments, and utilizing the results. Counselees are

to be actively involved in all steps of the model, which may be utilized for individual or group counseling.

QUESTIONS AND EXERCISES

1. What evidence can you give for the rationale that assessment results are used to enhance self-awareness?

2. By the use of an example illustrate how the model for using assessment results in this chapter is cyclical.

3. Why is the model of using assessment results only one part of the career decision process?

4. Why may it be necessary to retest an individual after two or three years?

5. How are assessment results used in the total-person approach to career decision-making?

3

Some Measurement Concepts

In this chapter several measurement concepts and methods of interpreting assessment results are discussed for the purpose of improving
the career counselor's skill in the selection and utilization of
standardized instruments. The reader will find numerous references
made to the material in this chapter when specific tests and inventories are described in the following chapters. Generally, the information found in this chapter is contained in separate chapters in most
textbooks. The purpose for combining this information here is, first,
to provide an overview of the common elements used in assessment interpretation; second, to provide the information necessary for comparing the strengths and weaknesses of currently used methods of score
reporting; third, to provide definitions of measurement concepts for
easy referral.

The first section of this chapter emphasizes methods of interpreting assessment results. Specifically, it describes the normal
bell-shaped curve and then discusses percentile equivalents, standard
scores, grade equivalents, and criterion-referenced measures. The second section discusses important measurement concepts: standard error
of measurement, standard error of differences between two subtests, and
expectancy tables.

TRANSFORMATION OF SCORES

Bell-Shaped Curve. Two of the most prominently used methods of interpreting assessment results are percentile equivalents and standard
scores. In order to obtain an understanding of the relationship between
these two reporting procedures, refer to the well-known normal, or
bell-shaped, curve in Figure 3-1. M represents the mean, or midpoint
(50th percentile), with four standard deviations on each side of the
mean. Starting at M, go to the right to +1 standard deviation and note
percentile equivalent of 84. Likewise, go to the left of M to -1 standard deviation and find the percentile equivalent of 16. You will notice
that other percentile points can be obtained for each standard deviation.
Understanding the relationship of percentile equivalents to standard
deviations and their relative positions on the bell-shaped curve helps

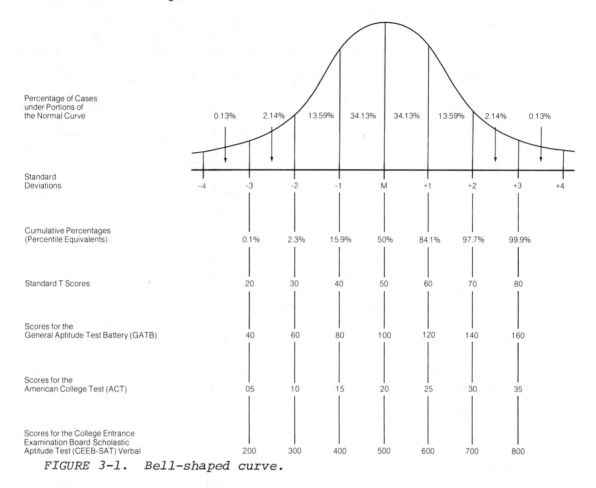

FIGURE 3-1. Bell-shaped curve.

in the interpretation of test scores. For example, a percentile score
of 98 is 2 standard deviations from the mean. A score equal to 2 standard deviations below the mean is approximately at the 2nd percentile.

Referring to Figure 3-1 you can see also that a GATB score of 120
is 1 standard deviation above the mean, or at the 84th percentile. An
ACT score of 25 is at the same relative position. These two scores
are not to be regarded as equal. The standard scores for each test
were developed using samples from different populations, and each test
may be quite different in content. However, two standard scores can be
compared by their relative position under the normal bell-shaped
curve. For example, an ACT score of 25 is at the same relative position within its reference group as a GATB of 120.

Percentile Equivalents. In Figure 3-2 a typical test profile is constructed to depict percentile equivalents. Note the heavy line representing the midpoint and the thinner lines representing the 25th
and 75th percentiles, the average range for this particular achievement test. The difference in scores between the 25th and 75th percentiles is not as great as may appear. Refer to the bell-shaped curve
in Figure 3-1 and notice that 50% of the scores are between the 25th
and 75th percentiles (often referred to as a *crowding*, or *closeness*,
of scores). To move several percentile points within the average band
does not take as great a performance as it does to move the same
number of percentile points beyond the 75th percentile. Thus, the

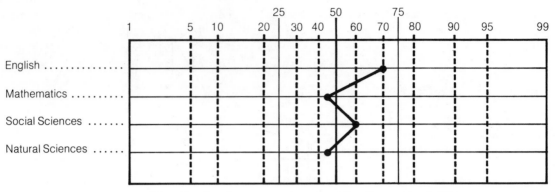

FIGURE 3-2. Profile depicting average band of percentile equivalents.

counselor needs to be cautious when interpreting differences in scores within the average range; the difference in performance within this range may not be as significant as it appears.

Percentile equivalents are direct and relatively easy to understand, which is the primary reason for their popularity. However, it is important to identify the norm reference group from which the percentile equivalents have been derived. Norm-referenced tests can be based on local, state, regional, or national data or on data for selected groups such as all seniors (nationally) who are attending college or all college seniors in the western region of the United States. Thus, in order to effectively communicate test results, the norm frame of reference should be established: "From a national sample, 60 out of 100 high school seniors who attended college scored lower than you did while 40 out of 100 scored higher."

Standard Scores. Normalized standard scores used in tests and inventories are based on standard deviation units in a normal distribution. Figure 3-1 shows the percentage of scores within each standard deviation unit and standard scores used by selected standardized tests. The first, the standard T score, has a range of 20 to 80 extending three standard deviations above the mean and three standard deviations below the mean. For all practical purposes, the entire range of scores of 99.72% of the cases will fall within +3 and -3 standard deviations. The middle 68% of the scores are within -1 and +1 standard deviations. Approximately 95% of scores will fall between ±1.96 standard deviation units. A T score of slightly less than 60 is in the top 20% for a given test. Such points of reference make the standard score a valuable tool for interpretation of assessment results. For example, a meaningful interpretation can be made of a score that is 1.5 standard deviation from the mean when normalized standard scores and their relationship to standard deviations are understood. Thus, the relative position of the standard score under the normal distribution provides a discernible point of reference for that score's variation from the average.

A frame of reference can easily be established for standardized tests by thinking of their scores in the same way. For example, a GATB score of 120 is one standard deviation from the mean, or at the 84th percentile. Likewise, one standard deviation below the mean (16th percentile) is equal to a GATB score of 80. The middle 68% of the scores are between the standard scores 80 and 120. A meaningful interpretation can thus be given to any standard score when the mean and standard deviation are known.

A *stanine* is a standard score on a scale with nine approximately equal units. The mean stanine is 5, and the standard deviation is 2. The advantage of the stanine is that scores are presented as a range rather than as points on a scale, as shown in Figure 3-3. In a

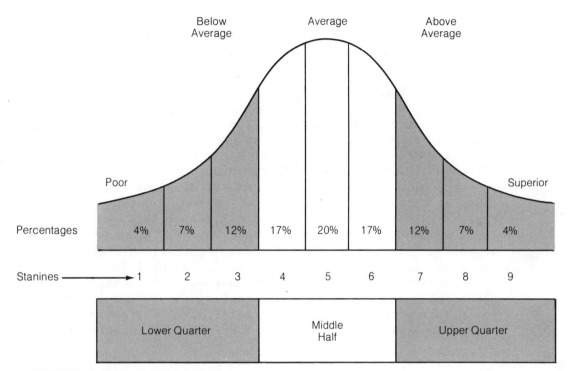

FIGURE 3-3. Stanines.

normal distribution the lower level, 1, represents the bottom 4% of the cases; stanine 5 represents the middle 20%; and stanine 9, the highest level, represents the top 4%. Thinking of a range rather than a point for score interpretation is more descriptive and deters emphasizing small differences. To be of practical significance the difference between stanine scores must be 2 or more.

Stanine scores may also be thought of in broader categories; as Figure 3-3 illustrates. For example, stanine scores 1, 2, and 3 are considered below average; stanine scores 4, 5, and 6 are considered average; and stanines 7, 8, and 9 are above average. Cumulative percentile points (Figure 3-3) provide further possibilities for interpreting stanines as lower quarter, middle half, and upper quarter.

Grade Equivalents. Because of the familiarity of grade placement and its frame of reference, grade equivalents are often used to interpret achievement test scores. Norms for grade equivalents are derived from average raw scores of students in each grade level. These equivalents are expressed by a number representing grade level and the ten months of the school year, September through June. For example, 10.0 represents the beginning of the tenth grade in September; 10.5 represents average performance in February of that academic year.

Because of the idea of placement within a grade, misinterpretation of grade equivalents can occur. For example, a score of 8.5 on a science test for a student currently in the sixth grade should not be interpreted to mean the student has mastered the science courses taught in the seventh grade and the first half of the eighth grade and can now be placed in the second half of the eighth-grade science class. No doubt, the student has performed admirably on the science test, but grade equivalent scores are not to be regarded as performance standards. Also, grade equivalents are not to be considered comparable for all scales. For example, in the fifth grade growth in learning a particular subject such as mathematics will be much greater than it will be in the ninth grade.

Criterion-Referenced Measures. In criterion-referenced measures an individual's score is interpreted by relative position within the distribution of scores obtained by the standardization sample or other groups of special interest. In other words, the interpretation of criterion-referenced test scores is based on how well the individual's performance matches a set of standards or external criteria judged by the test user to be suitable for the individual's grade level. The focus is on levels of performance within a limited range of specific skills or content. For example, criterion-referenced scores provide an index of how well an individual has mastered arithmetic computations or certain reading skills. In criterion-referenced tests specific information is provided as to what the individual is capable of doing: "The subject was able to subtract numbers with decimals." "The subject used the correct verb form in a sentence." Scales from a criterion-referenced test are used to determine an individual level of performance with reference to a specified content criteria.

ACCURACY OF MEASUREMENT

This section presents several concepts regarding the accuracy of measurements that should also aid the counselor in transforming assessment results into meaningful interpretations. First, in order to understand the relative position of a score, the counselor must be aware of inherent error, which is specific for particular tests. Second, significant differences that may exist between subtests on any one test greatly affect the interpretation that may be given to the test results as a whole. Finally, inaccuracy in interpreting assessment results for educational and vocational planning can be reduced by constructing locally based expectancy tables. In the paragraphs that follow, these concepts and their application to test interpretation are discussed and illustrated.

Standard Error of Measurement (s.e.m.). A score on a test should not be considered an exact point without any error. It is much more accurate to think of test scores as estimates of true scores. Thus, an individual's performance on a test can best be thought of as falling within a range or a band rather than as a point on a scale. The s.e.m. is an estimate of the amount of error in a particular test score; it is often provided in the test manual.

The traditional approach to using the s.e.m. is illustrated by the following example. An individual receives a score of 105 (observed score) on a test that has a reported s.e.m. of 5. We now want to obtain an estimate of the person's true score. Because of errors of measurement, observed scores are assumed to be normally distributed around the true score. Hence we can refer to standard deviation units to give us the limits of observed scores. In this example, the s.e.m. is used as a standard deviation (S.D.). Therefore, 105 ±1 S.D. (5) = 100-110. Over all individuals, according to the normal distribution, true scores lie within this band 68% of the time. With an S.D. of 2, however, 105 ±2 S.D. (10) = 95-115. Over all individuals, true scores lie within this band 95% of the time. Therefore, the probability is high that the true score for the student in the example is between 95 and 115 and the probability is somewhat lower that the true score is between 100 and 110.

Standard Error of Differences (SED) between Two Subsets. In career counseling it is often necessary to be certain when differences in subtest scores are of particular importance. The differences between scores can be ascertained by computing the SED. The following example illustrates this method.

A multiaptitude test battery reports T scores (mean = 50 and standard deviation = 10) for interpretation of subtest scores. On the abstract reasoning subtest scale a reliability coefficient of .89 is reported. Another scale has a reported reliability coefficient of .95. To find the SED between the two tests, the following formula is used:

$$SED = S.D. \sqrt{2 - r1 - r2}$$
$$SED = 10\sqrt{2 - .89 - .95}$$
$$SED = 4$$

where r1 = reliability of test 1; r2 = reliability of test 2.

To determine whether the difference between the individual's scores on the test is a real difference and not due simply to chance, the SED is multiplied by 1.96. Because ±1.96 standard deviation units on the normal distribution will include 95% of the cases, scores within that range will occur by chance only 5% of the time. In this case the result is obtained by multiplying 4 by 1.96, which is 7.84, or approximately 8 points. Thus, we can interpret a difference of 8 points or more between the two subtests in our example as being meaningful.

Expectancy Tables. In educational planning, a counselor often has to advise a student of chances of success in a particular college or university. An expectancy table constructed from the records of previous graduates and their performance at the university being considered provides relevant information. In Table 3-1 a sample expectancy table has been constructed from first-semester grade point averages and ACT composite scores.

The numbers that are not in parentheses are the number of students whose grade point averages are in the designated range. For example, two students whose ACT composite scores were in the range 26-28 earned grade point averages between 1.50 and 1.99. Seven students in this same ACT score range earned grade point averages between 2.00 and 2.49.

TABLE 3-1.   Sample Expectancy Table

American College Test (ACT) Composite Scores	First-Semester Grade Point Averages							
	0.00-0.49	0.50-0.99	1.00-1.49	1.50-1.99	2.00-2.49	2.50-2.99	3.00-3.49	3.50-3.99
32-35						(100) 1	(67) 1	(33) 1
29-31					(100) 1	(91) 2	(73) 4	(36) 4
26-28				(100) 2	(89) 7	(50) 4	(28) 3	(11) 2
23-25				(100) 5	(81) 9	(48) 6	(26) 6	(4) 1
20-22			(100) 6	(88) 13	(61) 15	(31) 12	(6) 3	
17-19		(100) 5	(92) 6	(83) 24	(46) 22	(12) 5	(5) 3	
14-16		(100) 5	(86) 9	(62) 13	(27) 8	(5) 2		
11-13	(100) 2	(92) 5	(72) 8	(40) 6	(16) 3	(4) 1		
8-10	(100) 2	(85) 4	(54) 5	(15) 2				
5-7	(100) 1							

The numbers in the parentheses are the cumulative percentages of in-dividuals within a particular ACT score range whose earned grades are in the corresponding grade point average cell or higher. For example, 88% of the individuals whose ACT composite scores were in the 20-22 range earned grade point averages between 1.50 and 1.99 or higher. Likewise, 92% of the individuals whose ACT composite scores were in the 11-13 range earned first-semester grade point averages of .50-.99 or higher.

To demonstrate the chances of success at the university being consid-ered, the ACT composite score provides an index of academic success. For example, 81 out of 100 individuals whose ACT composite scores were 23-25 made a 2.00 grade point average or higher. The chances that indi-viduals with the same ACT scores would make a 2.50 or higher grade point average are 48 out of 100.

SUMMARY

In this chapter several methods used to interpret assessment results have been discussed. These methods illustrate how assessment results can be transformed into meaningful information on characteristics and traits—information that can be used in career counseling. The concepts of measurement accuracy discussed illustrate further how tests must be interpreted to enhance the usefulness of information provided in career counseling.

QUESTIONS AND EXERCISES

1. From Figure 3-1, what are the approximate percentile equivalents for the following standard scores? GATB: 140, 61, 85; ACT: 15, 23, 36?

2. From Figure 3-1, what is the closest standard deviation to a standard score of 108 for a test that has a mean of 100 and a standard deviation of 10?

3. Why is it important to identify the norm reference group when using percentile equivalents to interpret assessment results? Illustrate your answer with an example.

4. What are the advantages of stanine scores over percentiles and grade equivalents?

5. Use the sample expectancy table (Table 3-1) to answer the following questions: (a) What would be the chances of Bob's making a 2.00 grade point average or better with an ACT score of 30? (b) What would be Joan's chances for a 2.00 grade point average or higher with an ACT score of 16? (c) What advice would you offer to Bob and Joan?

4
Using Ability Tests

Ability measures have been associated with career counseling since the time of the early trait-and-factor approach to career guidance (Parsons, 1909). Simply stated, the trait-and-factor approach matched the individual's traits with the requirements of a specific occupation. The key assumption of the trait-and-factor approach was that individuals have unique patterns of abilities or traits that can be objectively measured and that are correlated with the requirements of various types of jobs. Thus, appraising traits was the major task of the counselor. Williamson (1939, 1949) advocated the use of psychological testing in vocational counseling specifically for the purpose of analyzing an individual's potential in relation to requirements of training programs and occupations. Williamson considered a major role of the career counselor to be aiding individuals in assessing their assets and liabilities through an evaluation of test results. These early approaches to career counseling inspired the study of job descriptions and job requirements in an attempt to predict success on the job from the measurement of job-related traits.

The attention to specific job requirements revealed the need for multitrait measures. In particular, there was a need for a differential assessment of an individual's abilities. Multiaptitude test batteries evolved to fill this need. The statistical technique of factor analysis provided the tools for measuring individual abilities, and thus provided the foundation for multiaptitude test batteries. The growth of career counseling and the need for selection and classification of industrial and military personnel increased the demand for differential measures. The use of aptitude test results to select applicants for colleges and professional schools increased significantly with the growth in college enrollments after World War II. The armed forces have sponsored ongoing research programs to develop aptitude test batteries for their use. A number of multiaptitude test batteries have also been developed for career counseling (Anastasi, 1976). The use of aptitude test results remains a prominent part of career counseling.

In this chapter I concentrate on the use of aptitude tests in career counseling. I discuss three multiaptitude batteries and give examples of their use. I also describe the limitations of multiaptitude test batteries.

PURPOSE OF APTITUDE TESTS

An aptitude test is a measure of a specific skill or ability. There are two types of aptitude tests: multiaptitude test batteries and single tests measuring specific aptitudes. Multiaptitude test batteries contain measures of a wide range of aptitudes and combinations of aptitudes and provide valuable information that may be used in career decision making. Single aptitude tests are used when a specific aptitude needs to be measured, such as manual dexterity, clerical ability, artistic ability, or musical aptitude.

An aptitude is a specified proficiency or the ability to acquire a certain proficiency (Super & Crites, 1962). It also may be defined as a tendency or a capacity or an inclination to do a certain task. A common misconception is that aptitudes are inherited, unchangeable characteristics that need to be discovered and subsequently matched with certain job requirements. Such an assumption is misleading for the interpretation of aptitude test results (Bennett, Seashore, & Wesman, 1974). Rather, aptitude should be viewed as the result of both heredity and environment; an individual is born with certain capacities that may or may not be nurtured by the environment. In essence then, aptitude tests reflect the interaction of heredity and environment and predict the capacity to learn.

Within this frame of reference aptitude scores provide a broad measure of an individual's experience and ability at the time of testing. For example, academic aptitude reflects the entire array of skills needed to meet the demands of an academic curriculum. Mechanical aptitude reflects all the skills needed to do mechanical work.

Because aptitude scores are used to predict future performance in educational and vocational endeavors, they are a major element in career counseling. The probability of performing well on a job, in a training program, or in college is the kind of information the career counselor usually seeks. The matching of the individual's abilities to job requirements has long been the subject of research by government, industry, and job-planning specialists.

DIFFERENTIAL APTITUDE TEST (DAT)

The DAT is one of the better known and most widely researched aptitude tests on the market. Two new forms of the test, S and T, were developed from the previous forms, L and M.

There are eight subtests: verbal reasoning consists of analogies for measuring verbal thinking and understanding; numerical ability consists of arithmetic computation problems; abstract reasoning consists of problems requiring nonverbal reasoning ability; clerical speed and accuracy consists of clerical problems requiring a rapid response; mechanical reasoning consists of pictorial items requiring mechanical solutions; space relations consists of items requiring visualization of completed objects from parts and of how objects would appear if moved or rotated; spelling consists of items requiring recognition of correctly spelled words; language usage consists of items requiring recognition of errors in grammar.

Separate sex norms were derived from a stratified random sample of over 60,000 students. An impressive amount of validity data correlate test scores with a variety of course grades and achievement test scores. Sufficient evidence indicates that the test is a good predictor of high school and college grades. However, there are limited data concerning the ability of the test to predict vocational success. Consistently high reliability coefficients are reported by sex and grade level. Long-term consistency is supported by various studies, including a follow-up of 1700 high school students four years after graduation and a seven-year follow-up of a smaller sample. Cronbach (1970) suggests that differential ability patterns are fairly well stabilized by midadolescence.

INTERPRETING THE DAT

DAT forms S and T provide individual reports for interpretation. One type is a computer-produced profile, shown in Figure 4-1; and the other is a hand-plotted profile, shown in Figure 4-2. Both are interpreted in the same manner. The bar graph or row of Xs represents the range of percentiles (the individual's true score). The first step in interpreting the DAT is to observe whether the ends of bars or rows of Xs overlap. There is a significant difference between any two that do not overlap. Two bars or rows of Xs having an overlap of more than one-half their length are not significantly different. If the overlap is less than half their length, a difference should be considered as probable and should be specifically determined by retesting (Bennett et al., 1974).

The combination of verbal reasoning and numerical ability is a good index of scholastic aptitude. The verbal reasoning score is highly correlated with grades in a number of academic courses, especially English courses. The numerical ability score is highly correlated with grades in mathematics courses. Extensive research has been done with other combinations of DAT scores for predicting success in academic subjects and vocational courses (Bennett et al., 1974).

The DAT manual provides extensive information concerning individual DAT scores and predictors of course grades. Using this information the counselor can ascertain which aptitudes are required for certain courses and which aptitudes are useful in certain occupations. In addition, a regression equation for predicting College Entrance Examination Board Scholastic Aptitude Test scores from a combination of DAT form L scores is provided for counseling individuals considering college. These interpretive materials provide excellent guidelines for using the results of the test. A number of reviews have been published on the DAT including Bannatyne (1978), Bouchard (1978), Hanna (1978), Linn (1978), and Mastie (1978).

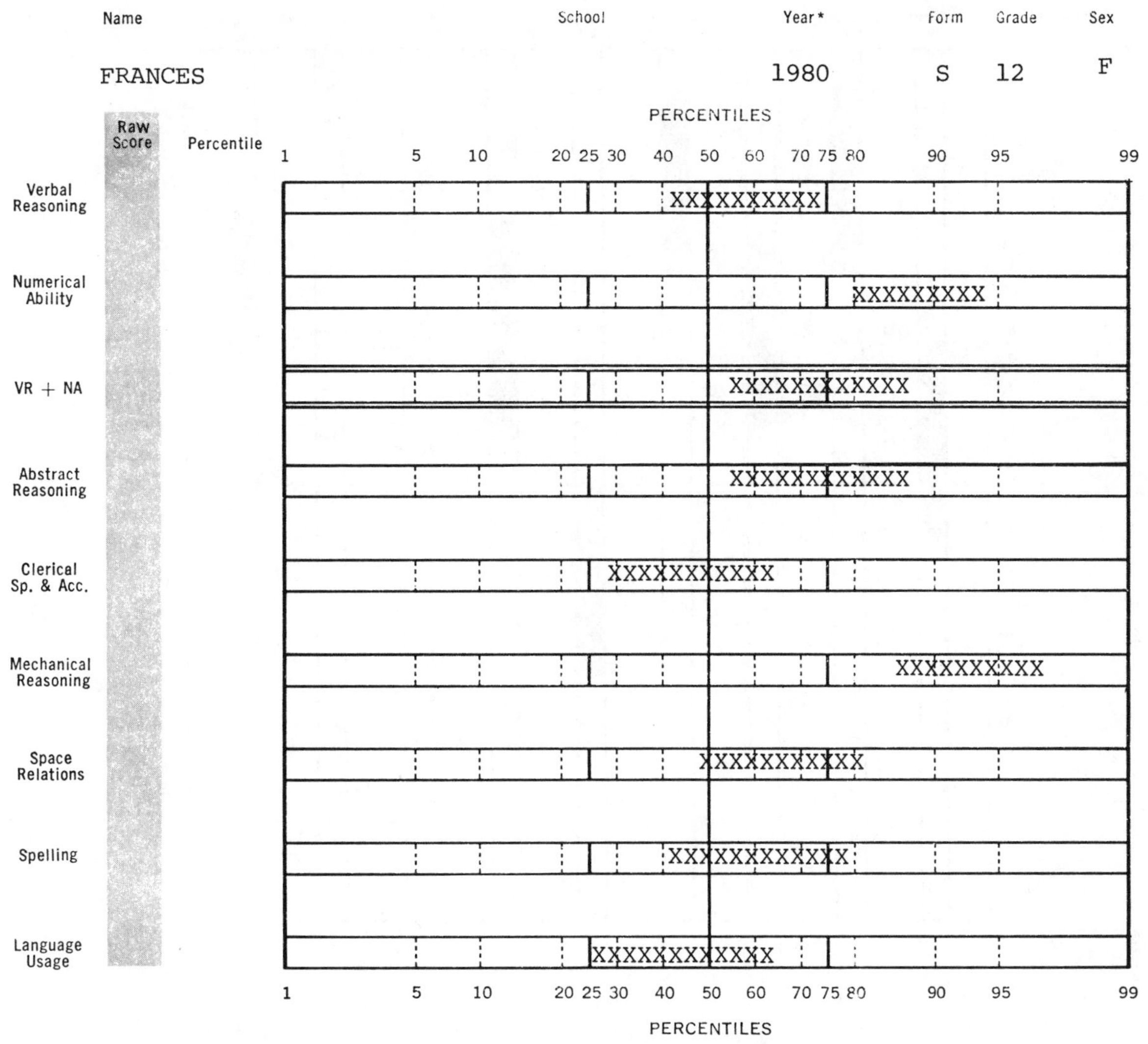
Name
School
Year*
Form
Grade
Sex
FRANCES
1980
S
12
F
PERCENTILES
Raw Score
Percentile
1 5 10 20 25 30 40 50 60 70 75 80 90 95 99
Verbal Reasoning
Numerical Ability
VR + NA
Abstract Reasoning
Clerical Sp. & Acc.
Mechanical Reasoning
Space Relations
Spelling
Language Usage
1 5 10 20 25 30 40 50 60 70 75 80 90 95 99
PERCENTILES

FIGURE 4-1. DAT computer-produced profile. From *Differential Aptitude Test* by G. K. Bennett, H. G. Seashore, and A. G. Wesman. Copyright © 1974 by The Psychological Corporation. Reprinted by permission.

Case of a Female High School Student Interested in Jobs Typically Held by Men.

Frances, a high school senior, came to the counseling center undecided about a career. Frances had three older brothers who had attended college and were fairly successful. Her academic record was good. Although she was not an honors student, she had excelled in mathematics and science courses. The counselor soon discovered that Frances had a background different from that of most female students whom she had talked with before. Frances was interested in working on automobiles; her brothers had taught her the fundamentals of auto mechanics, and she was known as one of the best mechanics in the school. She had rebuilt parts of her car with her older brothers' help. She

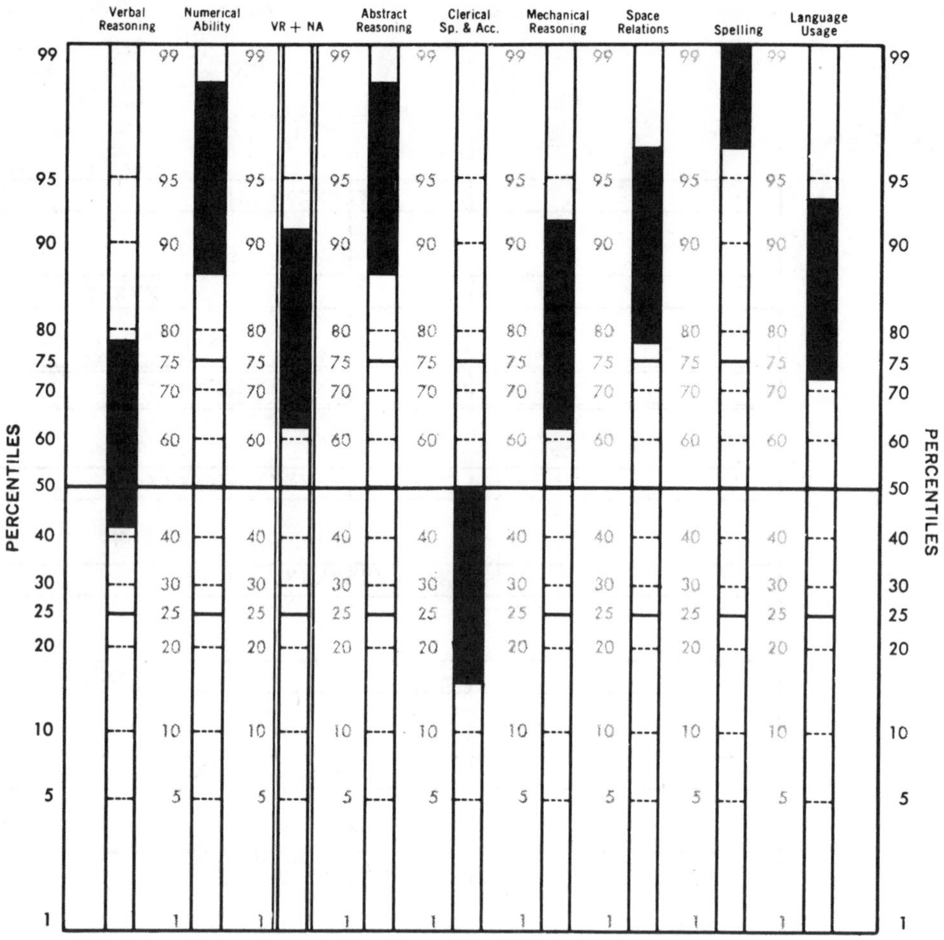

FIGURE 4-2. *DAT hand-plotted profile.* From *Differential Aptitude Test* by G. K. Bennett, H. G. Seashore, and A. G. Wesman. Copyright © 1974 by The Psychological Corporation. Reprinted by permission.

listed auto mechanics as a hobby of greatest interest, and she listed the sciences and mathematics as her favorite subjects. The counselor and Frances decided that it would be worthwhile for her to take tests that would provide specific information about her skills. They selected the DAT primarily because it provides both an index of scholastic aptitude and measures of specific skills.

The results of the test are shown in Figure 4-1. In discussing the results with Frances, the counselor discovered that Frances was almost embarrassed by the outcome of her test. She admitted that she did not consider herself as having interests typical of most girls her age. She stated that she should have done better in English and shouldn't have strong interests in auto mechanics and high scores in science and math. Frances also hesitated to express an interest in jobs typically for men.

Counselor: This profile indicates that you have very high scores in numerical ability and mechanical reasoning. Have you ever considered careers that require these skills?

Frances (hesitantly): But don't just boys go into those fields?

Counselor: Many boys do, but this does not mean that you shouldn't consider these areas as possible career choices. More and more women are going into careers that usually only men went into in the past.

The counselor encouraged Frances to consider any career she was interested in during this part of career exploration. She emphasized the increasing acceptance of women in positions that were once thought to be only for men. Frances began to express interest in a number of careers requiring numerical and mechanical skills. She seemed relieved that she was able to express herself freely. The counselor assured her that it was legitimate for her to have an interest in any career.

Frances zeroed in on the fact that most of her scores on the DAT pointed to an engineering degree. She became particularly interested in mechanical engineering. She mentioned that she had always been interested in machinery and what makes machines run. She decided to explore the requirements and particulars of this occupation in the career resource center.

DIFFERENTIAL APTITUDE TEST-CAREER PLANNING PROGRAM (DAT-CPP)

The DAT-CPP is a method of combining DAT scores with an individual's educational goals, expressed interest in specific school subjects, and expressed interest in specific jobs for the purpose of vocational planning. The program includes the use of the DAT (form S or T) and a Career Planning Questionnaire (CPQ). Both the DAT and the CPQ are computer scored for this program.

On the CPQ the student checks liked school subjects and activities listed under 18 different categories. Excluding the group for school sports, the student then picks the three groups liked best and records them on the form provided. Next, the student provides information concerning future educational plans or training plans and reports rank in class. Finally, the individual reviews 20 groups of jobs and occupations and picks the three groups most liked.

The final report contains two parts: a profile of DAT scores and a narrative report addressed directly to the student. The narrative report is designed to confirm the student's career choices or to suggest alternative plans. It reviews the data reported on the CPQ. Each occupational group indicated as a preference by the student is evaluated in the following way:

YOU INDICATED THAT YOUR FIRST CHOICE OF CAREER GOALS WAS IN THE GROUP CALLED: MEDICALLY RELATED
PEOPLE WHO CHOOSE THIS KIND OF WORK USUALLY LIKE THE SCHOOL SUBJECTS AND ACTIVITIES YOU LIKE, HOWEVER, THEY GET MORE EDUCATION THAN YOU ARE PLANNING TO GET. ALSO, THEY HAVE HIGHER SCORES ON SOME OF THE RELATED APTITUDE TESTS. IN VIEW OF THESE FACTS, YOU PROBABLY OUGHT TO RECONSIDER

THIS OCCUPATIONAL CHOICE AND TO THINK ABOUT OTHER OCCUPA-
TIONAL FIELDS MORE IN LINE WITH YOUR ABILITIES AND EDUCA-
TIONAL PLANS.[1]

The narrative ends with a summary statement such as this one:

CONSIDERING PRIMARILY YOUR TESTED APTITUDES, AND TO A
LESSER EXTENT YOUR SCHOOL SUBJECT AND ACTIVITY PREFERENCES,
YOU MAY WANT TO LOOK ALSO INTO THE FOLLOWING OCCUPATIONAL
GROUPS: ATTENDANTS, HELPERS, LOADERS. THIS IS ONLY A PAR-
TIAL LIST OF THE OCCUPATIONAL AREAS WHICH COINCIDE WITH
YOUR ABILITIES AND SCHOOL SUBJECT PREFERENCES.[2]

GENERAL APTITUDE TEST BATTERY (GATB)

The GATB is made up of 12 tests measuring nine factors. This test was
originally developed by the U.S. Employment Service. It requires approximately two and one-half hours to administer the entire battery. A
standard score (mean = 100, S.D. = 20) is used for interpretation.

The U.S. Department of Labor has conducted continuous studies on the
validity and reliability of the GATB. The manual reports on more than
450 studies involving over 25,000 individuals. Separate validity coefficients are given for minority group members. Reliability, ranging
from the .80s to the low .90s, has been determined primarily by equiva-
lent-form and retest methods.

The GATB measures these nine aptitudes: intelligence, or general
learning ability (G), is measured by three tests (vocabulary, arithmetic reasoning, three-dimensional space); verbal aptitude (V) is measured by a vocabulary test in which the individual is required to
identify words that have the same meaning or opposite meaning; numerical aptitude (N) is measured by problems requiring computation and
arithmetic reasoning; spatial aptitude (S) is measured by a three-
dimensional test requiring the individual to visualize how an object
would appear when moved or rotated; form perception (P) is measured by
a combination of two tests, one of which requires tool matching, the
other matching of geometric forms; clerical perception (Q) is measured
by a test requiring the matching of names; motor coordination (K) is
measured by one test requiring coordination of eyes, hands, or fingers
in making precise movements; finger dexterity (F) is measured by two
tests, the first requiring the individual to assemble rivets and wash-
ers and the other requiring the individual to disassemble them; manual
dexterity (M) is measured by two tests, the first requiring the individual to place pegs on a pegboard and the second requiring the individual to invert the pegs while transferring them to another board.

One of the limitations of the GATB is that all the tests must be
completed quickly (Anastasi, 1976). The strength of the GATB is in the
research that has been conducted in establishing validity and reliability. The GATB is one of the most thoroughly researched test batteries. The impressive validity data based on aptitude scores and

[1],[2]From *Differential Aptitude Test* by G. K. Bennett, H. G. Seashore, and A. G. Wesman. Copyright © 1974 by The Psychological Corporation. Reprinted by permission.

Occupational Ability Patterns (see below) provide credibility for the use of this test in career counseling. The GATB has been reviewed by Anastasi (1976), Cronbach (1970), and Weiss (1972).

Multiple Cutoff Strategy. The U.S. Employment Service utilizes multiple cutoff points on the GATB in occupational counseling programs. To determine the cutoff points for specific occupations, combinations of GATB factors are converted into standard scores. This strategy was developed by studying test scores, criterion correlations (job output, course grades, and so forth), and job analyses. The use of multiple cutoff points has been developed by extensive, ongoing research since 1947. Occupations found to have similar patterns of scores are combined into the work groups listed in the *Guide for Occupational Exploration* (U.S. Department of Labor, 1979a). The GATB aptitude scores found to be most significant are listed with the established cutoff scores (for adults, students in grade 10, and students in grade 9) for each of 66 work groups. The score patterns are known as Occupational Ability Patterns (OAPs). The OAP structure is used to guide individuals in career exploration. For example, an individual who is considering occupations in air and water operations should have the following minimum GATB scores: G 105, N 100, and S 100 (U.S. Department of Labor, 1979, p. 31). OAP numbers are cross referenced with the Dictionary of Occupational Titles (DOT) codes. This handy reference can thus be used for almost all kinds of work and for entry into professional careers.

A major criticism of the multiple cutoff method is that correlations are given for prediction of success by validity coefficients, but no data are reported on the probability of predicting an individual's success in an occupation.

Case of a Migrant Farm Worker Seeking a Stable Job

Jose had been a migrant farm laborer most of his life. His family would leave south Texas during harvest seasons and migrate to various sections of the country working in the farm fields. Jose dropped out of school when he was in the seventh grade. By the time he was 19 years old, his parents were no longer migrating to the farm fields because of age and illness.

Jose came to the rehabilitation counseling office to find a permanent job. He reported to the counselor that many times he attended school for only a few months out of the year because it was necessary for the family to move from one location to another. However, Jose did state that he had been able to obtain a reader and a math book from his older brothers and had studied on his own. He mentioned that his family relied on his skills in mathematics on many occasions. His knowledge of occupations was limited because he had been exposed to only a few.

In order to determine his skills Jose took a battery of tests including the GATB. Jose's score report for the GATB is shown in Figure 4-3. This profile reports the raw scores for each of the 12 parts of the test. Scores for the nine aptitudes are derived from these 12 scores. For example, raw scores from parts 3, 4, and 6 are converted to standard scores and totaled to give the G score. The standard

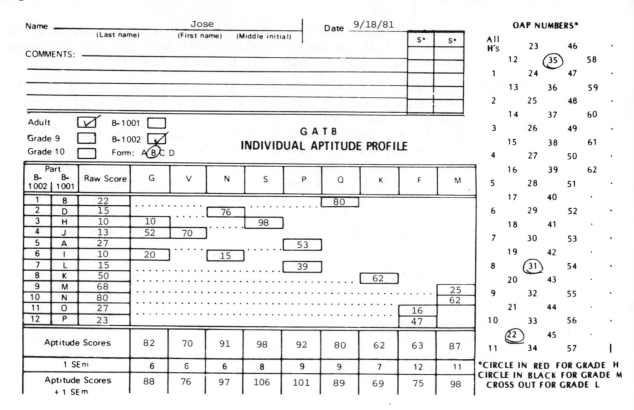

FIGURE 4-3.   *GATB profile for Jose.*

error of measurement is provided for each of the aptitude scores. On the far right of the report form the OAP numbers for high, medium, and low ratings are circled.

The counselor reported to Jose that his highest scores were in spatial aptitude, form perception, and manual dexterity. The counselor explained spatial aptitude as follows: "Jose, spatial aptitude measures how well you could visualize or form mental pictures of objects before they are built or how you might look at drawings that are used to guide people in the building trades, for example. This ability is used by architects and engineers and by anyone who needs to visualize work before building it. This skill is good for machinists, carpenters, and in many other types of occupations." The counselor also presented an explanation of form perception and manual dexterity. Jose listened intently, but it was evident that he did not grasp the full meaning of these measures.

The counselor then decided to look at the combination of the three high scores in relation to occupations. The counselor found that Jose had a high rating on OAP-31, production technology. After talking about this general occupational area, the counselor listed specific occupations: "These skills are used by assemblers, machine operators, and solderers." This list of jobs had little impact on Jose other than to confuse him further.

The counselor then decided on a different approach: "What this really means, Jose, is that you have aptitudes in certain areas that are necessary for a number of jobs that we can explore. I would like for you to think about jobs other than those you are familiar with at the present time. For example, a local industry needs machine operators. This is one of the jobs I mentioned before. We also have a number of other firms that hire people with the same kinds of skills you have. The next step should be to read descriptions of these jobs so that you will have a little better understanding of them. This should help you in deciding what you would like to do and will also introduce you to some jobs that you have never considered before."

Jose seemed delighted with the prospect of exploring different kinds of jobs. He still seemed uncertain about his future but was willing to investigate the jobs: "I never thought about any of these jobs before, and I didn't even know what went on in all those places. I always thought that I would have to be something like a janitor or a laborer. But this is what I really want, something that I can learn and be trained to do so that I can have a good job in one place for a long time."

Jose spent considerable time during the following weeks researching various careers. He eventually was placed as an apprentice machine operator in a local firm. He also wanted a high school equivalency diploma and so he enrolled in a local program to obtain it. His goal was to attend the local community college. In this case the aptitude test results provided a link to occupational information and to career options Jose had never considered before.

ARMED SERVICES VOCATIONAL APTITUDE BATTERY (ASVAB)

The ASVAB was developed to replace the separate Army, Navy, and Air Force classification batteries for selecting and classifying personnel. This battery is designed primarily for high school seniors. The armed services have developed cooperative programs with school systems for administering this battery, and they furnish test results at no cost. More than a million individuals take this test every year (Cronbach, 1979). Separate sex norms are available for grades 9, 10, 11, and 12. Testing time is approximately three hours.

The ASVAB form 5 consists of 12 tests that combine to yield five composite scores: verbal, ability to deal with written materials and verbal concepts; mathematics, ability to understand quantitative concepts; perceptual speed, ability to perform clerical activities; mechanical, ability to understand mechanical principles; trade technical, ability to perform automotive and electronic shop activities.

INTERPRETING THE ASVAB

The six composite scores can be used to counsel students concerning broad career fields. These scores are recorded on the profile by grade and sex. An example of the profile used is shown in Figure 4-4. Accompanying the profiles are explanations of the percentile scores, of what the aptitude tests measure, and of how to use the ASVAB results.

Sample job groupings provide examples of jobs recommended for each of the six composite scores. For example, under the math composite, the following sample jobs are listed: computer operator, data processor, inventory clerk, operations specialist, financial specialist, air

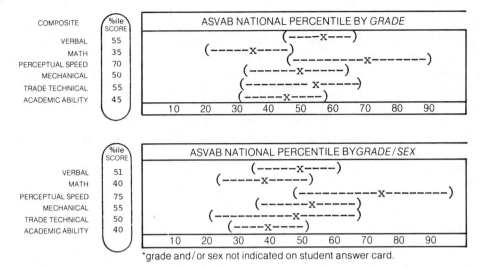

FIGURE 4-4.   ASVAB profile.

cargo specialist, purchasing agent, surveyor, communications technician, radio-teletype operator. The job areas were derived from training
course performance in the military but are suggested for consideration
in selecting civilian occupations.

Also provided to schools are gummed-label test-result printouts and
an alphabetical roster of students who took the test listing subtest
scores and percentiles by grade and sex.

The ASVAB has been closely scrutinized because of its wide use in
high schools. The reviews of Weiss (1978) and Cronbach (1979) should be
read before this instrument is used for advising high school students.
Cronbach (1979) suggests that the subtest scores are too unreliable to
be used separately and that the use of the test in general should be
limited. According to Weiss (1978), the reliabilities of subtest scores
are low primarily because the subtests are too short. Reliability coefficients reported in the manual were derived by internal consistency
and range from .91 to .67. The reliabilities for the composite scores
are higher than for the subtest scores, ranging from .88 to .92.

Validity data are based primarily on earlier forms of the test. However, there is only 50% content overlap with the earlier forms (Weiss,
1978). Correlations between form 2 and form 5 range from .56 to .76.
Correlations with the form 5 subtests and the DAT and GATB are .69 and
.83 for verbal, .67 and .86 for numerical, .55 and .78 for space perception, and .62 and .77 for mechanical comprehension.

Thus, sufficient data for determining the validity and reliability of
form 5 are not available (Cronbach, 1979; Weiss, 1978); the meaning of
the test scores is limited until additional validity data are generated. The composite scores appear to have face validity, but sufficient data are lacking to prove that the subtests measure what they
claim to measure. Despite the technical problems with form 5, the
career counselor may find this instrument useful in stimulating discussions concerning possible careers in the armed services.

Case of a High School Student Interested in the Armed Services

Corrina resided in a small rural community. The nearest city was 50 miles away. She had considered a career in the Army and took the ASVAB during her junior year in high school. Later, she decided she didn't want to leave home and dropped her plans.

When she was a senior, however, Corrina reported to the counselor that she was reconsidering the armed services because of a lack of jobs in her community and the nearby city. Because an Army recruiter was not available in the community, the counselor had been provided with ASVAB materials for counseling purposes. Figure 4-4 shows Corrina's profile. The counselor explained each of the scores in the following manner: "Your score on the verbal composite is at the 51st percentile. This means that 51 females out of 100 in the eleventh grade scored lower than you did, while 49 out of 100 scored higher than you did. The dashes on the profile indicate the range of your score. In other words, your true composite score for verbal is somewhere within this range. The verbal composite is a measure of your vocabulary, understanding of scientific principles, and ability to understand written materials. The tests used to measure the verbal composite are word knowledge (meanings of selected words) and general science."

Corrina wanted to know more about the significance of her high score in perceptual speed. Before responding directly to her question, the counselor explained that most jobs require a combination of abilities and even though she should consider jobs that depend heavily on speed and accuracy, she should consider other factors also. "Your perceptual speed score is related to occupations that require detail, accuracy, and numerical work. The occupations associated with this composite are administrative specialist, clerk-typist, court reporter, file clerk, keypunch operator, disbursing clerk, legal clerk, stock control clerk, and supply clerk. These occupations are usually found in the clerical, supply, and general administrative occupational groups."

After spending considerable time reviewing the sample occupations and occupational groups, Corrina decided she would like to consider the clerical groups. Specifically, she planned to visit an Army recruiter for more information about a career as a clerk-typist, file clerk, or supply clerk.

In Corrina's case the ASVAB results were used to stimulate career exploration. Associating several occupational groups with the results provided her with examples of occupations she could consider for a career. This information encouraged Corrina to relate her skills and interests to job opportunities in the armed services.

LIMITATIONS AND SUGGESTIONS FOR USE

Although multiaptitude tests provide differential measures of ability, expectations for the predictive value of the results may be too high. The scores from multiaptitude test batteries should not be expected to pinpoint careers. The tests cannot answer specific questions: "Will I be a good architect?" "Will I be a good mechanical engineer?" "Will

I be a good surgical nurse?" Only partial answers to these questions may be expected. For example, a space relation score on an aptitude battery should provide an index of the individual's ability to visualize the effect of three-dimensional movement, which is one of the aptitudes required of architects. However, many other factors, all of which cannot be measured by a multiaptitude battery, need to be considered by the prospective architect. It is therefore important to determine the individual's objectives before testing is accomplished.

"Should I consider being a mechanic?" "Do I have the aptitude to do clerical work?" "Is my finger dexterity good enough to consider assembly work?" Reasonable answers to these questions can be obtained from the results of aptitude tests. More important, however, a meaningful career search may begin once test results are evaluated. The results of multiaptitude test batteries provide valuable suggestions and clues to be considered along with other information in career decision making.

OTHER APTITUDE TESTS

In addition to the multiaptitude batteries discussed in this chapter, a number of other batteries are on the market. Here are four examples.

Primary Mental Abilities Test. This was one of the first factored aptitude batteries; it was restandardized in 1962. It can be scored for general intelligence and provides five specific factors for kindergarteners through adults: verbal meaning, number facility, reasoning, perceptual speed, and spatial relations. Scores are expressed as mental age, IQ, and percentile rank.

Academic Promise Test. Four tests provide information for predicting course grades and achievement test scores. The verbal test measures verbal reasoning and understanding of words. The numerical test measures quantitative ability. The abstract reasoning test measures nonverbal reasoning. The language test measures grammar usage.

Flanagan Aptitude Classification Test. This test consists of 16 subtests: inspection, coding, memory, precision, assembly, scales, coordination, judgment/comprehension, arithmetic, patterns, components, tables, mechanics, expression, reasoning, and ingenuity. Each test measures behaviors considered critical to job performance. Selected groups of tests may be administered. The entire battery takes several hours. This test is designed primarily for use with high school students and adults.

The Guilford-Zimmerman Aptitude Survey. This test consists of seven parts: verbal comprehension, general reasoning, numerical operations, perceptual speed, spatial orientation, spatial visualization, and mechanical knowledge. The tests are relatively independent and homogeneous. However, the norm population is not fully described in the manual.

SUMMARY

Early trait-and-factor approaches to career counseling utilized ability measures. Multiaptitude batteries evolved from a growing interest in intraindividual measurement. Ability measures may be used to stimulate discussion of personal characteristics and traits relevant for career decision-making.

An aptitude is a specific proficiency or an ability to acquire a certain proficiency. The aptitude tests discussed in this chapter measure a variety of skills and abilities.

QUESTIONS AND EXERCISES

1. Define aptitude and illustrate how aptitude scores are used in career counseling.

2. What are the major differences between the DAT and GATB? Give an example of a case and specify why you would choose one of these tests over the other to assess the individual's abilities.

3. Is it important for aptitude tests to provide separate sex norms? Why or why not?

4. Why are aptitude test scores generally better predictors of high school and college grades than of occupational success?

5. How would you prepare high school students to interpret the results of the ASVAB? Develop a list of major points you would cover for a presentation to a group or to an individual.

5
Using Achievement Tests

The career counselor has to be concerned with the academic achievement of each client. Levels of competence in reading, language usage, and mathematics may be the key to rejection or consideration of certain educational and vocational plans. In fact, most career planning in one way or the other is related to academic proficiency. The decision to obtain education and training beyond high school is often based directly on developed abilities as measured by achievement tests. And many vocations that do not require college training do require that the individual be able to read, do arithmetic, and write. Thus, achievement tests provide results that can be linked to most occupational requirements.

Career counselors should understand the difference between achievement tests and aptitude tests. Both measure learning experience. However, the achievement test measures learning of relatively restricted items and in limited content areas—that is, learning related to an academic setting. The aptitude test measures a specific skill, ability, or an achievement learned from a variety of experiences.

The choice of an aptitude test or an achievement test may be crucial in career counseling. Assessment of the purpose of the testing is the key. Both aptitude and achievement test results may be used as predictive and diagnostic information. However, aptitude tests are designed primarily as predictive tests, while achievement tests assess the present level of developed abilities. Thus, achievement tests measure the end product; they evaluate what the individual can do at the present time.

TYPES OF ACHIEVEMENT TESTS

Numerous achievement tests are on the market today. They are usually general survey batteries covering several subject matter areas or single subject tests. They can be criterion-referenced or norm-referenced or both. Achievement tests are usually identified by grade level. It is important to establish the specific purpose for giving an achievement test in order to decide what type to use. The following paragraphs relate purpose for testing to types of test.

The general survey battery should be chosen when comparisons of achievement in different content areas are needed. The survey battery provides a relatively limited sampling of each content area but, as the name implies, covers a broad spectrum of content areas.

The single subject test should be chosen when a precise and thorough evaluation of achievement in one subject is needed. More items and more aspects of the subject are usually covered in a single subject test than in a survey battery. In educational planning, it is often desirable to choose a single subject test when detailed information is necessary. The saving in testing time is also a major consideration in the decision to use a single subject test.

Both types of tests can be used as diagnostic instruments when measurement of specific skills or abilities such as reading, spelling, or arithmetic computation is needed. Knowledge of specific proficiencies can be a valuable tool for educational and career planning; individuals who are aware of their skills and proficiencies can relate them to occupational requirements. Detection of a specific deficiency is also valuable for referral to remedial programs.

This chapter first reviews and discusses two survey batteries and gives an example of the use of the survey battery in career counseling. It then reviews an achievement test designed to measure basic skills in arithmetic, reading, and spelling, and gives an example of its use. A criterion-referenced diagnostic achievement test is then reviewed with an example of its use. Finally, a single subject test of a basic skill is reviewed, and its use is illustrated.

CALIFORNIA ACHIEVEMENT TEST (CAT)

The CAT, a general survey battery, has two forms and ten levels (10-19). Level 10 is designed primarily as a readiness test for grade 1. Levels 11 through 19 (grade 12) have separate subtests for reading, spelling, language, mathematics, and reference skills. The tests may be machine scored or hand scored.

Reviews by Bryan (1978) and Womer (1978) give an overview of the development of this instrument, which was impressive. Over 100 textbooks and courses of study were evaluated in selecting item content. The norms for the CAT are kept current by standardizing the test two times a year. All test items have been reviewed for sex and ethnic bias. Alternate-form reliability coefficients for the total battery range from .86 to .96. For the subtests, the median reliabilities range from .44 to .84. Validity data include subtest intercorrelation coefficients and descriptions of how the items of the test were developed. Womer (1978) and Bryan (1978) suggest that there is ample evidence of content validity. The CAT is thus well documented as an evaluation tool for assessing student achievement in the basic content areas of reading, mathematics, and language.

INTERPRETING THE CAT

The CAT profile reports both norm-referenced and criterion-referenced results, as shown in Figure 5-1. The test results for the norm-referenced section are reported on the top part of the profile as follows: RS stands for raw score, OGE is the obtained grade

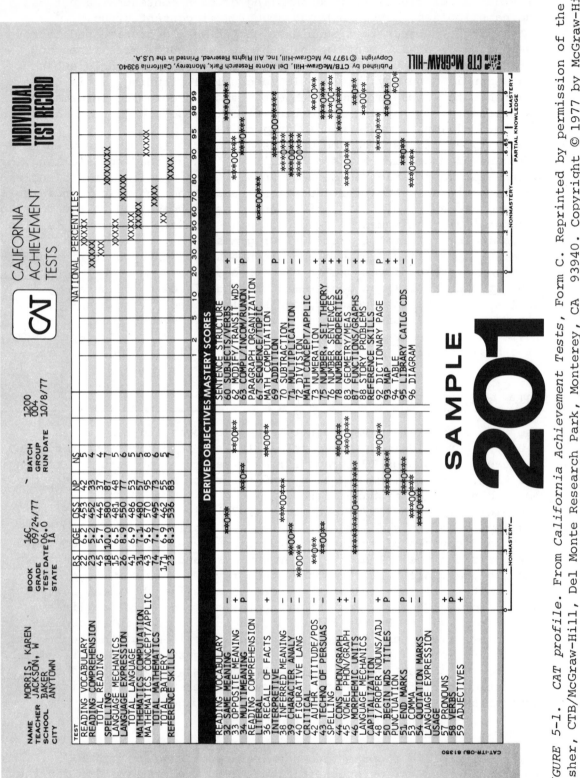

FIGURE 5-1. *CAT profile.* From *California Achievement Tests*, Form C. Reprinted by permission of the publisher, CTB/McGraw-Hill, Del Monte Research Park, Monterey, CA 93940. Copyright © 1977 by McGraw-Hill, Inc. All rights reserved. Printed in the U.S.A.

equivalent, OSS is the obtained scaled score, NP is the national percentile, and NS is the national stanine. The obtained scaled score has a range of 000-999 and is used primarily to measure growth by comparing current scores with those on previous tests. The norm-referenced profile is a handy, quick source of information on performance in the academic subject matter areas usually considered in educational and career planning. A review of the profile points out strengths and weaknesses in specific subjects, and a total battery score allows an overall evaluation of the individual's progress. Information on significant proficiency in certain subjects as well as deficiencies can be considered in the career planning process.

The criterion-referenced section provides a detailed account of the various skills measured by the CAT. Three points of reference are used for interpretation: nonmastery (-), partial mastery (P), and mastery (+). Subject matter is broken down into parts for a more comprehensive evaluation of specific skills. For example, under language mechanics, punctuation is listed: end marks, comma, and quotation marks. This particular part of the score report provides important information for someone considering a secretarial career. Other parts of the criterion-referenced report can be used in a similar manner.

FIGURE 5-2.   *CAL-STIK label.* From *California Achievement Tests,*
Form C. Reprinted by permission of the publisher, CTB/McGraw-Hill,
Del Monte Research Park, Monterey, CA 93940. Copyright © 1977 by
McGraw-Hill, Inc. All rights reserved. Printed in the U.S.A.

Another popular means for recording CAT results is by use of the CAL-STIK label, shown in Figure 5-2. This label can be easily attached to a cumulative folder. It reports results in grade equivalents, scaled scores, percentiles, and stanines. The interpretive materials thus provide many different score reports and adequate explanations of their use.

STANFORD ACHIEVEMENT TEST

The Stanford Achievement Test is another example of a survey battery. This test was first published over 50 years ago and has undergone numerous revisions. The test may be hand scored or computer scored. The publisher provides a comprehensive, computerized reporting service to assist local administrators with instructional planning and reporting to the public.

The first high school battery of the Stanford Achievement Test was published in 1965 (Adams, 1972). Developers of this test thoroughly reviewed textbooks and many different curriculum patterns. Items were edited by individuals from various minority groups and were evaluated in tryout programs involving 61,000 students in 1445 classrooms in 47 different school systems. Frequent revisions of the test have been made to stay abreast of changing curriculum patterns. The general use of the test is enhanced by several guides designed to aid in the interpretation of results. Because of the high level of the skills assessed, this test is particularly useful for helping individuals in making plans for college. Reviews by Elbel (1978), Passou and Schiff (1978), and Lehmann (1978) provide additional information for evaluating the development and use of this instrument.

Reliability established by split-half estimates for each subtest range from .87 to .95. Reliability estimates based on KR-20 range from .86 to .94. Content validity is well documented by a thorough explanation of the evaluation and editing process for test items. Construct validity is based on correlations with prior editions of the test, internal consistency of items, and evidence of the decreasing difficulty of items with progress in school.

INTERPRETING THE STANFORD ACHIEVEMENT TEST

Figure 5-3 is one of the profiles used for reporting individual performance. For each of the nine subject tests, results are reported by the number correct, scaled scores, grade equivalents, percentile ranks, and stanines. Percentile ranks and stanine scores may be based on tables for the beginning or end of the year. Total reading and total mathematics scores are also reported. A multiple-score report such as this one lends itself to meaningful interpretations for career counseling because the combination of scores displayed provides the counselor and counselee with an overview of achievement by subject.

	Number Right	Scaled Score	Grade Equiv.	%ile Rank*	STANINE*		
TEST 1: Vocabulary					1 2 3	4 5 6	7 8 9
TEST 2: Reading Comprehension					1 2 3	4 5 6	7 8 9
TEST 3: Math. Concepts					1 2 3	4 5 6	7 8 9
TEST 4: Math. Computation					1 2 3	4 5 6	7 8 9
TEST 5: Math. Applications					1 2 3	4 5 6	7 8 9
TEST 6: Spelling					1 2 3	4 5 6	7 8 9
TEST 7: Language					1 2 3	4 5 6	7 8 9
TEST 8: Social Science					1 2 3	4 5 6	7 8 9
TEST 9: Science					1 2 3	4 5 6	7 8 9
Total Battery (Test 1 through Test 9)					1 2 3	4 5 6	7 8 9
Total Reading (Test 1 + Test 2)					1 2 3	4 5 6	7 8 9
Total Mathematics (Test 3 + Test 4 + Test 5)					1 2 3	4 5 6	7 8 9

*Percentile Ranks and Stanines based on tables for Beginning □ End □ of Grade

FIGURE 5-3. Stanford Achievement Test profile. Reproduced from the Stanford Achievement Test by permission. Copyright © 1973 by Harcourt Brace Jovanovich, Inc. All rights reserved.

Particular attention should be given to the scaled scores, which provide an index for comparing growth from one grade level to another. Table 5-1, a part of the SAT scaled score table, illustrates how raw scores are converted to scaled scores. By using such a table, one can compare a raw score made on the reading comprehension section of the test in grade 9, for example, with the score made on the reading comprehension section in grade 12. However, the table should not be used to compare performance in one subject with performance in another. The advantage of the scaled score is that it provides equal units on a continuous scale for making comparisons.

TABLE 5-1. *Partial List of Scaled Scores for the Stanford Achievement Test*

Number Right (Raw Score)	Reading Comprehension Scaled Score	Number Right (Raw Score)	Reading Comprehension Scaled Score
42	184	21	149
41	184	20	148
40	183	19	145
39	182	18	142
38	180	17	138
37	179	16	137
36	176	15	131
35	175	14	128
34	174	13	126
33	173	12	121
32	171	11	116
31	169	10	114
30	168	9	110
29	166	8	105
28	164	7	101
27	162	6	95
26	161	5	93
25	158	4	88
24	157	3	86
23	155	2	84
22	154	1	81

Reproduced from the Stanford Achievement Test by permission. Copyright © 1973 by Harcourt Brace Jovanovich, Inc. All rights reserved.

Case of a High School Student Referred to a Counselor because of Poor Grades

Robert, a junior in high school, was referred to the career counselor by his English teacher, who reported that Robert was a poor student in English and, even with tutoring, had difficulty maintaining the level of performance necessary to pass her course. Earned course grades and comments from previous teachers reflected the same concerns. The teacher reported that Robert's parents were insisting that he attend college, and Robert was trying to meet their expectations of him. According to the teacher, Robert was making a maximum effort but with little success.

The counselor reviewed the results of an achievement test survey battery that had been administered during the current semester. A summary of Robert's scores is shown in Table 5-2. The counselor concluded that

TABLE 5-2.   Achievement Test Survey Battery Results for Robert

Test	National Percentile Equivalent	National Stanine
Reading comprehension	17	3
Vocabulary	20	3
Math reasoning	38	4
Math computation	57	5
Language usage		
Spelling	09	2
Grammar	11	3
Social science	19	3
Science	32	4

the reported weaknesses in language usage were certainly verified by the recent achievement test results. The counselor found that previous test data for Robert followed the same pattern—a weakness in language skills and average or better performance in mathematical computation.

Robert spoke softly and volunteered little information. He seemed proud of and at the same time somewhat threatened by the fact that his two older brothers were attending college. He reported that his father owned and operated a manufacturing firm. Both his parents were college graduates.

When the counselor asked Robert about his plans for the future, he answered with a well rehearsed "I want to be an accountant." The counselor acknowledged Robert's response positively, and explored in more detail Robert's interest in the field of business. During the course of the conversation, it became apparent that Robert possessed little knowledge about the activities of an accountant. To Robert the job was the same as bookkeeping. However, the counselor had established rapport with Robert and had been able to get him to project into the future and to talk about what he perceived as a good job.

Prior to the next counseling session, the counselor consulted Robert's math teacher. "Robert has good computational skills and really tries hard; he certainly is not my top student in mathematics, but he does well in applications." This information confirmed the results of the previous test data and of the recently administered achievement test. The counselor was encouraged, for now he could include some positive facts when giving Robert the test results.

At the next session, after a brief period of small talk designed to reinforce the rapport already established, the counselor suggested that they discuss the achievement test results. "Your score is at the 17th percentile on reading comprehension. This means that 17 out of 100 11th graders nationally scored lower than you while 83 out of 100 11th graders scored higher." The counselor explained the other scores in the same manner and then discussed groups of scores.

Robert was particularly sensitive to his low scores in language usage. He commented that he had always had problems with English courses. The counselor asked that he explain how this problem would affect his plans for educational training and a career. Robert acknowledged that he would have problems in college; his brothers had told him the English courses were difficult.

The counselor sensed that it was the right time to introduce encouraging information and an alternative potential career goal. "The field of business is broad and has many opportunities for you particularly with your good math skills. We can explore some careers that require math skills but that do not necessarily require a college degree. A couple of occupations that I can think of offhand are bookkeeping and bank teller." Robert was delighted with this information and in subsequent counseling sessions made reports on several careers he had researched in the career resource center. He seemed most interested in bookkeeping.

In a meeting with the counselor, Robert's parents expressed their appreciation for Robert's enthusiasm and interest in career exploration. They said they had hope that Robert could attend college as his brothers had, but they recently came to the realization that Robert was not as academically inclined. They now planned to encourage and support Robert's interest in alternative careers.

In this case the achievement test results were linked easily to educational planning and occupational information. Robert and his parents recognized that his weak English skills would make it difficult for him to be a successful college student but that his relatively higher skills in mathematics opened other occupational opportunities.

WIDE RANGE ACHIEVEMENT TEST (WRAT)

The WRAT, first standardized in 1936, is an example of an abbreviated achievement test measuring arithmetic, reading, and spelling. The arithmetic section can be given in approximately ten minutes. The examiner is required to orally present up to 46 words for the spelling section. The reading section requires the individual to pronounce from a list words that become progressively more difficult. The test can be given in a relatively short time when the arithmetic and spelling sections are given in a group setting. Each subtest is divided into two levels. Level I is for children ages 5 to 11 years. Level II is for individuals 12 years through adulthood.

Reliabilities for the WRAT subtests were obtained by the split-half method based on odd-even scores. The reported coefficients are high, ranging from .94 to .98. However, the information provided in the manual does not adequately describe the population sample on which the test was standardized in 1936. This same problem exists with the 1965 edition (Merwin, 1972). Intercorrelations between the subtests range from .69 to .94 for level I and .65 to .93 for level II. Validity was established by comparing WRAT subtest scores with scores on several widely used intelligence and achievement tests. Reviews by Merwin (1972) and Thorndike (1972) provide additional information on the development and use of this instrument.

INTERPRETING THE WRAT

The results are reported in percentiles, grade equivalents, stanines, standard scores, T scores, and scaled scores by age groups. The normative tables have a wide range; they are grouped by age from 5 years to 55-64 years. The standard scores have a mean of 100 and a standard deviation of 15.

The chief advantage of the WRAT is that it can be given in a relatively short time and can be used as a screening instrument for educational planning. It is particularly useful for testing individuals whose educational achievement is low; it gives an estimate of their developed abilities that can be used for vocational placement. Several case studies are reported in the manual to illustrate the use of the WRAT.

Case of a School Dropout Interested in Changing Jobs

Diana, 24 years old, dropped out of school when she was in the seventh grade. She had worked at a number of odd jobs but mainly as a dishwasher. She heard that there were opportunities for employment as a Licensed Vocational Nurse (LVN) and came to the career counseling center to find out what the requirements were. After reviewing the requirements, she asked the counselor whether there were some way of determining how she would do in LVN training and in classes that prepare individuals to obtain a high school equivalency diploma. The counselor suggested that she take an achievement test to give a rough estimate of her educational level in arithmetic, reading, and spelling. The WRAT was selected because it specifically measures basic achievement in those areas and can be quickly administered and scored.

The results of the WRAT for Diana are listed in Table 5-3. The

TABLE 5-3. WRAT Results for Diana

Test	Stanine	Percentile	Standard Score
Arithmetic	3	12	82
Reading	2	09	80
Spelling	2	08	79

counselor recognized Diana's disappointment with her performance. However, he pointed out that a high school diploma was not necessary to enter the local LVN training program. In discussing why she wanted to be an LVN, Diana expressed a sincere desire to help people.

Before Diana returned for her next appointment, the counselor reviewed the items on the test that she had missed. It was obvious that Diana's spelling skills were poor, but item analysis of the arithmetic test revealed that she made a number of careless mistakes. A review of the reading test revealed that Diana's word attack skills were poor but probably because she had not been exposed to many of the words she missed.

At the next counseling session, the counselor reviewed his item analysis of Diana's test results by pointing out careless mistakes and a lack of self-confidence in attempting words on the oral reading test. Diana appreciated being given concrete examples of her mistakes; she realized that she might do better with greater exposure to academic materials.

In subsequent meetings Diana agreed to enter a remedial program sponsored by the high school learning assistance center. When Diana was asked about the decision, she stated "I've always been afraid of tests. Now—could you believe it?—the test scores helped me see the light!"

Diana's career exploration was enhanced in a number of ways by the test. First, she was encouraged to upgrade her vocational skills by further academic training. Secondly, she gained self-confidence by diagnosing the mistakes on her test. By encouraging her to upgrade her skills through educational programs, the counselor helped to make other work opportunities available to Diana.

MASTERY: SURVIVAL SKILLS TEST (SST)

The SST is a criterion-referenced test designed to measure mastery of essential reading and math skills. The reading test assesses performance of such tasks as reading telephone books, following simple directions, and reading a street map. The mathematics test assesses performance of such tasks as determining correct change, calculating budgets, and itemizing expenses. Each test can be administered in one hour or less. The two editions of the test are designed for grades 6-12 (school edition) and for grades 11-adult (adult edition). The test can be locally scored or computer scored. Several options of computer scoring are available.

INTERPRETING THE SST

Figure 5-4 is an individual student profile. The profile contains the following information: a list of objectives for each test, performance on individual items and objectives for each test, and overall performance on each test. There are 20 specific objectives for each test with three items for each objective. The profile gives scores for each item so that test results can be evaluated in detail. In addition, a review of the specific objectives reveals information that can be used in career planning. For example, mastery of the objective of making change can be directly related to requirements for certain jobs. Tests such as this one, which are designed to measure mastery of specific skills, provide information of inestimable value for counseling students in middle grades through high school on planning future instruction and for adults on skills needed in daily living.

Case of a Counselee with Limited Educational and Vocational Experience

Rita was referred to the career counselor by a local social service agency. She had been deserted by her husband after ten years of marriage and left with three children. She had little work experience. Her school grades were poor; and she had dropped out of school while in the seventh grade to get married. One of her immediate problems was managing personal expenditures because her husband had paid the mastery: an evaluation tool

SRA CRITERION-REFERENCED MEASUREMENT PROGRAM

REPORT FOR WESTRICK EDWARD /FAIRVIEW HIGH
GROUP SOPHOMORE
2232

SUBJECT SURVIVAL SKILLS-MR GRADE 10-1
GROUP I.D. 180HURON DATE 05/04/77
TEST # 002232-5254
CODE #
TAPE NO 72431 52 7-2272

OBJECTIVE: (LEARNER WILL (IDENTIFY)...)

OBJ CATALOG NO / DIA PROBE NOS	OBJ MST	ITEM RIGHT		
1 KNOW HOW TO MAKE CHANGE — MM1	Y	1 +	2 +	3 +
2 FIND TOTAL INCOME FROM AVG WEEKLY INCOME — MM2	Y	4 +	5 +	6 +
3 CALCULATE WAGES FROM HOURLY RATE AND HOURS — MM3	Y	7 +	8 +	9 −
4 DETERMINE AND COMPARE UNIT COSTS — MM4	N	10 +	11 +	12 +
5 FIND TAKE HOME PAY FROM SALARY AND DEDUCTION — MM5	Y	13 +	14 +	15 +
6 FIGURE DAILY AMOUNTS FROM WEEKLY BUDGET — MM6	Y	16 Ⓑ + 17 +		18 +
7 FIND MULTIPLES OF ITEMIZED WEEKLY EXPENSES — MM7	Y	19 +	20 +	21 +
8 COMPUTE A SALES SLIP, INCLUDING TAX — MM8	Y	22 +	23 +	24 +
9 ESTIMATE WEEKLY SAVINGS TO BUY AN ITEM — MM9	Y	25 +	26 +	27 +
10 CALCULATE WEEKLY WAGES FROM PIECEWORK RATE — MM10	Y	28 +	29 +	30 +
11 COMPUTE MONTHLY RATE TO REPAY DEBT IN A YEAR — MM11	Y	31 +	32 +	33 +
12 COMPUTE TOTAL AND AVERAGE SCORES IN SPORTS — MM12	Y	34 +	35 +	36 +
13 FIND TOTAL MATERIALS COST FROM UNIT COSTS — MM13	N	37 +	38 +	39 +
14 DETERMINE RECIPE AMOUNTS FOR DIFF SIZE GROUP — MM14	Y	40 +	41 +	42 +
15 CALCULATE DISTANCE FROM TIME AND RATE — MM15	Y	43 +	44 +	45 +
16 COMPUTE UTILITIES COST AND COMPARE WITH BILL — MM16	N	46 +	47 +	48 +
17 FIND AMOUNT OF FLOOR COVERING NEEDED FOR ROOM — MM17	Y	49 +	50 +	51 +
18 FIGURE DISTANCE, TIME, AND GAS COST FOR A TRIP — MM18	N	52 +	53 +	54 +
19 COMPUTE COST OF PET CARE OVER NUMBER OF YEARS — MM19	Y	55 +	56 +	57 +
20 FIND AMOUNT OF MATERIAL NEEDED TO MAKE AN ITEM — MM20	N	58 +	59 −	60 +

OBJECTIVE: (LEARNER WILL (IDENTIFY)...)

OBJ CATALOG NO / DIA PROBE NOS	OBJ MST	ITEM RIGHT		
1 UNDERSTAND MEDICAL TERMS AND INSTRUCTIONS — MR1	Y	1 +	2 +	3 +
2 UNDERSTAND CAUTION LABELS ON BOTTLES, ETC. — MR2	Y	4 +	5 +	6 +
3 SELECT USE OF ITEMS BASED ON CONSUMER TERMS — MR3	Y	7 +	8 +	9 −
4 RESPOND PROPERLY TO ROAD SIGNS — MR4	N	10 +	11 +	12 +
5 FOLLOW SIMPLE DIRECTIONS — MR5	Y	13 +	14 +	15 +
6 UNDERSTAND COMMON INFORMATION SIGNS — MR6	Y	16 Ⓓ + 17 +		18 +
7 USE BUILDING FLOOR Ⓒ PLAN AND SCHEDULE — MR7	Y	19 +	20 +	21 +
8 RECALL FACTS FROM HANDBOOK ON SAFETY — MR8	Y	22 +	23 +	24 +
9 KNOW HOW TO USE A STREET GUIDE AND ITS MAP — MR9	Y	25 +	26 +	27 +
10 BE ABLE TO FILL IN BLANKS ON A FORM — MR10	Y	28 +	29 +	30 +
11 SELECT USE OF PRODUCT BASED ON INGREDIENTS — MR11	Y	31 +	32 +	33 +
12 KNOW HOW TO USE TELEPHONE DIRECTORY — MR12	Y	34 +	35 +	36 +
13 KNOW HOW TO USE A BUILDING DIRECTORY — MR13	N	37 +	38 +	39 +
14 IDENTIFY ITEMS FROM A BUSINESS STATEMENT — MR14	Y	40 +	41 +	42 +
15 KNOW HOW TO USE AN ENTERTAINMENT GUIDE — MR15	Y	43 +	44 +	45 +
16 ORDER A MEAL FROM A MENU AND FIGURE THE BILL — MR16	N	46 −	47 +	48 +
17 IDENTIFY FACTS IN AD AND JUDGE ITS SINCERITY — MR17	Y	49 +	50 +	51 +
18 USE A PLANE SCHEDULE TO DEVELOP A TRAVEL PLAN — MR18	Y	52 +	53 +	54 +
19 IDENTIFY CONDITIONS OF A CONTRACT — MR19	Y	55 +	56 +	57 +
20 FOLLOW AND IDENTIFY PARTS OF A CONCERT PROGRAM — MR20	Y	58 +	59 +	60 +

% OF OBJ MASTERED 15 NO OBJ MASTERED
Y = YES, MASTERED OBJ N = NO, DID NOT MASTER OBJ
SCIENCE RESEARCH ASSOCIATES, INC.

© 1974, Science Research Associates, Inc. All rights reserved.
% OF OBJ MASTERED 75 NO OBJ MASTERED 17
+ = RIGHT ANSWER − = WRONG ANSWER 0 = OMISSION

PRINTED IN THE UNITED STATES OF AMERICA
% OF OBJ MASTERED 85

Ⓐ LIST OF OBJECTIVES FOR FIRST CRT Ⓑ STUDENT PERFORMANCE ON ITEMS AND OBJECTIVES FOR FIRST CRT Ⓒ LIST OF OBJECTIVES FOR SECOND CRT
Ⓓ STUDENT PERFORMANCE ON ITEMS AND OBJECTIVES FOR SECOND CRT Ⓔ OVERALL STUDENT PERFORMANCE ON BOTH CRTs

FIGURE 5-4. SST individual student profile. From Mastery: Survival Skills Test, Science Research Associates Staff. Copyright © 1974, Science Research Associates. Reprinted by permission.

bills and handled the money. The counselor decided to administer a skills test that would provide information for making a decision about prevocational training by identifying Rita's specific deficiencies in managing money—for example, problems in developing a budget, computing bills, and doing comparative shopping.

The results of the test chosen, the SST, indicated that she had not mastered the following objectives: estimating the weekly savings needed to buy an item; computing the monthly payment necessary to repay a debt in a year; determining recipe amounts for different size groups; computing the cost of utilities and comparing the cost with the bill; figuring distance, time, and cost of gas for a trip; finding the amount of material needed to make an item; understanding caution labels on bottles; selecting items based on consumer information.

The first step for Rita was placement in a prevocational training program designed to help her overcome the problems identified by the SST. Specifically, instruction included information on financial planning, budgeting, comparative shopping, food preparation, and other home-related tasks.

The results of the test also revealed that Rita had the math skills necessary for making change correctly. She had been given responsibility for handling money by her parents, who sent her to stores to make purchases, and she expressed confidence in her abilities in this area. When the counselor asked her to relate this skill to a job opportunity, she replied "Check-out clerk or store clerk." The counselor realized that this source of immediate employment could help Rita supplement her income while considering other employment opportunities.

In this case the SST not only provided information that could be used to identify personal needs for home management but also provided clues for employment, both now and in the future. The counselor was aware that problems in the home, if not resolved first, would eventually affect Rita's ability to function on a job.

A WRITERS SKILLS TEST

The Basic Skills Assessment Program, consisting of tests of reading, mathematics, and writing skills, was developed by Educational Testing Service (ETS) with a national consortium of school districts. The tests may be administered as a battery, or individual tests may be selected as needed. Each test can be administered in approximately 45 minutes. They can be machine or hand scored. One of these tests, A Writers Skills Test, illustrates the use of a single subject achievement test.

A Writers Skills Test consists of 75 multiple-choice items covering spelling, punctuation, capitalization, logic, and evaluation. In addition the test uses four exercises to measure an individual's writing ability: writing a job application letter, completing a form, conveying information or directions, and writing creatively. A well-prepared manual is provided for evaluating the writing sample by an analytical or holistic scoring procedure.

Reliability estimates computed by KR-20 for total scores on A Writers Skills Test are high (.95). Subtest reliabilities range from .73 to .89. Content validity appears well established from the description

of the development of specifications for the test. Concurrent validity
was established by reporting the relationship of teachers' judgments
of a student's need for remedial work to scores on the test.

INTERPRETING A WRITERS SKILLS TEST

A scaled score (mean = 150, S.D. = 25) and the percentage of scores
below a given score for grades 8, 9, and 12 are provided for interpretation. In addition, means and standard deviations for each grade are
reported. A list of individual item responses is optional.

A Writers Skills Test is unique in that it provides an evaluation of
actual writing proficiency. The writing exercise portion scored by an
analytical system provides results as yes/no (pass/fail) for each exercise. The criteria used to determine a yes score are established by the
user based on local standards. For example, the user decides the relative emphasis to be put on spelling, punctuation, and legibility.
Results from the holistic scoring method are reported in numbers; 4
(superior), 3 (meets minimal local standards), and 2 (does not meet
minimal local standards), and 1 (is extremely weak).

There may be some argument about the validity of the scoring procedures for the writing exercises. But the manual carefully explains
the standardized scoring procedures adopted. In addition, ETS offers
consultant/workshop packages for helping users improve their scoring
skills. As these procedures are refined and validated, an increasingly
accurate appraisal of an individual's writing ability will be available.

Case of Counselee Aspiring to a Specific Job

For ten years Joan took care of her parents. After their deaths,
Joan, now 28, needed to find a job to support herself. She told the
counselor that she made average grades in high school but dropped out
during her junior year to care for her parents. She had never seri-
ously considered a career. Reading had been her primary pastime during
these years, and she had developed an interest in newspaper work. Specifically, she expressed a desire to write or edit for the hometown
newspaper. The counselor recalled a recent conversation with the owner
of the paper inquiring about qualified individuals in the community.
However, he did not know whether Joan had the skills necessary, although he observed that she expressed herself well verbally. The counselor and Joan decided that a writing and grammar test would help them
decide whether an interview with the newspaper owner was warranted at
this time.

The counselor wanted a test that would provide an index of Joan's
basic skills in capitalization, punctuation, logic, and spelling as
well as a writing sample. A Writers Skills Test from the Basic Skills
Assessment Program was selected. The counselor obtained the assistance
of the high school English department in scoring the writing sample
by the analytical method. He asked the scorers to score the writing
sample on the basis of 12th grade norms.

The results indicated that Joan's primary weakness was in punctuation, but she received pass scores on all other criteria. The scorers
recommended a remedial program for upgrading her punctuation skills.
The counselor and Joan decided that she would complete the recommended

program and then apply for a job with the local newspaper. In this case, the results of the test and particularly the writing sample were used to identify both weaknesses and strengths related to the requirements of the job under consideration.

OTHER ACHIEVEMENT TESTS

Because many published achievement tests are currently available, the following list is far from complete. The first three examples given are survey batteries; the next two are diagnostic tests; and the last four are separate subject tests.

Comprehensive Test of Basic Skills. This survey battery is designed primarily to measure basic skills in reading, language, mathematics, reference, science, and social studies. The reading, language, and mathematics subtests are further divided into parts.

Iowa Test of Basic Skills. Five major areas are tested by this survey battery: vocabulary, reading comprehension, language skills, work study skills (reading graphs and maps and using reference material), and mathematics. Some item overlap exists across grades. Scores are provided as grade equivalents and grade percentile norms.

Metropolitan Achievement Test High School Battery. Skills in language, reading, arithmetic, science, social studies, and study techniques are measured by this survey battery. Three or four forms are available for each level—primer through advanced. Four scores are reported for each subtest: standard score, grade equivalent, stanine, and percentile rank.

Diagnostic Reading Scales. This test is designed to measure reading disabilities. It contains reading passages, word recognition lists, and phonetics tests.

Stanford Diagnostic Arithmetic Test. This test has two levels. Level 1 (grades 2.5-4.5) covers concepts of numbers, computation, and number factors. Level 2 (grades 4.5-8.5) covers concepts of numbers, number factors, computation with whole numbers, with common fractions, with decimal fractions, and with percents.

Cooperative Mathematics Test. This series of nine tests measures performance in arithmetic, structure of number systems, algebra I, algebra II, algebra III, geometry, trigonometry, analytic geometry, and calculus.

Cooperative English Test. This test provides measures of reading comprehension and English expression.

Cooperative Social Studies Test. This test measures achievement in American history (grades 7-12), American government (grades 10-12), modern European history (grades 10-12), and world history (grades 10-12).

Cooperative Science Test. This test measures achievement in general science (grades 7-9), advanced general science (grades 8-9), and high school biology, chemistry, and physics.

SUMMARY

Academic achievement is a primary consideration in educational and vocational planning. For educational planning there is a direct relationship, and almost all jobs are linked to achievement of basic skills. Compared with aptitude tests, achievement tests measure much narrower content areas and more limited learning experiences. Aptitude tests measure broader areas of abilities and experiences. There are two types of achievement tests: general survey batteries, and single subject tests. Achievement test results are reported as norm-referenced scores or criterion-referenced scores or both.

QUESTIONS AND EXERCISES

1. Explain the difference between achievement and aptitude tests. Illustrate your explanation with an example of a case in which you would use one or the other kind of test.

2. What is the difference between a norm-referenced and a criterion-referenced test? What circumstances would indicate when to use one or the other?

3. Describe cases in which you would use a general survey battery, a single subject test, and a diagnostic test.

4. Give an example of how you would interpret a scaled score to an individual and then illustrate how you would interpret a scaled score to a high school class.

5. Would you choose a norm-referenced or a criterion-referenced achievement test for a 54-year-old, Black mother of four who has never worked? Why?

6
Using Career Maturity Inventories

The concept of career maturity has evolved from developmental approaches to career guidance and career education programs. Ginzberg, Ginsburg, Axelrad, and Herma (1951), Havighurst (1953), Super (1953, 1974), Tiedeman and O'Hara (1963) have made significant contributions toward an understanding of the importance of developmental approaches in career counseling. Super (1953) especially has emphasized that career choice is a continuous process throughout life. At different stages of life different developmental tasks must be accomplished to reach maturity.

The degree of an individual's career maturity is determined by the individual's location in the developmental process. To determine the particular stage of development, Super (1974, p. 13) identifies six dimensions. He feels these dimensions are relevant to and appropriate for adolescents, but they have become the basis for all career maturity inventories: orientation to vocational choice—an attitudinal dimension determining whether the individual is concerned with making a vocational choice; information and planning—a competence dimension concerning the specificity of career information the individual has and the amount of planning the individual has done; consistency of vocational preferences—a dimension providing an index of an individual's consistency of preferences; crystallization of traits—a dimension indicating an individual's progress toward forming a self-concept; vocational independence—a dimension indicating an individual's independence in making decision about work; and wisdom of vocational preferences—a dimension concerning the individual's ability to make realistic preferences consistent with personal goals. Individuals who score high on all dimensions are considered to be vocationally mature. In addition, for career counseling purposes the counselor is provided with an index of career maturity based on several dimensions.

The concept of career maturity covers not only these individually accomplished developmental tasks but also the behavior manifested in coping with the tasks of a given period of development—choosing certain courses, engaging in certain extracurricular activities, obtaining work experience. Career maturity inventories therefore measure the degree of vocational development, vocational attitude, and competence in coping with vocational developmental tasks. Knowing when individuals are competent and attitudinally ready to undertake career-related activities and to make important decisions concerning their education or vocation is an important part of career counseling and career education programs.

Just as in an individual's vocational development, there are critical decision points in career education programs. Program evaluations are needed to make the appropriate decisions. One of the major uses of career maturity inventories is in making these assessments of the effectiveness of career education programs.

In this chapter four career maturity inventories are reviewed. For each inventory, the career maturity dimensions are identified and the use of the results for career counseling and career education programs is emphasized.

CAREER MATURITY INVENTORY (CMI)

The CMI, formerly called the Vocational Development Inventory, is divided into two parts: an attitude scale and a competence scale. Both scales are applicable to males, females, minorities, and other special groups and can be hand or computer scored. Normative data for both scales cover grades 6-12. (Norms are also available for grade 13.) The two scales can be administered and interpreted separately; however, the author suggests the use of both scales for maximum usefulness in assessing career maturity.

The attitude scale is designed to measure whether the individual is concerned about making a vocational choice. The attitude section of the inventory is in a true-false format and consists of a screening form (A-2) and a counseling form (B-1). The screening form yields only one total score; the counseling form yields a score for each of five subscales: decisiveness in career decision-making, involvement in career decision-making, independence in career decision-making, orientation to career decision-making, and compromise in career decision-making. The reading level for the attitude scale is approximately sixth grade. The suggested time limits are 20 minutes for the screening form and 30 minutes for the counseling form. The attitude dimensions measured are listed in Table 6-1 which provides sample items and defines the variables for each dimension. The information contained in this table is not only valuable for understanding what is being measured by the attitude section but also valuable for interpreting the attitude dimensions for career counseling and for career education program evaluations.

Internal consistency for the attitude scale was calculated by the KR-20 for item data from grades 6-12 and yielded ranges from .65 to .84 with a mean coefficient of .74. A test-retest (one-year interval) measure of stability yielded a coefficient of .71 for grades 6-12. Content validity was established by evaluation of items by ten expert judges. Criterion-related validity was established by comparing scores on the attitude scale with other criteria of career maturity such as Super's indices of vocational maturity (1974) and Gribbons and Lohnes's description of readiness for vocational planning (1968). The author concludes that criterion-related validity should be considered as tentative because the number of cases in the study was small.

TABLE 6-1. *Variables in the Attitude Scale of the CMI**

Dimension	Definition	Sample Item
Involvement in the choice process	Extent to which individual is actively participating in the process of making a choice	"I seldom think about the job I want to enter."
Orientation toward work	Extent to which individual is task- or pleasure-oriented in attitudes toward work and values placed on work	"Work is dull and unpleasant." "Work is worthwhile mainly because it lets you buy the things you want."
Independence in decision-making	Extent to which individual relies on others in the choice of an occupation	"I plan to follow the line of work my parents suggest."
Preference for career choice factors	Extent to which individual bases choice on a particular factor	"Whether you are interested in a job is not as important as whether you can do the work."
Conceptions of the choice process	Extent to which individual has accurate or inaccurate conceptions about making a career choice	"A person can do any kind of work as long as he or she tries hard."

*From *Career Maturity Inventory* devised by John O. Crites. Reprinted by permission of the publisher, CTB/McGraw-Hill, Del Monte Research Park, Monterey, CA 93940. Copyright © 1973, 1978 by McGraw-Hill, Inc. All rights reserved. Printed in the U.S.A.

The competence test measures the specificity of information the individual has concerning careers and the planning skills needed for career decision-making. It contains items in multiple-choice format and consists of five parts: knowing yourself, knowing about jobs, choosing a job, looking ahead, and solving problems. Internal consistency for the competence scale was calculated by the KR-20 for each subtest for grades 6-12. The reported range was .72 to .90 with the exception of the problem-solving scale for the sixth and seventh grades. Few data are reported for establishing the validity of this scale. However, the author contends that content validity is ensured by the detailed analysis of the items selected.

The format of the competence subtest knowing yourself, which requires individuals to judge and appraise hypothetical characters, poses an interesting question. Can we assume that individuals who are capable of appraising others or judging what others should do are good self-appraisers? Because this appears to be the basic assumption of the author, data should be reported to support this assumption.

The results of a study by Westbrook, Cutts, Madison, and Arcia (1980) do not support the multidimensional structure of the CMI. Their findings suggest that the variables measured by the CMI are positively related to each other. Until further research is done, counselors are warned to use this inventory with some caution.

INTERPRETING THE CMI

The results of the CMI are provided on a profile as shown in Figure 6-1. One of the limitations of the inventory is the single score yielded by the attitude subtest (Westbrook and Mastie, 1973). Because this scale measures several indices of attitudinal development, meaningful results could be communicated by additional part scores.

The degree of career maturity may be determined by evaluating responses to the inventory and from each scale score report. This information can be used for counseling purposes. For example, if a review of the responses on the attitude scale indicates an individual lacks independence in career decision-making, counseling programs designed to encourage independent thought and recognition of personal assets should be considered. Likewise, a finding of a lack of occupational information (competence scale 2) or poor planning skills (competence scale 4) suggests specific counseling procedures.

Patterns on the CMI profile also provide relevant information for evaluating career maturity and deciding on counseling approaches. For example, an individual may be relatively high on the attitude scale but low on the competence scale for looking ahead. In this case, the individual may be ready to make a career decision but does not have the planning skills necessary to follow through.

Individual responses may also be evaluated for counseling considerations. For example, individuals who have difficulty in assessing their assets and liabilities might profit from counseling sessions in which they can clarify their characteristics and traits.

The CMI can be administered to a wide range of individuals, which increases its utility. The items have been drawn primarily from actual counseling cases. The author acknowledges that longitudinal research is needed to provide further measures of career development aspects. For an in-depth review of this instrument refer to Katz (1978), Zytowski (1978a), and Sorenson (1978).

Evaluation of a Prevocational Training Program

A prevocational training program was designed for adults residing in small towns and rural areas within a 50-mile radius of a university in south central Texas. The major purpose of the program was to assist disadvantaged adults in preparing for employment.

The instructor was interested in knowing which components of the program were most effective in improving perceptions of and dispositions toward the world of work and in improving knowledge of occupations and planning skills. The CMI was selected as an evaluation tool because it could answer these questions. Garcia, Zunker, and Nolan

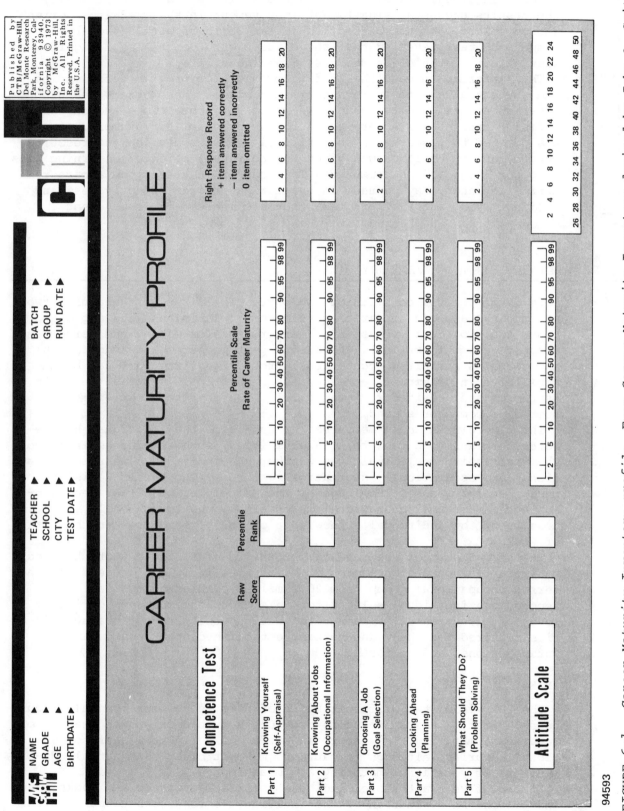

Published by CTB/McGraw-Hill, Del Monte Research Park, Monterey, California 93940. Copyright © 1973 by McGraw-Hill, Inc. All Rights Reserved. Printed in the U.S.A.

NAME ▲
GRADE ▲
AGE ▲
BIRTHDATE ▶

TEACHER ▲
SCHOOL ▲
CITY ▲
TEST DATE ▶

BATCH ▲
GROUP ▲
RUN DATE ▶

CAREER MATURITY PROFILE

Competence Test

	Raw Score	Percentile Rank

Right Response Record
+ item answered correctly
− item answered incorrectly
0 item omitted

Percentile Scale
Rate of Career Maturity

Part 1 — Knowing Yourself (Self-Appraisal)

1 2 5 10 20 30 40 50 60 70 80 90 95 98 99

2 4 6 8 10 12 14 16 18 20

Part 2 — Knowing About Jobs (Occupational Information)

1 2 5 10 20 30 40 50 60 70 80 90 95 98 99

2 4 6 8 10 12 14 16 18 20

Part 3 — Choosing A Job (Goal Selection)

1 2 5 10 20 30 40 50 60 70 80 90 95 98 99

2 4 6 8 10 12 14 16 18 20

Part 4 — Looking Ahead (Planning)

1 2 5 10 20 30 40 50 60 70 80 90 95 98 99

2 4 6 8 10 12 14 16 18 20

Part 5 — What Should They Do? (Problem Solving)

1 2 5 10 20 30 40 50 60 70 80 90 95 98 99

2 4 6 8 10 12 14 16 18 20

Attitude Scale

1 2 5 10 20 30 40 50 60 70 80 90 95 98 99

2 4 6 8 10 12 14 16 18 20 22 24

26 28 30 32 34 36 38 40 42 44 46 48 50

94593

FIGURE 6-1. Career Maturity Inventory profile. From *Career Maturity Inventory* devised by John O. Crites. Reprinted by permission of the publisher, CTB/McGraw-Hill, Del Monte Research Park, Monterey, CA 93940. Copyright © 1973, 1978 by McGraw-Hill, Inc. All rights reserved. Printed in the U.S.A.

(1980) report that pretest and posttest scores on the CMI showed changes in a positive direction on the attitude scale. Specifically, the results suggested significant improvement in the graduates' orientation toward work and perception of the world of work. However, the competence test revealed that the classes were not having a significant effect on the class members' planning skills.

This information made the instructor aware of program deficiencies and suggested ways to improve certain parts of the program. Learning experiences designed to enhance knowledge of occupations and career decision-making skills were added to the program. For example, time was devoted to research in the university career development resource center, and information was given to individual clients concerning jobs in general and in the community. This case illustrates how a career maturity inventory may be used in evaluating program effectiveness and in identifying parts of programs that are in need of improvement.

CAREER DEVELOPMENT INVENTORY (CDI)

Form IV of the CDI consists of two parts. The first part measures two attitudinal aspects of career development (planfulness and exploration) and two cognitive aspects (career decision-making and career and occupational information). The second part measures knowledge of the individual's preferred occupational group. The first part can be administered in 40 minutes and the second part in 20 minutes. Separate sex norms are provided for grades 9-12. The inventory can be machine scored or computer scored.

The planfulness scale measures how much time the individual has devoted to planning career-related activities, such as courses in school. The exploration scale indicates whether the individual has used educational and occupational information resources. The career decision-making scale measures knowledge of the principles of career decision-making. Career and occupational information, the fourth scale, is a measure of the individual's knowledge of and perspectives on the world of work.

The second part of the inventory consists of a single test, knowledge of preferred occupational groups. First, the individual selects a preferred occupational group from 20 families of kindred occupations. Second, the individual selects for this group the most appropriate level of education or training, the duties, the personal characteristics required for entry and getting established, the rewards and satisfactions, and so forth.

INTERPRETING THE CDI

The CDI yields two different kinds of data useful for counseling purposes. First, a composite score provides a multidimensional measure of vocational maturity. This score is useful as a single measure of vocational maturity, although the authors make it clear that not all dimensions of vocational maturity are measured.

Second, five trait scores indicate specific strengths and weaknesses and provide an evaluation of the individual's readiness to make career decisions. These scores are useful for determining further developmental experiences necessary to increase readiness for decision-making.

The CDI is useful as a diagnostic measure in that it indicates an individual's readiness to make educational and occupational choices. The results provide an index of attitudes toward career planning, knowledge of occupations, and skills necessary for career decision-making. Curriculum and guidance programs may also be evaluated using the CDI for their effectiveness in supporting attitudes and in teaching skills necessary in the career decision-making process. Earlier forms of this instrument have been reviewed by Bingham (1978), Borgen (1978), and Ricks (1978).

Use of Test Questions in Group Counseling

The career counselor in a high school and one of the teachers reviewed the results of the CDI that had recently been administered to juniors and seniors in their school. Their major goal was to establish programs for students based on needs indicated by the CDI results. Typical of the programs was the one developed for students with particularly poor scores on the planning section of the inventory. The students volunteered for participation in the program.

Both the teacher and the counselor were concerned with the students' lack of knowledge of working environments and their naive and nonchalant attitudes concerning the world of work. They wanted to provide a program that would help these students take a realistic approach to career planning. They agreed on a group counseling approach in order to reach all these students in a short period of time. The strategy was to use selected items from the CDI section measuring planfulness to stimulate group discussion. Several specific tasks were identified as the major objectives: clarify career planning attitudes, evaluate time spent thinking about and planning careers, identify courses associated with potential career plans, increase awareness of relevant activities associated with career planning, clarify reasons for considering postschool education and careers, clarify reasons for considering work environments in relation to careers. The following dialogue illustrates how the strategy of using CDI questions was employed to meet the specific objectives.

> *Counselor:* The major goal of this counseling session is to encourage each of you to devote more time to career planning. We will begin our session by discussing some of the questions in the CDI. Each of you has an inventory booklet for this purpose. [The counselor continued by presenting sample questions that she had previously identified. One of the questions dealt with the purpose of learning about actual working conditions of jobs being considered.]
>
> *Jan:* If you don't know anything about a job, how can you be expected to choose it?
>
> *Roberto:* Yeah, you have to know what the requirements are to make a decision about it.
>
> *Tom:* You should also know where you will be working—I mean, what places and how.

Rosa: I remember that my brother told me he never would have taken the job he has if he had known more about it. He gets all dirty, and the other guys talk rough and threaten him. He is trapped in that job, and he can hardly wait to find another job.

Counselor: Very good! You have illustrated why it is important to thoroughly investigate the requirements of occupations you may be considering and the kind of people you will be associating with in those occupations. Now, let's look at another question. Jan, what was your answer for question 1: "Taking classes that will help me decide what line of work to go into when I leave school or college"?

Jan: I'm not sure but I believe I answered "Not giving any thought to doing this." [Pause.] I really haven't thought about it much. I guess I'm just enjoying myself now and not considering the future.

Bertha: I heard that more and more women are going to have to work to support their families, so I believe we have to plan for jobs in the future like the boys do.

Rosa: I agree. The sooner we get started thinking about the jobs the better prepared we will be.

Tom: Well, if you gals are going to start planning for jobs, we guys had better get started too!

The counselor provided the opportunity for each member of the group to respond to other key questions from the CDI. After the implications of the questions were discussed, the counselor reiterated the need for thinking about and planning various career-related activities. This case illustrates the use of inventory questions to create discussion topics related to identified goals and specific tasks.

NEW MEXICO CAREER EDUCATION TEST SERIES (NMCETS)

The NMCETS is a good example of a vocational maturity test designed to assess specific objectives for career education programs for grades 9-12. This criterion-referenced test consists of six subtests, five competence scales and one attitude scale: attitude toward work, career planning, career-oriented activities, knowledge of occupations, job application procedures, and career development. Each test has general objectives and subobjectives stated in behavioral terms. Questions were derived from a review of the objectives of a national sample of career education programs.

The range of the subtest coefficients for grades 9 and 12 was .52 to .87 with the average near .66. According to Bodden (1978) these reliabilities are low primarily because of the small number of items used in the subtests. The authors claim validity on the basis of gains in the students' vocational readiness in grades 9-12. Independent T tests of 9th and 12th grade means were statistically significant, which lends support to the author's claim that the inventory assesses incremental program effects.

Because this test is relatively new, it should be considered experimental. There are some limitations to the test. The authors fail to provide adequate information on the counseling implications of the test results. In addition, the norms on this test are based completely on samples of students drawn from the public schools in New Mexico. The test is in need of further research and comprehensive normative data. Finally, the philosophical basis of the attitude scale should be scrutinized and its appropriateness for the target population carefully analyzed. The correct responses on this scale appear to be based on the authors' particular philosophy without sufficient evidence of validity. This instrument has been reviewed by Bodden (1978), Prediger (1978), and Westbrook (1978).

INTERPRETING THE NMCETS

Percentile and stanine norms for each of the six tests are provided for 9th and 12th grades. These scores aid in use of the test as a diagnostic tool for counseling. However, the authors suggest this test may be best used as a criterion-referenced measure of the effectiveness of career education programs in reaching established goals. Another important use of the NMCETS is in needs assessments for career education programs. This instrument seems to have great potential for prescribing specific activities. The dimensions measured by this instrument provide a solid foundation on which to base career education programs.

COGNITIVE VOCATIONAL MATURITY TEST (CVMT)

The CVMT is primarily a cognitive test of an individual's knowledge of occupations. Specifically, it measures knowledge of how to make realistic occupational choices; knowledge of work conditions, training requirements, and duties of various occupations; knowledge of sources of career information, planning skills, occupational and industrial trends, and employment-seeking skills. The authors emphasize that the test does not attempt to measure attitudes toward work (Westbrook & Parry-Hill, 1973). The test consists of 120 multiple-choice items; administration time is approximately 60 minutes. The reading levels for the subtests range from 1.4 to 2.2.

The test is divided into six subtests: fields of work (knowledge of occupations), job selection (knowledge of individual characteristics required for jobs), work conditions (knowledge of characteristics of work environments), education required (knowledge of educational requirements of jobs), attributes (knowledge of specific requirements of jobs), and duties (knowledge of duties performed in jobs). Each subtest yields its own score.

Internal consistency was established by KR-20 for all subtests grade 6-9. The coefficients range from .67 to .91. The criterion validity was based on data from a sample of ninth graders whose vocational choices were in their fields of interest and whose aptitude scores were considered appropriate for their career choice. These students tended to score higher on the subtests than did their counterparts, whose career choices were not in accord with their interests or aptitudes.

INTERPRETING THE CVMT

Westbook and Mastie (1973) suggest that the CVMT has value as a diagnostic test. It is also appropriate for evaluating needs for career education programs and the effectiveness of career education programs that have objectives that match the six areas measured. However, their general evaluation of the CVMT suggests that the instrument is in need of further research, and the current norm table should be used with a great deal of caution. In addition, content and construct validity of the subtests need to be researched and established. More data are also needed on the stability of the test. The measures of cognitive domain need refinement and expansion.

In the meantime, the CVMT may be used effectively as a criterion-referenced measure. For example, the CVMT may be used to assess individual readiness for career planning by evaluating the difference in scores obtained and projected or expected scores. It may also be used for assessing career program needs.

Needs Analysis for Program Development

The counselor at Jones High School received permission to participate in a follow-up survey of graduates sponsored by a national testing firm. The survey included those students who had graduated from Jones High within the last five years. The results of the survey pointed to a general weakness on the part of the high school in preparing students for making career decisions and in general in preparing them for the world of work. The counselor presented these results to the administration and later in a faculty meeting. He gained the support of the faculty and the administration for developing programs to prepare students for entering the labor market.

Although the committee formed to develop these programs was aware of the results of the recently completed survey, the members unanimously agreed that an analysis of current student needs would provide guidelines for building developmental programs. The CVMT was chosen primarily because of its six criterion-referenced measures. The committee agreed that this instrument could serve both as an indicator of needs and as an evaluation tool when used as a posttest. Financial limitations dictated that the test could be administered only to the freshman class.

The results of the CVMT indicated a general weakness among students in fields of work, work conditions, and attributes required. The committee decided to concentrate their efforts on these identified needs. Specifically they decided to sponsor specially designed seminars and to solicit the help of a selected group of teachers in developing modules that could be incorporated into classroom instruction. An example of a counseling component designed to enhance the students' knowledge of occupations had these technique options: published printed materials, microfiche systems, computer information systems, files. The specific tasks to be accomplished were: identify sources of occupational information, identify work worlds and how they relate to lifestyle, identify and assess occupational opportunities, relate identified skills and work experience to specific occupational requirements, evaluate how well occupations fulfill needs, relate identified goals to occupational choice, identify educational/training needs for specific occupations, identify expectations of future work and lifestyle.

The case of Jones High illustrates how the CVMT can identify specific needs of individuals—information that can then be used to develop programs. As an evaluation tool for program effectiveness the CVMT identifies weaknesses and strengths of the strategies used.

SUMMARY

The career maturity of adolescents, according to Super, is a stage of development with six dimensions: orientation to vocational choice, information and planning, consistency of vocational preferences, crystallization of traits, vocational independence, and wisdom of vocational preferences. These dimensions have become the foundation on which career maturity inventories are built. Thus, career maturity inventories measure degree of vocational development, attitudes toward work, and competence in coping with vocational developmental tasks. Career maturity inventories provide measures of the individual's readiness to enter certain career-related activities and are used to assess the effectiveness of career education programs.

QUESTIONS AND EXERCISES

1. What are career maturity inventories designed to measure?

2. Why is career maturity difficult to measure?

3. When can career maturity inventory results be used in career counseling programs? Illustrate with three examples.

4. How would you justify the use of a career maturity inventory to evaluate career education programs?

5. What are the advantages of using questions taken directly from a career maturity inventory to stimulate group discussion?

7

Using Interest Inventories

In one way or another almost everyone has been involved in the exploration of interests in deciding which activities to pursue for leisure
or in a career or both. To help in this exploration, interest inventories have long been associated with career guidance. Fryer (1931)
found, however, that asking people directly about their interests produced unreliable and often unrealistic results. His findings led to the
common pattern of taking an indirect approach to differentiate interests. The instruments reviewed in this chapter are based on this approach.

Because sex bias in interest assessment has received considerable
attention, I present a summary of this issue at the beginning of the
chapter. This summary is followed by a discussion of two widely used
interest inventories—the Strong-Campbell Interest Inventory and the
Kuder Occupational Interest Survey. Other, more recently developed inventories reviewed are the Self-Directed Search (Holland, 1973), the
Harrington/O'Shea Systems for Career Decision-Making (Harrington &
O'Shea, 1976), and the Non-Sexist Vocational Card Sort (Dewey, 1974).
Several examples of the use of interest inventories are provided.

SEX BIAS AND SEX FAIRNESS IN INTEREST ASSESSMENT

In recent years a considerable body of literature has concerned sex
bias and unfairness in career interest measurement. A number of the
most relevant articles have been compiled by Diamond (1975) under the
sponsorship of the National Institute of Education (NIE). The NIE pub-
lishes guidelines that identify sex bias as "any factor that might influence a person to limit—or might cause others to limit—his or her
consideration of a career solely on the basis of gender" (Diamond,
1975, p. xxiii).

According to Diamond, the guidelines have led to some progress in
reducing sex bias in interest inventories by calling for fairness in
the construction of item pools ("Items such as statements, questions,
and names of occupations used in the inventory should be designed so
as not to limit the consideration of a career solely on the basis of
gender"), fairness in the presentation of technical information ("Tech-

nical information should include evidence that the inventory provides career options for both males and females"), and fairness in interpretive procedures ("Interpretive procedures should provide methods of equal treatment of results for both sexes"). Generally, the guidelines are aimed at encouraging both sexes to consider all career and educational opportunities and at eliminating sex-role stereotyping by those using interest inventory results in the career counseling process.

Harmon (1975) suggests that sex bias is prevalent in most currently used interest inventories primarily because they assume that work is dichotomized into man's work and woman's work. This argument raises the issue of the kind of norms that should be used for interest measurement—that is, should there be separate or combined sex norms?

One answer to this question is given by Prediger & Johnson (1979). According to them, a method of reducing sex bias in interest inventories is the use of sex-balanced scales such as those provided in the unisex edition of the American College Test Interest Inventory. In this inventory, which uses combined sex norms, items are sex balanced because "they capture the essence of a work-related activity preference while minimizing sex-role connotations" (Prediger & Johnson, 1979, p. 11). The rationale is that combined sex norms can be used because sex-balance items elicit similar responses from men and women. The authors argue that different sets of occupational scales for men and women perpetuate sex-role stereotyping in that such items suggest the typical kinds of work performed by members of each sex.

Johansson (1975), however, believes separate norms should be used because he considers sex bias in interest inventories to be a result of our socialization process—that is, male/female stereotypes are an integral part of our society. Therefore, he recommends the use of separate sex norms for interpretive purposes until further research on sex bias in our society can be done. He points out that both the Strong-Campbell Interest Inventory and the Kuder Occupational Interest Survey employ separate sex norms.

Along the same lines, Holland (1975) suggests that vocational aspirations of men and women differ primarily because of their histories. As women's lives are changed in a society free of sex-role stereotyping or by counseling programs designed to minimize the effects of sex-role stereotyping, different patterns of interest will emerge. Holland argues that attention should be directed toward achieving an androgynous society rather than toward attacking interest inventories, which reflect early socialization and conditioning.

Conversely, Cole and Hansen (1975) suggest that we do not have to wait for a society free of sex-role stereotyping to evolve in order to broaden the interest patterns of women. They contend that presenting expanded career options for women in interest inventories will encourage exploration of a wide range of careers and thus provide increased opportunities. Within this frame of reference interest inventories should indeed be criticized if they do not provide equal options for men and women.

Birk (1975) suggests that the problem lies in the interpretation of interest inventory results. She believes that the lack of instructions for interpreting interest inventories to women perpetuates sex bias in career counseling programs. Because counselors may have to rely heavily on information contained in the test manual, she recommends that interest inventory manuals discuss problems of occupational stereotyping and other issues of sex bias and sex fairness. For example, the counselor should be informed that all jobs are available to any individual regardless of sex, that the purpose of interest inventories is to generate career options for both males and females, and that false notions concerning sex-role stereotyping among women need to be discussed and clarified. Furthermore, a summary of Title IX of the 1972 Educational Amendments of Higher Education should be provided. In essence, Birk suggests that revising the interest inventory manuals is the way to overcome the limitations of inventories caused by sex-role stereotyping.

In addition, Birk (1975) suggests that interpretation formats and materials should include guidelines for using score results to counsel women. Case studies of women in a variety of occupations would provide the counselor with representative examples of both sexes in the work force. Also, the same interpretation format should be used for both sexes. Interpretive materials should thus clearly establish that both men and women are to be encouraged to consider all occupations and college majors.

As Diamond (1975) points out, changes in interest inventory approaches may be slow. In the meantime, the career counselor has to rely heavily on manuals and research reports that describe limitations in the use of interest inventory scores for women. As more research becomes available, better guidelines for sex-fair interest inventories will be developed.

STRONG-CAMPBELL INTEREST INVENTORY (SCII)

The SCII replaced the well-known Strong Vocational Interest Blank (SVIB). The SVIB was based on empirical information gathered over several decades. Strong (1943) made no proper assumptions concerning the specific interest patterns of workers in the occupational groups he researched. Strong postulated that an individual who has interests that are similar to those of persons working in a given occupation is more likely to find satisfaction in that particular occupation than is a person who does not have common interests with those workers.

Several major changes were made with the publication of the SCII. Unlike its predecessor, the SCII uses Holland's (1973) theoretical framework to provide a system for interpretation of scores. In addition, the SCII has a single inventory for males and females. All items judged to be sexually biased were eliminated. Occupational titles were rewritten to be gender neutral, and new scales were developed so that both sexes could be evaluated on all scales (Campbell, 1974).

Despite these changes, the SCII has been attacked for its sex bias. Steinhaurer (1978) argues that differences between the interests of men and women with respect to work are not great enough to warrant separate treatment on an interest inventory. She concludes that such separate treatment promotes sex differences in career choices. Lunneborg (1978) agrees with this conclusion. The general opinion of these two reviewers is that combined scales should be developed.

The SCII is divided into seven parts with a total of 325 questions. On Parts I-V individuals indicate whether they like, are indifferent to, or dislike specific occupations, school subjects, activities, amusements, and types of people. On Part VI individuals indicate preference for a number of activities. On Part VII individuals choose statements that describe them. The reading level of the inventory is junior high school (Campbell, 1974). The SCII answer sheet is computer scored.

The reliability and validity studies for the SCII are comparable to those reported for the well-researched SVIB scales (Johnson, 1978). The stability of the SCII is well documented. Test-retest reliability studies include correlation coefficients (.50 and up) of 16-year-olds tested 35 years later. Other studies of shorter time intervals are also reported and indicate acceptable levels of reliability with correlation in the .90s. See reviews by Crites (1978), Dolliver (1978), Johnson (1978), Lunneborg (1978), and Steinhaurer (1978).

Dolliver, Irvin, and Bigley (1978), however, point out that the manual fails to provide relevant data for interpretation and research. Specifically, it should report mean and standard deviations for criterion groups (both men and women) on all occupational scales. However, Dolliver (1978, p. 1626) concludes that despite these limitations the SCII appears to be the best vocational interest inventory available.

Another major criticism of the SCII concerns its predictive validity. The results of a 12-year follow-up study of 220 clients counseled in the University of Missouri Counseling Center (Dolliver et al., 1978) revealed that the predictive validity of the SVIB was considerably less than that reported by Strong. However, Cronbach (1970) points out that many factors determine what field a person will enter. Interest inventories are not to be used to predict career choices but as measures for forecasting satisfaction in a career. If one is seeking a prediction of success, interest inventories combined with ability tests provide excellent measures (pp. 472-476).

The strength of the SCII is the variety of data generated on the interpretive report form. These data are useful in counseling and provide information that is usually not found on interest inventory profiles. In addition, the SCII has a well-documented history, which increases confidence in using this instrument.

INTERPRETATION OF THE SCII.

The interpretation process proceeds from a review of the general occupational themes scores, which provide a general overview of interest patterns, to the increasingly specific basic interest scores, and finally to measures of interests for specific occupations. Two of the companies that provide computer-generated profiles for the SCII are National Computer Systems (NCS) and Mincomp Corporation. Let us look first at a profile from NCS (Figure 7-1) for general occupational themes. This profile is structured around Holland's (1973) six occupational modal personal styles. Each of the six themes is reported by a standard score (mean = 50, S.D. = 10), indicating whether the interest level is considered very low, low, average, high, or very high. Shaded bars indicate norms for men; open bars indicate norms for women; asterisks indicate standard scores.

The basic interest scales focus on subdivisions of the general occupational themes—subdivisions from which career groups or clusters of occupations can be derived. For example, the R theme, shown in Figure 7-2, focuses on agriculture, nature, adventure, military activities, and mechanical activities. A standard score and norms are given for each scale. In this example, the individual has an average interest in adventure and low to very low interests on other scales for R theme.

Specific occupational scales are also grouped according to Holland's six themes (see Figure 7-3). Standard scores and male and female norms

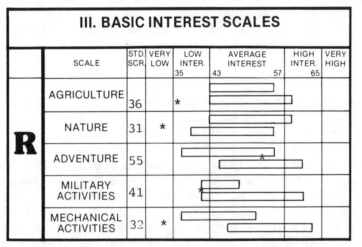

II. GENERAL OCCUPATIONAL THEMES

	SCALE	STD. SCR.	VERY LOW	LOW INTER. 35	AVERAGE INTEREST 43 57	HIGH INTER. 65	VERY HIGH
R	REALISTIC	30*					
I	INVESTIGATIVE	35	*				
A	ARTISTIC	59			*		
S	SOCIAL	43		*			
E	ENTERPRISING	36	*				
C	CONVENTIONAL	23*					

FIGURE 7-1. *SVIB-SCII profile*. From *Strong-Campbell Interest Inventory*, Form T325 of the STRONG VOCATIONAL INTEREST BLANK by Edward K. Strong, Jr. and David P. Campbell with the permission of the publishers, Stanford University Press. Copyright © 1974, 1981 by the Board of Trustees of the Leland Stanford Junior University.

III. BASIC INTEREST SCALES

	SCALE	STD. SCR.	VERY LOW	LOW INTER. 35	AVERAGE INTEREST 43 57	HIGH INTER. 65	VERY HIGH
R	AGRICULTURE	36		*			
	NATURE	31	*				
	ADVENTURE	55			*		
	MILITARY ACTIVITIES	41		*			
	MECHANICAL ACTIVITIES	32	*				

FIGURE 7-2. *R theme on SVIB-SCII profile*. From Strong-Campbell Interest Inventory, Form T325 of the STRONG VOCATIONAL INTEREST BLANK by Edward K. Strong, Jr. and David P. Campbell with permission of the publishers, Stanford University Press. Copyright © 1974, 1981 by the Board of Trustees of the Leland Stanford Junior University.

FEM. CODE	MALE CODE	OCCUPATION	FEMALE SCALE	MALE SCALE	VERY DISS. 15	DISSIMILAR 25	AVERAGE 44	SIMILAR 54	VERY SIM.	
S	S	ELEMENTARY TEACHER	24	37						
SEC	SCE	GUIDANCE COUNSELOR	20	18						
	S	LICENSED PRAC. NURSE		48						
SA	SIE	MINISTER	20	29						
SR	SR	PHYSICAL ED. TEACHER	10	21						
SRE	SRE	RECREATION LEADER	34	38						
SI		REGISTERED NURSE	33							**S**
SE	SE	SCHOOL ADMINISTRATOR	27	25						
SEC	SEC	SOCIAL SCIENCE TEACHER	31	32						
SA	SA	SOCIAL WORKER	31	41						
S	S	SPECIAL ED. TEACHER	48	39						
SA	SA	SPEECH PATHOLOGIST	48	50						
SE	SE	YWCA/YMCA DIRECTOR	23	35						

FIGURE 7-3. S occupational scale on SVIB-SCII profile. From Strong-Campbell Interest Inventory, Form T325 of the STRONG VOCATIONAL INTEREST BLANK by Edward K. Strong, Jr. and David P. Campbell with permission of the publishers, Stanford University Press. Copyright © 1974, 1981 by the Board of Trustees of the Leland Stanford Junior University.

are reported on a profile that indicates whether the subject's interests are very dissimilar, dissimilar, average, similar, or very similar for each of the occupations.

Eleven administrative indices are reported on the SCII profile. Among these are an infrequent response index, which indicates whether the individual has marked a significant number of rare or uncommon responses. In this event, a negative score is reported and responses should be carefully checked. In some cases individuals may have become confused when filling out the answer sheet and answered the items in the wrong order. Other individuals may have purposely marked false choices. Still others may have unique interests.

The academic comfort scale (ACS) indicates the degree to which the individual likes academic work, such as reading, writing, and doing research. This scale should be checked for individuals considering higher education as follows: B.A. students should have a mean score of 50, M.A. students 55, and Ph.D. students 60 on this scale. A comprehensive list of these scores for male and female occupations is in the manual.

The introversion-extroversion (IE) index is an indicator of the individual's preference for working with things or with people. This scale thus provides an index to preferences for people-oriented occupations or non-people-oriented occupations.

Another index reports the percentages of like (LP), indifferent (IP), and dislike (DP) responses for each section of the inventory. Unusual responses can be determined by comparing these percentages with those in the table provided in the test manual (see Page 90 of the manual). These percentages provide important information for the counselor. For example, high percentages on dislike indicate that an individual may be strongly committed to a specific interest area; in other words, the individual has narrowed interests or likes to one or a few occupational areas. An individual with few like responses to occupational choices may also have intensely focused interests or that individual's interests may not have crystallized yet. The counselor will want to explore these possibilities by further analysis of responses to various items on the SCII.

On the back of each SCII profile is a detailed explanation of all the scores, scales, and administrative indices and a brief summary of the theoretical orientation from Holland (1973). Most individuals can interpret their own scores by carefully reading this material. Technical descriptions of scales and references are provided for the counselor's information.

In order to make maximum use of the information on the SCII profile, a systematic evaluation is recommended. For this purpose a SCII summary evaluation form such as Table 7-1 can be devised. The counselor begins by checking the number of total responses. If there are fewer than 310, the results of the inventory should be considered questionable. Items 2-5 concern the administrative indices and should be completed as outlined.

The pattern, or the general occupational themes, should be reviewed next. This pattern is a reflection of the counselee's general occupational preferences, or modal personal styles. An individual whose highest standard scores are 61 for C theme, 50 for I theme, and 45 for E theme has a summary code of CIE. This person's primary modal personal style (C) is conventional, which indicates a practical, rather conservative individual according to Holland's (1973) typology. The occupation associated with this style is general office work, such as that done by an accountant or credit manager. Information on the secondary modal personal style (I) and information on the overall pattern (CIE) also provide clues for the career counseling process.

The highest scores on the basic interest scales should also be carefully reviewed. Particular attention should be given to the career groups reported as high or very high. An interest in a career group or cluster may be the key to further exploration if a specific occupation cannot be identified.

The occupational scales provide specific information for a career search. A score of 45 or higher on an occupational scale indicates interests that are similar to those of individuals in that occupation. A score of 55 or higher indicates a very similar interest pattern. Scores of 45 and higher should be carefully reviewed as possible career choices.

The Mincomp Corporation of Denver provides two computer-generated SCII profiles. One is similar to the NCS profiles in that identical information is provided. The form of presenting the data is different in that the Mincomp form groups the information generated for each theme together. Another difference in this form is that scores on opposite-sex measures are provided. The summary evaluation form shown in Table 7-1 can be used to compile information from this Mincomp report.

The other Mincomp SCII report is in narrative form. The report begins with a printout of the individual's scores on the six general occupational themes followed by a brief description of how to interpret them. The report then gives a detailed explanation of the individual's highest rated theme and other themes with high scores or moderately high scores. Included with the description of each theme are scores on the basic interest scales with *Dictionary of Occupational Titles* (DOT) (U.S. Department of Labor, 1977) and *Occupational*

TABLE 7-1. SCII Summary Evaluation Form*
_____

Steps

1   Responses—less than 310—(stop for checking)
2   Infrequent responses—(minus number)—check manual
3   ACS—(BA mean score of 50, MA mean score of 55, Ph.D. mean
        score of 60)
4   IE—(considered extroverted if 40 or under, introverted if
        60 or over)
5   LP, IP, DP (boundary 5-60)

        Record section which is outside of limits and refer to Page
        90 of manual.

        _____   _____   _____

6   Summary code for three highest General Occupational Themes
        and two examples of variation of theme.

        _____   _____   _____

        _____   _____   _____

        _____   _____   _____

7   Record Basic Interest Scales shown as high and very high.

        -

        -

        -

8   Record Occupational Scales with scores from 45-55.

        _____

        _____

        _____

        _____

9   Record Occupational Scales with scores of 55 and higher.

        _____

        _____

        _____

        _____
_____

    *Used with *Strong-Campbell Interest Inventory*, Form T325 of the
STRONG VOCATIONAL INTEREST BLANK by Edward K. Strong, Jr. and David P.
Campbell with permission of the publishers, Stanford University Press.
Copyright © 1974, 1981 by the Board of Trustees of the Leland Stanford
Junior University.

Outlook Handbook (OOH) (U.S. Department of Labor, 1978-1979) numbers. The occupational scales are reported by grouping the three highest general occupational themes and by combining the highest scored themes (IRS, IR, IA, I). DOT and OOH numbers are also included with specific training times. The next part of the report is an evaluation of the individual's high-interest occupations.

The remainder of the report includes the scores made by the individual on the general occupational themes, the basic interest scales, and the occupational scales. The administrative indices are also reported. This portion of the report form can serve as a summary of scores for the entire inventory. The individual is reminded to spend time reviewing the low scores reported on the profile primarily for an indication of the kind of work that should not be considered in the career exploration process. The SCII narrative report by Mincomp Corporation is straightforward and should be easily interpreted by most individuals who are capable of completing the inventory.

Case of a College Freshman Undecided about a Career

Al, a second-semester freshman in college, told the career counselor that he needed help in determining his interests. He added that none of the college courses he had taken so far had stimulated him to consider a specific career. As a result he felt as though he were drifting. His father, successful in business, was putting pressure on Al to make up his mind. Al appeared to be serious about wanting to determine his interests for career considerations.

Counselor: We will gladly administer and interpret an interest inventory for you. However, I want you to understand that the results of the inventory may not pinpoint a career for you to consider.

Al: Oh! I thought it would tell me what I should do for the rest of my life.

Counselor: Many students share your belief. They have high expectations of interest inventories and are disappointed when they get their results. Realistically, we can expect to find some occupations for you to explore further or an occupational group you may wish to investigate. I should add that we also often find that a student will simply have his or her interests confirmed by a test.

Al: Okay, that's fair enough. I need some information to help me get started toward making a career decision.

The counselor continued with an explanation of the career decision process. After he was satisfied that Al understood that interest inventory results are to be used with other factors in career exploration, the counselor discussed the selection of an interest inventory. "The SCII provides a comparison of your responses to responses of individuals in a number of career fields. With these results you can determine how similar your interests are to those of individuals who have made a commitment to a specific career. You will also be able to identify some of your general occupational interests and some of your basic interests." The counselor and Al selected the SCII because it includes many careers that require a college degree and suggests many occupational groups for further exploration. Al's results from the SCII were compiled as shown in Figure 7-4.

The counselor began the interpretation session with a review of the career decision process. He then presented Al with the profile of the results. He explained the occupational themes designated by certain letters: "The first is the R theme, which stands for realistic. Individuals who have high scores on this theme generally prefer to work with objects, machines, or tools. Examples are those in the skilled trades such as plumbers, electricians, and machine operators. Other examples are photographers and draftsmen. You have a low score for this theme." The counselor continued to explain each theme in a similar manner.

The counselor directed Al's attention to the summary code of his three highest general occupational themes. He emphasized the importance of considering combinations of interests as opposed to considering just one high interest area. In Al's case the AES summary code suggested an interest in occupations that involve art, writing, sales, and management, and that are service oriented. The counselor suggested that consideration be given to different combinations of the summary code: EAS, SAE, and so on.

The counselor then went to the next part of the report and explained that the basic interest scales are also grouped according to one of the six themes. Al's highest scores were noted, and specific occupational scales were discussed. Finally, the counselor pointed out occupational scales with scores from 45 to 55. Several of the occupations seemed to interest Al.

The counselor suggested that they review the results of the SCII by having Al summarize what he learned about himself: "I seem to be interested in artistic kinds of work. At least this was my highest general occupational theme. I also have an interest in enterprising activities and socially related activities. I guess I like working with people to some extent particularly in influencing or persuading them. Specific occupations that interest me are advertising and sales work. I would like to explore the advertising and public relations occupations."

FIGURE 7-4. SCII summary evaluation form for Al.

<u>Steps</u>

1   Responses - less than 310 - (stop for checking) **325**

2   Infrequent responses - (minus number) check manual *none*

3   ACS - (BA mean score of 50, MA mean score of 55, Ph.D. mean score of 60) **52**

4   IE - (considered extroverted if 40 or under, introverted if 60 or over) **31**

5   LP, IP, DP (boundary 5-60) *none*

Record section which is outside of limits and refer to Page 90 of manual.

_____   _____   _____

6   Summary code for three highest General Occupational Themes and two examples of variation of theme.

A	E	S
E	A	S
S	A	E

7   Record Basic Interest Scales as shown as high and very high.

  - A - *art and writing*
  - E - *merchandising, sales, business management*
  - S - *social service*

8   Record Occupational Scales with scores from 45-55.
art teacher, photographer, interior decorator,
life insurance agent

_____

9   Record Occupational Scales with scores of 55 and higher.
advertising executive, artist, sales manager

_____

_____

_____

The counselor was satisfied with this summary, as Al was able to link the inventory results with potential career fields. The counselor encouraged Al to refer to the interest inventory results for other options if he was not satisfied with his career search.

KUDER OCCUPATIONAL INTEREST SURVEY (KOIS)

Kuder (1963) identified clusters of interest by administering questionnaires listing various activities to individuals employed in different occupational areas. Items that were highly correlated with each other were grouped together in descriptive scales. Groups of items that had lower correlations with each other were formed into nine clusters and designated as broad areas of interest. In this system a specific occupational interest is determined by common factors or traits found within a broad area.

TABLE 7-2. Four Kuder Inventories

Preference Schedule or Interest Survey	Form	Target Population	Scoring
Kuder Preference Record—Vocational	CP and CM	High school students and adults	CP—Hand scored CM—Machine scored
Kuder Preference Record—Personal	AH	High school students and adults	Hand scored
Kuder General Interest Survey	E	Junior and senior high school students	Hand scored
Kuder Occupational Interest Survey	DD	Students in grades 9-12, college students, and adults	Computer scored

From the *Kuder Occupational Interest Survey*, Form DD, Interpretive Leaflet © 1979, 1974, 1970, 1966, G. Frederic Kuder. Reprinted by permission of the publisher, Science Research Associates, Inc.

Kuder developed four inventories as shown in Table 7-2. The most recent inventory, the KOIS, is illustrated here to provide an example of the use of the inventories for career counseling. The format of the inventories requires the individual to respond to triads of items by indicating the most liked and least liked activity. The following scales are used in the Kuder surveys: outdoor, mechanical/computation, scientific, persuasive, artistic, literary, musical, social service, and clerical. A list of specific occupations correlated with each scale is provided. None of the inventories has a time limit, but each can usually be taken in 30 to 40 minutes. The KOIS requires computer scoring.

The KOIS report form for females is shown in Figure 7-5. The first two columns report occupational scales by sex and indicate whether the scales are twin scales—that is, whether scores are reported in both the male and female columns. The third column reports college major scales. An asterisk indicates a top score or significant score, and the individual is directed to give greatest consideration to those scales.

Report of Scores   Kuder Occupational Interest Survey   Form DD

NAME HARRIS SANDRA   FEMALE   65760   DATE 08/15/79

OCCUPATIONAL SCALES	NORMS M	NORMS F	OCCUPATIONAL SCALES	NORMS M	NORMS F	COLLEGE MAJOR SCALES	NORMS M	NORMS F
OFFICE CLERK		.50*	>DENTIST	.32		>PHYSICAL EDUC		.46*
STENOGRAPHER		.48*	ENGINEER, ELEC	.32		HOME ECON EDUC		.44*
>BOOKKEEPER		.47*	ENGINEER, MECH	.32		>MATHEMATICS		.43*
>FLORIST		.47*	MATHEMATICIAN	.32		BUS ED & COMMERC		.42*
BANK CLERK		.46*	POLICE OFFICER	.32				
DEPT STORE SALES		.45*	PHOTOGRAPHER	.31		>MUSIC & MUSIC ED		.40*
PRIMARY SCH TCHR		.45*	VETERINARIAN	.31		AGRICULTURE	.40*	
BEAUTICIAN		.44*	DEAN OF WOMEN		.30	ANIMAL HUSBANDRY	.40*	
HOME DEMONST AGT		.44*	NUTRITIONIST		.30	>ELEMENTARY EDUC		.39
AUTO MECHANIC	.43*		SOC WORKR,SCHOOL		.30	HEALTH PROFES		.39
CARPENTER	.43*		>MATH TCHR,HI SCH	.30		NURSING		.38
NURSE		.42	>PHYS THERAPIST	.30		DRAMA		.37
SECRETARY		.42	SALES ENG,HT/AIR	.30		>FOREIGN LANGUAGE		.37
ELEM SCHL TCHR	.42*		>COUNSELOR,HI SCH		.29			
>INTERIOR DECORAT	.42*		HOME EC TCHR COL		.29	>BIOLOGICAL SCI		.36
POSTAL CLERK	.42*		>SOC WORKER,GROUP		.29	>ART AND ART EDUC		.35
WELDER	.42*		ARCHITECT	.29		ENGINEERNG,CIVIL	.35*	
>MATH TCHR,HI SCH		.41	>COMPUTR PROGRAMR	.29		FORESTRY	.35*	
OCCUPA THERAPIST		.41	OPTOMETRIST	.29		>HISTORY		.33
BRICKLAYER	.41*		REAL ESTATE AGT	.29		ENGINEERING,MECH	.33	
MACHINIST	.41*		RELIGIOUS ED DIR		.28	SOCIAL SCI, GENL		.32
>DENTIST		.40	>SOCIAL CASEWORKR		.28	TCHG CATH SISTER		.32
>PHYS THERAPIST		.40	SOC WORKER,MEDIC		.28			
>X-RAY TECHNICIAN		.40	>AUDIOL/SP PATHOL	.28		>MUSIC & MUSIC ED	.32	
ELECTRICIAN	.40*		PEDIATRICIAN	.28		>PHYSICAL EDUC	.32	
PLUMBER	.40*		PHYSICIAN	.28		>ELEMENTARY EDUC	.31	
>LIBRARIAN		.39	>SCIENCE TCHR, HS	.28		ENGINEERING,ELEC	.31	
>FLORIST	.39*		>SOC WORKER,PSYCH		.27	>FOREIGN LANGUAGE	.31	
PAINTER, HOUSE	.39*		OSTEOPATH	.27		>SOCIOLOGY		.30
>COMPUTR PROGRAMR		.38	PHARMACIST	.27		>ART AND ART EDUC	.30	
DENTAL ASSISTANT		.38	RADIO STATON MGR	.27		>PSYCHOLOGY		.29
FORESTER	.38*		CHEMIST	.26				
DIETITIAN,SCHOOL		.37	ENGINEER, INDUS	.25		>ENGLISH		.28
>BOOKSTOR MANAGER	.37*		JOURNALIST	.25		ARCHITECTURE	.26	
TRUCK DRIVER	.37*		YMCA SECRETARY	.25		BUS MANAGEMENT	.26	
>BOOKSTOR MANAGER		.36	>LAWYER		.24	AIR FORCE CADET	.26	
>PHYSICIAN		.36	PSYCHOLOGIST		.24	MILITARY CADET	.26	
BANKER	.36		>PSYCH, CLINICAL		.24	>POLITICAL SCI		.25
>BOOKKEEPER	.36		>LAWYER	.24		BUS & MARKETING	.25	
BLDG CONTRACTOR	.36		>ACCT,CERT PUBLIC	.23		ENGINEERING,CHEM	.25	
FARMER	.36		MINISTER	.23				
PLUMBING CONTRAC	.36		PERSONNEL MANAGR	.23		>MATHEMATICS	.25	
SUPERVSR,INDUSTR	.36		PSYCHIATRIST	.23		BUS ACCT AND FIN	.24	
BUYER	.35		SCHOOL SUPT	.23		PHYSICAL SCIENCE	.24	
ENG,HEAT/AIR CON	.35		>COUNSELOR,HI SCH	.22		>BIOLOGICAL SCI	.22	
PLANT NURSRY WKR	.35		PHARMACEUT SALES	.22		>SOCIOLOGY	.21	
>X-RAY TECHNICIAN	.35		PODIATRIST	.22		ECONOMICS	.20	
>ACCOUNTANT		.34	>SOCIAL CASEWORKR	.22		>ENGLISH	.20	
DIETITIAN, ADMIN		.34	>SOC WORKER,PSYCH	.22		>HISTORY	.20	
COUNTY AGRI AGT	.34		STATISTICIAN	.22				
ENGINEER, CIVIL	.34		>PSYCH, CLINICAL	.17		PREMED/PHAR/DENT	.19	
INSURANCE AGENT	.34		PSYCH, INDUSTRIAL	.17		LAW-GRAD SCHOOL	.18	
PRINTER	.34		PSYCHOLOGY PROF	.17		>PSYCHOLOGY	.17	
TRAVEL AGENT	.34		>SOC WORKER,GROUP	.17		>POLITICAL SCI	.14	
TV REPAIRER	.34		PSYCH,COUNSELING	.15				
>AUDIOL/SP PATHOL		.33	UNIV PASTOR	.15				
CLOTHIER, RETAIL	.33							
ENG,MINING/METAL	.33							
>LIBRARIAN	.33							
METEOROLOGIST	.33							
>INTERIOR DECORAT		.32						
>SCIENCE TCHR, HS		.32						
AUTO SALESPERSON	.32							

```
                    V    55

          M    .39      S    .38

          MBI -.12      F    .34

          W    .46      D    .42

          WBI -.13      MO   .42
```

Your scores are reported to you in rank order, on all scales. They show to what extent the choices you marked were like those typical of satisfied people in the occupations and college majors listed. Your top scores are followed by an asterisk (*). (For additional information and for an alphabetical list of scales, see the other side of this report.)

> INDICATES TWIN SCALES, WITH SCORES IN M AND F COLUMNS.

© 1979, 1970, 1968, 1965. Science Research Associates, Inc. All rights reserved   Printed in the United States of America   7-3870

FIGURE 7-5. KOIS report form. From the *Kuder Occupational Interest Survey,* Form DD, Interpretive Leaflet © 1979, 1974, 1970, 1966, G. Frederic Kuder. Reprinted by permission of the publisher, Science Research Associates, Inc.

In the lower right corner of the report form, the verification (V) scale is used to determine whether the individual is sincere or capable of responding to the survey. A V score of 44 or less calls into question the validity of the scale scores. Questionable survey results may be the result of carelessness, faking, or poor reading ability. If the V score is below 44, the counselor should make a determination of the cause before continuing the interpretation. (Specific instructions for determining the cause of low scores are provided in the manual.) The eight experimental scales offer only tentative information and should be reviewed in the test manual.

The relationship of the individual's responses to the response patterns of a given occupational group is determined by a special correlation technique. Over three-fourths of the individuals in the 30 occupational groups compiled by Kuder scored .45 or over on the items for their groups. Thus, a score of .45 or more indicates an occupational scale that should be considered in a career search. A word of caution: some high school students may score low on the occupational scales because of their lack of experience in and awareness of the world of work. Conversely, because of their current academic experiences, some high school students may score high on college major scales.

Occasionally profiles have most coefficients below .31. These low scores may be a consequence of immaturity and a lack of experience and may thus indicate interests have not been crystallized. Low scorers may also have misunderstood the directions or may simply have marked responses in a careless, random manner. At any rate, if only a few coefficients reach .32–.39 caution should be used in the interpretation of the scores (Kuder, 1979).

Scores on opposite-sex scales should be given consideration especially by females when female norm scales are not available. Significantly high scores reported for females on male norms indicate possible areas to consider in the career search. Broad patterns should also be considered, as many individuals have not crystallized their interests.

Two types of reliability are reported in the KOIS manual. Test-retest reliabilities (two-week interval) for students in grades 12 and in college had stable coefficients in that the median coefficient was .90. Other test-retest studies involving male high school seniors and female college seniors yielded coefficients in the .90s. One long-term study (approximately three years) of engineering students yielded a test-retest coefficient of .89. Concurrent validity was established by studying errors of classification of six validation groups. The findings suggested that the KOIS is able to discriminate between various criterion groups (W. B. Walsh, 1972). There is a need for more data on the predictive validity of this instrument.

The KOIS interpretive material is straightforward and easily used. The separation of occupational scales and college major scales adds to the flexibility and usefulness of this inventory. The KOIS has been reviewed by W. B. Walsh (1972), Stahmann (1972), and Brown (1972).

Case of a High School Senior Rebelling against Parental Expectations

Ann, a high school senior, had been the topic of conversation during many coffee breaks in the teachers' lounge at City High School. The major concern of the teachers was her complete lack of interest in academic courses. Yet Ann's parents were well educated and were prominent members of the art and music groups in the city. Ann's grades reflected her lack of interest, and she had successfully resisted receiving any counseling assistance. Her parents finally convinced her to see the school counselor. As expected, Ann approached the counselor in a casual manner and quickly admitted that the visit was her parents' idea. The counselor spent several sessions with Ann attempting to get her to respond positively. Ann responded with enthusiasm only when the counselor brought up the subject of future plans.

The counselor decided that she might be able to win Ann's confidence through career exploration. Ann had taken the KOIS during her junior year. A review of the results revealed that only a few of the coefficients reached .36 and .39. The counselor remembered that the manual mentioned that such scores should be used with caution. However, she decided to discuss the results with Ann. Ann said, "I didn't care about that test. What's the use of taking an interest inventory when you don't have many choices in the first place?"

The counselor asked Ann to explain her remarks. Ann indicated that she had marked the inventory haphazardly without even reading some of the options. When the counselor asked her to explain her statement about not having many choices, Ann was rather hesitant. After a brief pause she responded "Nobody cares or understands so why bother?" Ann eventually revealed that she felt hemmed in and unable to identify with her parents' expectations. She expressed a negative view of their lifestyle and emphasized that she wanted something different. She felt her parents were unaccepting of her needs and interests. Ann summed up her feelings: "So what's the use of saying what I want?"

In the sessions that followed the counselor encouraged Ann to express her interests and individuality. Nevertheless, Ann remained confused about a career. Ann agreed to retake the KOIS but with a changed attitude and a different approach to responding to the choices.

When the counselor received the results of the KOIS, she began by observing the V score. Because that score was well above .44, the scores were considered valid. Next, she reviewed Ann's high scores (Table 7-3).

TABLE 7-3. KOIS Scores for Ann

Occupational Scales		College Major Scales	
Social caseworker	.60	General social science	.59
Social worker, psychiatric	.58	Psychology	.57
Social worker, school	.56	Sociology	.54
Nurse	.55	Nursing	.53
X-ray technician	.51		

Ann seemed eager to discuss the results when she arrived for the counseling session. The counselor cautioned Ann that these scores would not solve all her problems but would provide vital information that could be used for career exploration. The counselor then explained the scores, and Ann pointed out those above .45. Although Ann seemed interested in the results of the KOIS, this was the first time she had given serious thought to exploring a career on her own, and she needed reinforcement by the counselor. She expressed an interest in working with people in some capacity but also recognized that her knowledge of careers and working environments was extremely limited. She agreed to become a part of a career decision group, which she entered armed with several occupational considerations provided by the KOIS. The counselor was pleased with Ann's progress, particularly in expressing her individual needs and interests.

SELF-DIRECTED SEARCH (SDS)

The SDS is based on Holland's (1973) theory of career development. It can be self-administered, self-scored, and self-interpreted. Individuals begin by making a list of occupational aspirations, then indicate likes or dislikes for certain activities. Next they indicate activities that they can perform well or competently and identify occupations that appeal to or interest them. Finally, they evaluate themselves on 12 different traits based on previous experience. Individuals calculate their scores according to easily understood directions and subsequently record the three highest scores in order. The three highest scores are determined by adding scores of responses to most liked activities, activities done most competently, interest in occupations, and self-estimates of traits. These scores are organized to reveal a summary code of three letters representing the personality styles in Holland's typology—realistic, investigative, artistic, social, enterprising, and conventional.

The following information can be obtained for each summary code: primary modal personal style, primary occupational environment, specific occupations, and DOT numbers of specific occupations (from Viernstein, 1972) for cross-reference. Individuals are then able to compare their occupational codes to occupational aspirations and to codes for 495 occupations provided in *The Occupations Finder* (Holland, 1979a) booklet. A portion of the information found in *The Occupations Finder* is shown in Figure 7-6.

If, for example, an individual's summary code is RSC, the occupations listed under this code are primary occupations for further exploration. In the Holland system the more dominant the primary modal personal style, the greater the likelihood of satisfaction in the corresponding work environment (Holland, 1973). In order to investigate other career possibilities, the individual is required to list related summary codes. In the above example, different combinations of the summary code RSC should be explored: SRC, SCR, CRS, CSR, and RCS.

Internal consistency was calculated by KR-20 and yielded coefficients ranging from .67 to .94 from samples of 2000 to 6000 college freshmen. Of that group, coefficients for men ranged from .63 to .88 and for women from .53 to .85. Test-retest reliabilities (3-4-week intervals) for high school students yielded a median coefficient of

REALISTIC OCCUPATIONS (CONTINUED)

CODE: RSE (cont.)	ED
Waiter/Waitress (311.677-010)	3
Parking-Lot Attendant (915.473-010)	2
Soda Clerk (319.474-010)	2
Warehouse Worker (922.687-058)	1

CODE: RSC	ED
Exterminator (389.684-010)	3
Elevator Operator (388.663-010)	2
Stock Clerk (222.387-058)	2
Kitchen Helper (318.687-010)	1

CODE: RSI	ED
Vocational Agriculture Teacher (091.227-010)	5
Appliance Repairer (637.261-018)	4
Weaver (683.682-038)	3
Knitter (685.665-014)	2

CODE: REC	ED
Supervisor, Natural-Gas Plant (542.130-010)	4

CODE: REI	ED
Ship Pilot (197.133-026)	4
Shop Supervisor (638.131-026)	4
Supervisor, Paper Machine (539.132-010)	4

CODE: RES	ED
Fish and Game Warden (379.167-010)	5
Cattle Rancher (410.161-018)	4
Locomotive Engineer (910.363-014)	4
Crater (920.484-010)	3
Braker, Passenger Train (910.364-010)	3
Construction Worker (869.664-014)	3
Fisher (442.684-010)	2
Track Layer (s869.687-026)	2

CODE: RCI	ED
Surveyor, Geodetic (018.167-038)	5
Carpenter (860.381-022)	4

CODE: RCI (cont.)	ED
Instrument Mechanic (710.281-026)	4
Motion-Picture Projectionist (960.362-010)	4
Office-Machine Servicer (633.281-018)	4
Signal-Tower Operator (Railroad Trans) (910.362-010)	4
Supervisor, Painting (840.131-010)	3
Surveyor Helper (869.567-010)	3

CODE: RCS	ED
Furrier (783.261-010)	4
Tailor (785.261-010)	4
Telephone Repairer (822.281-022)	4
Bus Driver (913.463-010)	3
Sewage-Plant Operator (955.362-010)	3
Blaster (859.261-010)	3
Bricklayer (861.381-018)	3
Cement Mason (844.364-010)	3
Dressmaker (785.361-010)	3
Furnace Installer (862.361-010)	3
Garment Cutter (781.584-014)	3
Mail Carrier (230.367-010)	3
Meter Reader (209.567-010)	3
Miner (939.281-010)	3
Paperhanger (841.381-010)	3
Plasterer (842.361-018)	3
Sailor (911.687-030)	3
Tile Setter (861.381-054)	3
Industrial-Truck Operator (921.683-050)	2
Spinner (682.685-010)	2

CODE: RCE	ED
Crane Operator (921.663-010)	3
Lumber Inspector (669.587-010)	3
Tractor Operator (929.683-014)	3
Tractor-Trailer-Truck Driver (904.383-010)	3
Truck Driver, Light (906.683-022)	3
Fork-Lift Truck Operator (921.683-050)	2

FIGURE 7-6. Portion of The Occupations Finder. From *The Occupations Finder* for use with *The Self-Directed Search* by John L. Holland, copyright © 1978. Consulting Psychologists Press, Inc. Reprinted by permission.

.81 for boys and a median coefficient of .83 for girls. A sample of 65 college freshmen yielded test-retest reliability coefficients ranging from .60 to .84 over a seven- to ten-month interval. There appears to be sufficient evidence of content validity from item content. A number of studies supporting the predictive validity of the SDS have been compiled and are reported in the SDS manual (Holland, 1979b).

The SDS is designed to furnish the individual with a model of systematic career exploration. Although the SDS can be self-interpreted, the individual should be stimulated to seek further career guidance. Many individuals will want to clarify their interests with a counselor who can provide additional information for career decision-making. The SDS provides results that can be easily incorporated into group and individual career counseling programs.

One of the major criticisms of the SDS centers around a need for monitoring the self-scoring of the instrument. Also, individuals often need assistance in using *The Occupations Finder* according to Dolliver and Hansen (1978). Finally, more data are needed and should be reported in the manual on the use of the SDS for women, minority groups, and adults. Extensive reviews of the SDS include those by Crites (1978), Brown (1978), Seligman (1978), Cutts (1978), and Dolliver and Hansen (1978).

Holland is to be commended for encouraging people to consider their careers by using a straightforward format. The popularity of the SDS demonstrates the need for this type of format. His theoretical approach to personality development as a primary consideration in career decision-making has greatly influenced methods for presenting results on a number of widely used interest inventories.

Group Program in a Community College

A community college counseling center regularly offered seminars in career exploration. A major component of the program involved interest identification. In one all-male group, the SDS was administered with the counselor monitoring the scoring.

After each student had recorded his SDS code, the counselor explained Holland's six modal personal styles and their corresponding codes, then grouped students according to their personal styles. Using *The Occupations Finder*, each group was assigned the responsibility of writing and presenting at the next session a description of its primary modal personal style and of one or more specific occupations that matched this style.

In the next counseling session, the counselor gave each member a copy of *The Occupations Finder*. The counselor explained the use of this booklet for locating specific occupations by summary codes. The counselor noted that DOT codes as well as educational levels were listed for each of the summary codes. When the counselor was sure that everyone understood how to use the booklet, he made this assignment: "Each of you is to use the career resource center library and write a description of two more occupations under your summary code using our career planning notes to record your comments. Bring these completed forms with you to our next session." Figure 7-7 gives examples for draftsman (RIE) and pharmacist (IES).

During the next group meeting the counselor encouraged members to relate problems encountered with locating careers according to their summary codes and to ask questions concerning their career exploration. Each member was encouraged to investigate other combinations of his SDS code. For example, the counselor suggested that the individual who made the report on drafting, RIE, investigate occupations under IRE, IER, and other combinations. Each member was requested to share his career planning notes with other members in his group. All group members were invited for individual counseling sessions and were encouraged to evaluate other occupations they were considering including an evaluation of the educational/training requirements and potential for employment.

FIGURE 7-7. *Career Planning notes completed by community college students.*

1. Occupation _Draftsman_
2. Source of Information _Encyclopedia of Career and Vocational Guidance, Vol II_
3. Educational Requirements _Some college and technical training_
4. Personal Requirements _Good hand-eye, visual-motor coordination. Be able to work with detailed plans and lay-out sketches. Be able to visualize objects in three-dimensional form._

5. Salary Range _$10,000 to $15,000_
6. Outlook _Favorable although employment is affected by general business year._
7. Other Notes _Conditions of work are good, that is, usually work is well-lighted, air-conditioned buildings._

1. Occupation _Pharmacist_
2. Source of Information _Opportunities in Pharmacy Careers_
3. Educational Requirements _5 years of college, 4 years of college and 1 year in pharmacy._
4. Personal Requirements _Be good in sciences, particularly in chemistry. Be willing to keep precise records and work with precise measures._

5. Salary Range _$12,000 to $20,000 and up_
6. Outlook _Good work available with firms, drug chains, or on your own._
7. Other Notes _Pharmacists usually work long hours and are respected in the community._

HARRINGTON/O'SHEA SYSTEMS FOR CAREER DECISION-MAKING (CDM)

The CDM (Harrington & O'Shea, 1976) can also be self-administered and self-interpreted. Holland's (1973) theory of career development is the framework on which the system has been constructed. Five of Holland's six occupational types have been given different names: realistic has been changed to crafts, investigative has been changed to scientific, artistic has been changed to the arts, social remains as is, enterprising has been changed to business, and conventional has been changed to clerical (Harrington & O'Shea, 1976). Care was taken to make all items in the system applicable to both men and women. The results are reported independently of sex.

The format requires the individual to list occupational preferences, choose favorite school subjects, indicate future educational plans, choose four job values from a list, estimate four strongest abilities, and indicate interests and activities by responding to "like," "can't make up my mind," or "dislike."

There are three CDM systems: S, I, and P. System S is a self-scoring form. Individuals are instructed to find their two highest combined raw scores, such as social-crafts or business-clerical, and then to match these career codes with career clusters. For example, an individual having a career code of social-crafts has the following career cluster: personal service, social service, and customer service. An interpretive folder provides general information on career decisions, defines the six scales used in the system, and provides 12 steps for interpreting the results of the survey. Information on the 18 career clusters includes typical jobs, related school subjects, training, values, abilities, DOT numbers, and OOH page and reference numbers.

System I provides a comprehensive, computer-generated interpretation of the CDM. This narrative covers information on the interpretation of scores, career choices, career cluster, educational preferences, abilities, training, job values, and national employment outlook. Some individuals may indicate a preference for career areas for which they do not have high scores on the survey. In this event the narrative report also covers these career areas for the individual.

INTERPRETING YOUR SCORES

YOU SHOULD BE AWARE THAT MOST PEOPLE DO NOT FALL INTO ONLY ONE AREA. INSTEAD, COMBINATIONS OF A PERSONS HIGHEST TWO OR THREE SCORES ARE MOST USEFUL IN SUGGESTING APPROPRIATE OCCUPATIONS FOR EXPLORING. WE HAVE DIVIDED UP THE WORLD OF WORK INTO 18 CAREER AREAS. EACH AREA CONTAINS JOBS THAT ARE VERY SIMILAR IN THAT ALL THE JOBS IN THE AREA INVOLVE THE SAME COMBINATION OF OCCUPATIONAL INTERESTS. FOR EXAMPLE, MEDICAL-DENTAL JOBS HAVE BEEN GROUPED TOGETHER BECAUSE THEY CALL FOR SCIENTIFIC AND SOCIAL SERVICE ACTIVITIES AND INTERESTS. THUS, A PERSON WHOSE HIGHEST SCORES ON THIS SURVEY ARE SCIENTIFIC AND SOCIAL SERVICE WILL HAVE THE MEDICAL-DENTAL FIELD SUGGESTED AS ONE AREA FOR CLOSE STUDY.

ABILITIES

THE ABILITIES YOU RATED ON THE SURVEY AS YOUR STRONGEST WERE:

MATH ABILITY   -SOLVING MATH PROBLEMS AND UNDERSTANDING ARITHMETIC REASONING.
SCIENTIFIC ABILITY -DOING LABORATORY EXPERIMENTS AND UNDERSTANDING SCIENTIFIC PRINCIPLES.

MANUAL ABILITY   -PREFERRING TO WORK WITH YOUR HANDS AS
                       IN PHYSICAL WORK OR SEWING AND KNIT-
                       TING.
SOCIAL ABILITY   -ABILITY TO WORK WITH PEOPLE, CONSID-
                       ERED FRIENDLY BY OTHERS.

   LETS SEE HOW WELL YOUR SELF-RATINGS AGREE WITH WHAT
MEDICAL AND DENTAL WORK DEMANDS. FOR MOST CAREERS IN THIS
AREA A HIGH LEVEL OF SCIENTIFIC ABILITY, MATH ABILITY,
LANGUAGE ABILITY, SOCIAL ABILITY,AND SPATIAL ABILITY IS
NECESSARY. MANUAL ABILITY IS REQUIRED IN SEVERAL OF THE
OCCUPATIONS, FOR EXAMPLE, DENTIST AND CHIROPRACTOR. IF YOU
HAVE NOT RATED YOURSELF HIGH ON MOST OF THESE ABILITIES
AND ARE CONSIDERING A CAREER IN MEDICINE OR DENTISTRY, YOU
MIGHT WANT TO DISCUSS THIS WITH A COUNSELOR.
   IN THE SPACES BELOW WRITE IN THE MEDICAL-DENTAL JOBS
WHICH AGREE MOST WITH YOUR ABILITIES.

_____   _____   _____

_____   _____   _____

JOB VALUES

   MEDICINE AND DENTISTRY PROVIDE AN OPPORTUNITY TO REALIZE
MANY VALUES AND SEVERAL IN PARTICULAR: PRESTIGE, GOOD
SALARY, HIGH ACHIEVEMENT, VARIETY, CREATIVITY, WORK WITH
THE MIND, JOB SECURITY, WORKING WITH PEOPLE, LEADERSHIP AND
INDEPENDENCE. COMPARE THESE VALUES WITH THOSE THAT YOU SAID
IN THE SURVEY YOU PRIZE MOST HIGHLY, THAT IS:

JOB SECURITY   -HAVING A STEADY JOB FROM WHICH YOU ARE
                     UNLIKELY TO BE FIRED.
GOOD SALARY   -BEING WELL PAID FOR YOUR WORK.
ROUTINE ACTIVITY -WORK THAT IS UNCOMPLICATED AND ORGANIZED
                     WITH THE TASKS REPEATED OVER AND OVER.
WORK WITH PEOPLE -WORKING IN CLOSE CONTACT WITH PEOPLE, BE-
                     ING ABLE TO COMFORT AND ASSIST OTHERS.

   REMEMBER THAT VALUES ARE HIGHLY PERSONAL. HOWEVER, IF
YOUR VALUES ARE DIFFERENT FROM THOSE THAT ARE MOST OFTEN
REALIZED IN THE MEDICAL-DENTAL FIELD, THEN YOU MIGHT NOT
FIND SATISFACTION IN IT.
   NOW GO BACK TO THE LIST OF JOBS GIVEN ABOVE AND IN THE
SPACES BELOW WRITE IN THOSE CAREERS WHICH SEEM MOST IN
AGREEMENT WITH YOUR VALUE SYSTEM.

_____   _____   _____

_____   _____   _____

NATIONAL EMPLOYMENT OUTLOOK

   ENTRY INTO MANY HEALTH OCCUPATIONS IS RESTRICTED BY THE
LIMITED NUMBER OF OPENINGS IN THE VARIOUS TRAINING SCHOOLS.
THUS COMPETITION AMONG THE MANY QUALIFIED APPLICANTS IS
STRONG. THE EMPLOYMENT OUTLOOK IS VERY GOOD FOR PHYSICIANS,
DENTISTS, AND OSTEOPATHIC PHYSICIANS. FAVORABLE OPPORTUNI-
TIES EXIST FOR OPTOMETRISTS, VETERINARIANS, AND PODIATRISTS.

THERE WILL BE A FAVORABLE DEMAND FOR SPEECH PATHOLOGISTS
AND AUDIOLOGISTS WHO EARN A MASTERS DEGREE; HOWEVER, THERE
MAY BE GROWING COMPETITION AS LARGE NUMBERS OF GRADUATES
ENTER THE FIELD. THE INCREASING EMPHASIS ON THE MASTERS
DEGREE WILL LIMIT OPPORTUNITIES FOR THOSE WITH A BACHELORS
DEGREE. ENROLLMENTS IN CHIROPRACTIC COLLEGES ARE GROWING
RAPIDLY AS THE PROFESSION GAINS ACCEPTANCE. AS A RESULT,
OPPORTUNITIES FOR CHIROPRACTORS MAY BECOME MORE RESTRICTED.

MEDICAL-DENTAL

MEDICAL-DENTAL IS THE CAREER AREA THAT YOUR SCALE SCORES
WOULD SUGGEST FOR PRIMARY CONSIDERATION. IN GENERAL, JOBS
IN THIS AREA INVOLVE ACTIVITIES OF A SCIENTIFIC AND TECH-
NICAL NATURE TO FURTHER THE HEALTH AND WELL BEING OF
OTHERS. MEDICAL CAREERS DEMAND A GREAT DEAL OF DECISION-
MAKING BASED ON PERSONAL JUDGMENT OF THE FACTS IN THE CASE.
LETS SEE WHAT SOME OF THE TYPICAL JOBS ARE IN THIS AREA,
WHAT THESE JOBS INVOLVE, AND THE PREPARATION AND ABILITIES
THEY DEMAND.

JOBS	JOB ACTIVITIES	REQUIREMENTS
ANESTHESIOLOGIST	APPLIES KNOWLEDGE	SUPERIOR INTELLEC-
OBSTETRICIAN	OF MEDICAL OR	TUAL CAPACITY AND
PEDIATRICIAN	DENTAL SCIENCE	ACHIEVEMENT IN
PSYCHIATRIST	TO THE DIAGNOSIS,	SCHOOL; ANALYTICAL
RADIOLOGIST	PREVENTION AND	ABILITY IN DIAGNO-
OSTEOPATHIC	TREATMENT OF	SIS; VERBAL ABILITY
PHYSICIAN	HUMAN AND ANIMAL	TO USE MEDICAL
DENTIST	DISEASE, DISORDERS	TERMINOLOGY; SPA-
VETERINARIAN	AND INJURIES.	TIAL PERCEPTION TO
AUDIOLOGIST		USE X-RAYS; FINGER
CHIROPRACTOR;		AND MANUAL DEX-
PODIATRIST		TERITY; MOTOR CO-
SPEECH		ORDINATION; NUMERI-
PATHOLOGIST		CAL ABILITY FOR
OPTOMETRIST		STUDY OF BASIC SUB-
PHYSICIAN		JECTS SUCH AS CHEM-
ORTHODONTIST		ISTRY; ABILITY TO
		WORK AND MAKE DECI-
		SIONS UNDER HEAVY
		STRESS; STAMINA TO
		MAINTAIN ALERTNESS,
		CONCENTRATION, AND
		PERFORMANCE FOR
		LONG PERIODS; 8 TO
		9 YEARS OF PREMED-
		ICAL OR PREDENTAL
		AND MEDICAL OR
		DENTAL TRAINING
		PLUS 3 TO 6 YEARS
		IN MANY OF THE
		AREAS TO DEVELOP
		SPECIALIZED SKILLS;
		STATE LICENSE

SEE OCCUPATIONAL OUTLOOK HANDBOOK PAGES 365, 372, 373, 374, 376, 378, 4Ø5; WORK GROUP Ø2.Ø3[2]

The system P profile provides almost the same information as and has the same format as system S with the exception of the score report, which is a computer printout. System P is different from system I in that it does not have a narrative report. System P can only be computer scored. The first part of the profile for system P lists scales in rank order. The second part of the profile lists career areas and typical jobs suggested by the score report. In addition, the profile reports stated occupational preferences, school subject preferences, future plans, values, and abilities. Further classifications of the results of the survey are also provided.

Coefficients of internal consistency for the six interest scales for high school and college males ranged from .86 to .90 and for females from .84 to .90. Test-retest reliability coefficients (30-day interval) for high school students ranged from .75 to .88 for males and from .78 to .90 for females. Test-retest reliability coefficients (30-day interval) for graduate students in social science ranged from .76 to .94 for males and from .78 to .88 for females. These measures of reliability appear to be sufficient, although the number of cases (24-75) was small.

The authors have accumulated impressive evidence of construct and concurrent validity primarily by comparing the CDM scales with corresponding SCII and SDS scales. Predictive validity is not attempted because the authors suggest that the CDM is designed for self-exploration, not for predicting the occupation an individual will enter. More data are being collected and will be reported in a revised manual. For further evaluation of this instrument refer to the review by Willis (1978).

The CDM provides a comprehensive model for career decision-making. It can best be used for those in junior high school and older subjects (including adults). Minority group norms are available, and the authors claim the test has no sex bias. Although scores can be self-interpreted, the authors recommend seeing a professional for continuation of career planning. Again, the major purpose of the CDM is to provide data that will encourage self-exploration in the career decision process.

NON-SEXIST VOCATIONAL CARD SORT (NSVCS)

One promising method of exploring women's interests is the NSVCS, developed by Dewey (1974). This instrument was derived from a modified version of the Tyler's vocational card sort method (Tyler, 1961) by Dolliver (1967). The NSVCS is described as a nonsexist method in that the same occupational options are presented to both sexes, occupational titles have been neutralized (salesperson rather than salesman), and sex-role biases are confronted and discussed. The NSVCS consists

[2]*The System for Career Decision-Making*, by T. G. Harrington & A. J. O'Shea. Distributed by Chronicle Guidance Publications, Inc., Moravia, New York. Reprinted by permission.

of seventy-six 3 × 5 cards containing occupational titles derived from male and female forms of the SVIB and KOIS. Each occupation is coded according to Holland's classification system as discussed earlier.

Administration of the NSVCS has four steps. First, the individual sorts the cards into three piles: "would not choose," "in question," and "might choose." Second, the individual discusses with the counselor occupations in the category "would not choose," giving reasons for placing occupations in this category; some of the remarks are recorded by the counselor. The individual then cites reasons for placing occupations in the other two categories. Third, the individual selects and rank orders ten occupations based on their personal appeal, fantasy of associated lifestyle, and perceptions of associates on the job. The counselor encourages the individual to also consider such factors as values and abilities. Fourth, the individual and the counselor discuss the remarks recorded in earlier sessions, and the individual describes perceptions of certain occupations. During this time women are encouraged to discuss sex-role biases associated with occupations and to clarify their own positions in regard to sex-role stereotyping.

Dewey suggests that the NSVCS encourages women to form new self-perceptions and attitudes about themselves and to confront the issue of sex-role stereotyping in career decision-making. Although she does not claim that these procedures and techniques will completely solve the problem of sex-role stereotyping, they do provide women with the opportunity to enhance their career potential.

The NSVCS and other card-sort programs are viable alternatives to standardized interest inventories for women. After comparing the impact of the SCII and the VCS, Cooper (1976) concludes that the VCS is more effective than the SCII for encouraging career exploration among women. Dolliver (1967) suggests that a major advantage of the card sort is that client attitudes and self-perceptions are elicited during the sorting process. This process encourages women to confront the issues of sex-bias and sex-role stereotyping in the career decision process.

Case of a Woman Dissatisfied with Secretarial Work

Jackie, a 23-year-old woman, was employed as a secretary even though she had a B.A. in psychology. She was considering enrolling in graduate school as a way of escaping the monotony of her low-paying job. After administering the NSVCS, the counselor noted several themes: "I am depressed; I feel wasted and angry. I want to be involved in a kind of work which is socially relevant but do not want to work directly with people. I want to be able to express my creativity and to have the freedom to choose the directions I develop toward. While I want autonomy, I am really afraid of being in a leadership position with a lot of responsibility."

Because the counselor was familiar with this last fear—having a lot of responsibility—she pointed out to Jackie that many women lower their vocational aspirations as a result of this fear. The session that followed dealt with how easy it was for Jackie to accept the limits that she had internalized as a result of the female socialization process without ever testing them out for herself. She told of an experience in adolescence that fit this theme. She had wanted to run for student government president in her high school but had been encouraged by her advisor, her mother, and female friends to seek the vice-presidency instead. She recalled other times when she had set goals for herself that others had sabotaged by redirecting her to a different goal. The counselor acknowleged Jackie's anger and resentment and pointed out that women are taught in many subtle ways that they function best in supportive, nurturing, or secondary roles.

One field Jackie chose to explore further was parapsychology, a field that both challenged and excited her. She had given up her interest in it before in response to her parents' notion that it was weird. Through the NSVCS experience, Jackie began to get some notion of how she could separate her own feelings, values, and experiences from those of her family and friends. She was thus able to begin the process of redirecting her energy toward fulfilling her own needs.[3]

OTHER INTEREST INVENTORIES

The following are examples of other interest inventories currently being used. This list is far from complete, as a considerable number of interest inventories are published today. Some measure general interests, while others measure interests in specific occupational fields.

Ohio Vocational Interest Survey. This survey is for students in grades 8-12. Testing time is between 60 and 90 minutes. The 24 interest scales are related to people, data, and things. This survey is designed primarily to measure general interests.

Brainard Occupational Preference Inventory. This inventory is designed for use in grades 8-12. Testing time is approximately 30 minutes. Scores are expressed in percentiles for men and women. Scores yield individual preference for six broad fields: commercial, mechanical, professional, aesthetic, scientific, agriculture (men only), and personal service (women only). These measured preferences provide guidelines for career exploration.

Career Assessment Inventory. This computer-scored inventory can be administered in 45 minutes. It is for individuals 15 years and older. There are three types of scales provided. One is a general occupational theme scale providing a measure of an individual's orientation to work. Basic attitude scales provide measures of interest and their relationship to specific careers. This inventory is designed to be used primarily with individuals who are not planning on going to college.

Minnesota Vocational Interest Inventory. This inventory is designed for men 15 years and older. There are 21 occupational scales and 9 general interest scales. Standard T scores (mean = 50, S.D. = 10) are reported. This inventory is useful for measuring interest in nonprofessional occupations.

[3]Adapted from the *Non-Sexist Vocational Card Sort*, by C. R. Dewey. Copyright © 1976 by Cindy Rice Dewey. Reprinted by permission.

SUMMARY

Interest inventories have a long association with career counseling. Strong and Kuder were pioneers in the interest measurement field. More recently Holland's theory of careers greatly influenced the presentation of interest inventory results. The NIE guidelines on sex bias (Diamond, 1975) have led to some reduction in sex biases on interest inventories. However, we need to reevaluate our entire approach to interest measurement.

QUESTIONS AND EXERCISES

1. In what instances would you choose the SCII over the KOIS? Give reasons for your choice.

2. How would you explain to a high school senior that measurements of interests do not necessarily indicate how successful one would be in an occupation?

3. A college student states he knows what his interests are but can't decide on a major. How would you justify suggesting that he take an interest inventory?

4. How would you interpret an interest inventory profile that has no scores in the above-average category? What would you recommend to the individual who took the inventory?

5. Defend or criticize the following statements: Interests are permanent over the life span. An individual will have the same interests in 1905 as in 1985.

8
Using Personality Inventories

The term *personality* can cover a multitude of perceptions. For example, the statement "She has the personality to be a good sales representative" suggests that the individual has such traits as gregariousness, friendliness, aggression, strong drive, and is well-adjusted. All of these are the kinds of characteristics and traits a career counselor is interested in measuring to some degree. Counselors turn to personality inventories to measure individual differences in social traits, motivational drives and needs, attitudes, and adjustment—vital information in the career exploration process.

A number of career theorists have stressed the importance of considering personality factors and characteristics in career guidance. Super, Starishevsky, Matlin, and Jordaan (1963) emphasize the importance of self-concept in career counseling. Holland (1973) relates modal personal style to work environments. Roe (1956) stresses the influence of early personality development on vocational direction. Tiedeman and O'Hara (1963) emphasize the role of total cognitive development in decision-making. Despite this emphasis on the relationship between personality development and career development, personality inventories have not been used extensively in career counseling. The current trend toward the use of computer-interpreted personality inventories could provide a much needed impetus for improving the quality and increasing the quantity of personality measures and for promoting their use in career counseling.

Cronbach (1970, p. 550) suggests that personality measures are to be used like interest measures—that is, "as a mirror to help the individual examine his view of self." Like interest inventories, personality measures provide topics for stimulating dialogue. Through discussion the individual confirms or disagrees with the results and comes to understand the relationship of personality characteristics to career decisions.

Four computer-scored measures of personality are presented in this chapter along with one non-computer-scored inventory. In addition examples are provided that illustrate the use of personality inventories in career counseling.

EDWARDS PERSONAL PREFERENCE SCHEDULE (EPPS)

The EPPS measures 15 personality variables based on Murray's (1938) manifest needs. The instrument was designed to measure "normal" personality variables for research and counseling purposes. The inventory is untimed, can be taken in approximately 40 minutes, and is hand or computer scored. These 15 personality variables are measured by the EPPS (Edwards, 1959): achievement—a need to accomplish tasks well; deference—a need to conform to customs and defer to others; order—a need to plan well and be organized; exhibition—a need to be the center of attention in a group; autonomy—a need to be free of responsibilities and obligations; affiliation—a need to form strong friendships and attachments; intraception—a need to analyze behaviors and feelings of others; succorance—a need to receive support and attention from others; dominance—a need to be a leader and influence others; abasement—a need to accept blame for problems and confess errors to others; nurturance—a need to be of assistance to others; change—a need for variety and novel experiences; endurance—a need to follow through on tasks and complete assignments; heterosexuality—a need to be associated with and attractive to members of the opposite sex; aggression—a need to express one's opinion and be critical of others.

The inventory consists of pairs of statements that are related to needs associated with each variable. Individuals are required to choose the statement more characteristic of them. Some of the paired statements require the individual to indicate likes and dislikes, as shown by this example:

A. I like to talk about myself to others.
B. I like to work toward some goal that I have set for myself.

Other paired statements require the individual to describe feelings, as shown by this example:

A. I feel depressed when I fail at something.
B. I feel nervous when giving a talk before a group.[1]

As individuals select these statements, they are indicating needs as measured by this instrument. Thus, someone choosing statements associated with the achievement variable may have a strong need to be successful, to be a recognized authority, to solve difficult problems. Likewise, someone choosing statements associated with the succorance variable may have a strong need to have others provide help and to seek encouragement from others.

INTERPRETATION OF THE EPPS

Results are reported as percentiles (Figure 8-1). Percentile tables are provided for college students and general adult groups with separate sex norms. A consistency variable is used to determine whether the answering pattern is consistent enough to be considered valid.

---

[1]From *Edwards Personal Preference Schedule*, by A. L. Edwards. Copyright 1954, © 1959 by The Psychological Corporation. Reprinted by permission.

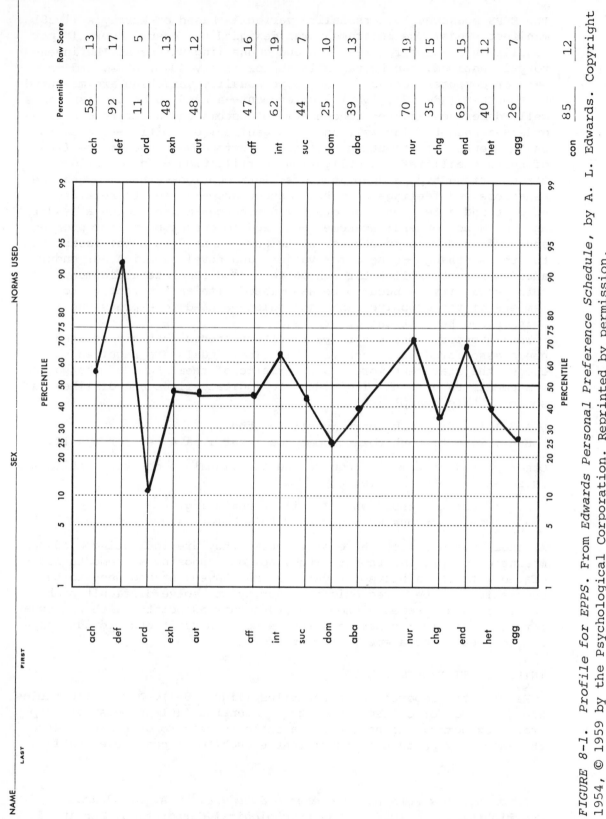

NAME _____
LAST   FIRST

SEX _____

NORMS USED _____

	Percentile	Raw Score
ach	58	13
def	92	17
ord	11	5
exh	48	13
aut	48	12
aff	47	16
int	62	19
suc	44	7
dom	25	10
aba	39	13
nur	70	19
chg	35	15
end	69	15
het	40	12
agg	26	7
con	85	12

FIGURE 8-1. Profile for EPPS. From *Edwards Personal Preference Schedule*, by A. L. Edwards. Copyright 1954, © 1959 by the Psychological Corporation. Reprinted by permission.

Although the EPPS is not widely used at the present time, it can provide useful information for career counseling. For example, a significantly high score on the deference scale indicates that the individual prefers to let others make decisions and does not have a strong need to be placed in a leadership role. By the same token, an individual with a significantly low score on the order scale would probably not enjoy a job requiring neatness and organization. This individual should probably not be directed to office work that has highly structured procedures and strict rules and regulations.

Combinations of needs can also be explored for their relationship to careers. A combination of achievement and dominance, for example, indicates that an individual needs to be recognized as an authority and prefers to direct the actions of others. Such an individual may be task oriented, may strive to become a recognized authority, and may tend to dominate others. These personality traits are desirable in many managerial and sales positions.

A word of caution: an individual's needs do not always have the same priority—that is, an individual's preferences may change over the life span. EPPS results indicate current preferences, needs, and personal orientation and should be considered as only one factor in career decision-making.

Split-half reliabilities for the 15 scales of this inventory range from .60 to .87; test-retest reliabilities (one-week interval) range from .74 to .88. Few validity data are reported in the manual. Independent validation studies have yielded inconclusive results (Anastasi, 1976). According to Anastasi (1976, p. 513) the EPPS is in need of "(a) revision to eliminate certain technical weaknesses particularly with regard to item form and score interpretation, and (b) properly conducted validation studies." For further evaluation of this instrument see reviews by Heilbrun (1972) and McKee (1972).

Although the EPPS has questionable validity, the needs measured by this instrument are a viable consideration in career counseling. The results can be used effectively to explore an individual client's currently dominant needs in relation to less dominant ones. Thus, this instrument is recommended for promoting discussion of personal needs and their relationship to careers.

Case of a College Sophomore Undecided about a Specific Career Area

Mary, a college sophomore, was interested in a business career but could not decide on the area of business that would be best for her. Past academic performance and previous achievement test data indicated that Mary was a capable college student. Following the counselor's suggestions she collected information on a variety of careers through conferences with faculty members from the school of business and in the career resource center.

In the next conference with the counselor she reported that she was able to eliminate some careers through her research but remained interested in several possibilities including accounting, insurance, marketing, and management. The counselor asked Mary whether she had ever considered need fulfillment in relation to a career. The idea of meeting personal needs in the business field intrigued Mary, and she became interested in learning more about her needs. The EPPS was

selected and administered primarily because it measures manifest
needs. The counselor's strategy was to have Mary identify her needs
and relate them to the work environments of the occupations she was
considering.

Mary's three highest scores were on the change, exhibition, and
dominance scales. Her lowest scores were on the deference and abasement scales. The counselor asked Mary to read the explanation of the
manifest needs associated with her three highest scores and two lowest
scores in the manual.

Mary summarized the results: "I like variety and change in daily
routine. I also have a need to live in different places. I like to experiment and experience the excitement that goes with it. This I agree
with wholeheartedly! I can't see myself sitting in an office every day,
month after month. I also cannot see myself doing the same thing over
and over again. Yes, I have a need for change and variety.

"The exhibition scale worried me at first. But I have to agree. I do
have a need to be considered witty by others, and I like being clever
and the center of attention. I guess I've always wanted to be popular
and be around people.

"I definitely agree with the dominance scale. I have a strong need to
be a leader. In fact, I have always striven for a leadership position.
To be a leader is important to me. This seems to verify my low-order
needs as measured by this inventory—deference (deferring to others)
and abasement (feeling inferior to others). I'm just the opposite."

The counselor praised Mary for her summary and asked her how these
identified needs could be translated into a career choice. The counselor suggested she review the information she had compiled from researching occupations and relate this information to need satisfaction.
She responded that she could probably satisfy her need to be a leader
in almost all the careers she had considered in business. However,
after some thought, she came to the conclusion that management and marketing would provide greater opportunities for variety and change than
would accounting and insurance.

Mary and the counselor continued their discussion of management and
marketing. They concluded this session with an agreement on the next
step in the career exploration process: Mary was to gather additional
information on the current and projected job market for the two careers before making a final decision.

SIXTEEN PERSONALITY FACTOR QUESTIONNAIRE (16PF)

The first form of the 16PF was published in 1949 (Cattell, Eber, &
Tatsuoka, 1970). There are now six forms for measuring the same 16
personality dimensions in individuals 16 years and older. Four forms
(A, B, C, D) have an adult vocabulary level; two forms (E, F) are for
low-literacy groups.

The 16 personality characteristics, or factors, measured are shown
in Table 8-1. These 16 primary factors are source traits, or combinations of traits considered to be components of an individual's personality. Items in the test were selected because they correlated
highly with a particular factor, but a given item may also correlate

TABLE 8-1. *Primary Source Traits Covered by the 16PF*

Factor	Low Sten Score Description (1-3)	High Sten Score Description (8-10)
A	Reserved, detached, critical, cool, impersonal Sizothymia	Warmhearted, outgoing, participating, interested in people, easy-going Affectothymia
B	Less intelligent, concrete-thinking, Lower scholastic mental capacity	More intelligent, abstract-thinking, bright Higher scholastic mental capacity
C	Affected by feelings, emotionally less stable, easily upset, changeable Lower ego strength	Emotionally stable, mature, faces reality, calm, patient Higher ego strength
E	Humble, mild, accommodating, easily led, conforming Submissiveness	Assertive, aggressive, authoritative, competitive, stubborn Dominance
F	Sober, prudent, serious, taciturn Desurgency	Happy-go-lucky, impulsively lively, enthusiastic, heedless Surgency
G	Expedient, disregards rules, feels few obligations Weaker superego strength	Conscientious, persevering, proper, moralistic, rule-bound Stronger superego strength
H	Shy, restrained, threat-sensitive, timid Threctia	Venturesome, socially bold, uninhibited, spontaneous Parmia
I	Tough-minded, self-reliant, realistic, no-nonsense Harria	Tender-minded, intuitive, unrealistic, sensitive Premsia
L	Trusting, adaptable, free of jealousy, easy to get on with Alaxia	Suspicious, self-opinionated, hard to fool, skeptical, questioning Protension
M	Practical, careful, conventional, regulated by external realities Praxernia	Imaginative, careless of practical matters, unconventional, absent-minded Autia
N	Forthright, natural, genuine, unpretentious Artlessness	Shrewd, calculating, socially alert, insightful Shrewdness
O	Unperturbed, self-assured, confident, secure, self-satisfied Untroubled adequacy	Apprehensive, self-reproaching, worrying, troubled Guilt proneness
Q_1	Conservative, respecting established ideas, tolerant of traditional difficulties Conservatism of temperament	Experimenting, liberal, analytical, likes innovation Radicalism
Q_2	Group oriented, a "joiner" and sound follower Group adherence	Self-sufficient, prefers own decisions, resourceful Self-sufficiency
Q_3	Undisciplined self-conflict, careless of protocol, follows own urges Low integration	Controlled, socially precise, following self-image, compulsive High self-concept control
Q_4	Relaxed, tranquil, torpid, unfrustrated Low ergic tension	Tense, frustrated, driven, restless, overwrought High ergic tension

From *Handbook for the Sixteen Personality Factor Questionnaire (16PF)* by R. B. Cattell, H. W. Eber, M. M. Tatsuoka, 1970. Institute for Personality and Ability Testing. Reproduced by permission of the copyright owner.

with other factors (Cattell et al., 1970). Thus a combination of items measures each distinct factor, but parts of that factor may be correlated with parts of other distinct factors. Understanding this principle aids in the interpretation of this instrument.

The first 12 traits in Table 8-1 are designated by letters used for identifying these personality factors within a universal standard system. This alphabetical identification system is widely used by professional psychologists when referring to personality factors. In communicating the meaning of the personality factors to the general public, more descriptive terms are used. The factors Q_1 through Q_4 have been given these labels because they are unique to the 16PF at this time (Cattell et al., 1970).

Attention should be directed to factor B, which is considered to be an intelligence scale. This scale has been designed to give equal weight to fluid and crystallized ability factors (Cattell, 1963) and to provide a dimension of general ability. It is suggested that this scale be supplemented with other intelligence tests when providing career counseling for occupations requiring high ability levels.

INTERPRETING THE 16PF

The 16 personality factors shown in Table 8-1 make up the profile and are reported by the use of stens. A bipolar description is provided for each source trait to make the interpretation of scores meaningful.

A major part of the research on the 16PF has been devoted to identifying vocational personality patterns and occupational fitness projections. In the handbook (Cattell et al., 1970) over 70 occupational patterns are reported by sten units. Specific occupations are arranged in 24 occupational groups. For example, the group air industry personnel contains reports on airline hostesses, pilots, engineers, and apprentices. Table 8-2 provides a description of two occupations as an example of the information the career counselor will find useful.

TABLE 8-2. Two 16PF Occupation Descriptions

Group	Specific Occupations	Significant Characteristics
Air industry personnel	Aircraft engineering apprentice	High ego strength and high self-discipline, preference for technical, realistic orientation, low sophistication.
Executive and industrial supervisors	Supermarket personnel	Interpersonal warmth, raised level of anxiety, paying attention to detail, mediocre general ability.

Note. Adapted from 16PF Manual by IPAT Staff, 1972, 1979, Institute for Personality and Ability Testing, Inc. Reproduced by permission of the copyright owner.

The 16PF can be hand scored or computer scored. The hand-scored forms report scores for 15 personality factors and an intelligence measure as shown in Table 8-1. The computer-scored narrative interpretation form provides an abundance of information in addition to the personality profile. An example of a narrative report form follows:

PRIMARY PERSONALITY CHARACTERISTICS OF SIGNIFICANCE
CAPACITY FOR ABSTRACT SKILLS IS HIGH.
HIS REACTION TO SITUATIONS IS SOBER, SERIOUS, AND CAUTIOUS.
AS A PERSON, HE IS TENDER-MINDED AND AESTHETICALLY SENSI-
TIVE. HE IS INCLINED TO BE IMAGINATIVE, TO DISREGARD PRAC-
TICAL, CONVENTIONAL MATTERS, AND TO BE ABSORBED IN IDEAS.
IN THIS RESPECT HE IS EXTREMELY HIGH. BEING SELF-SUFFI-
CIENT, HE PREFERS TACKLING THINGS RESOURCEFULLY, ALONE.
PRODUCES A CASUALNESS IN THIS PERSON.
BROAD INFLUENCE PATTERNS
HIS PERSONALITY ORIENTATION IS INTROVERTED. THAT IS, HIS
ATTENTION IS DIRECTED INWARD TO THOUGHTS AND FEELINGS.
THIS TENDENCY IS HIGH (7.7).
TASKS AND PROBLEMS ARE APPROACHED WITH EMPHASIS UPON
EMOTIONAL RELATIONSHIPS. LESS ATTENTION IS PAID TO RATIONAL
AND OBJECTIVE CONSIDERATIONS. THIS TENDENCY IS ABOVE AVER-
AGE (6.5).
HIS LIFE STYLE IS INDEPENDENT AND SELF-DIRECTED, LEADING TO
ACTIVE ATTEMPTS TO ACHIEVE CONTROL OF THE ENVIRONMENT. IN
THIS RESPECT, HE IS ABOVE AVERAGE (6.5).
CLINICAL OBSERVATIONS
NEUROTIC MALADJUSTMENT IS ABOVE AVERAGE (7.4).
ANXIETY LEVEL IS AVERAGE (5.8).
EFFECTIVENESS OF BEHAVIOR CONTROLS IS BELOW AVERAGE (3.9).
TREATMENT CONSIDERATIONS
THE INFLUENCE OF A CONTROLLED ENVIRONMENT MAY HELP. SUG-
GESTIONS INCLUDE EMPHASIS UPON PLANS AND THEIR EXECUTION
TO DEVELOP SELF-DISCIPLINE
VOCATIONAL OBSERVATIONS
AT CLIENT'S OWN LEVEL OF ABILITIES, POTENTIAL FOR CREATIVE
FUNCTIONING IS EXTREMELY HIGH (10.0).
POTENTIAL FOR BENEFIT FROM FORMAL ACADEMIC TRAINING, AT
CLIENT'S OWN LEVEL OF ABILITIES, IS VERY HIGH (8.7).
IN A GROUP OF PEERS, POTENTIAL FOR LEADERSHIP IS LOW (2.7).
NEED FOR INTERPERSONAL ISOLATION, AT WORK, IS VERY HIGH
(8.9).
NEED FOR WORK THAT TOLERATES SOME UNDEPENDABILITY AND IN-
CONSISTENT HABITS IS ABOVE AVERAGE (6.7).
POTENTIAL FOR GROWTH TO MEET INCREASING JOB DEMANDS IS
ABOVE AVERAGE (6.7).
THE EXTENT TO WHICH THE CLIENT IS ACCIDENT PRONE IS ABOVE
AVERAGE (6.7).[2]

Occupational fitness projections provide a comparison of the individual's profile with a sample of occupational profiles as shown on
the next page.

[2]From 16PF by R. B. Cattell, H. W. Eber, and M. M. Tatsuoka, 1967.
Institute for Personality and Ability Testing, Inc. Reproduced by
permission of the copyright owner.

OCCUPATIONAL FITNESS PROJECTIONS
TO PROVIDE A STRONGER FOUNDATION FOR VOCATIONAL PREDICTIONS
FROM THESE PERSONALITY SCORES, THE CLIENT'S PROFILE HAS
BEEN COMPARED TO A SAMPLE OF OCCUPATIONAL PROFILES. ALL OF
THE FOLLOWING PROJECTIONS MUST BE MADE RELATIVE TO THE CLI-
ENT'S SPECIFIC ABILITIES AND MOTIVATIONAL LEVEL. CONSE-
QUENTLY, THEY MUST BE REGARDED AS TENTATIVE RATHER THAN
CONCLUSIVE. FOR CONVENIENCE, THE SPECIFIC PROFILES HAVE
BEEN GROUPED INTO SEVERAL CATEGORIES.
1. ARTISTIC PROFESSIONS
       ARTIST   EXTREMELY HIGH
       MUSICIAN   ABOVE AVERAGE
       WRITER   EXTREMELY HIGH
2. COMMUNITY AND SOCIAL SERVICE
       EMPLOYMENT COUNSELOR   EXTREMELY HIGH
3. SCIENTIFIC PROFESSIONS
       BIOLOGIST   ABOVE AVERAGE
       CHEMIST   AVERAGE
       ENGINEER   HIGH
       GEOLOGIST   AVERAGE
       PHYSICIST   ABOVE AVERAGE
       PSYCHOLOGIST   ABOVE AVERAGE
4. TECHNICAL PERSONNEL
       AIRLINE PILOT   LOW
       COMPUTER PROGRAMMER   AVERAGE
       ELECTRICIAN   LOW
       MECHANIC   BELOW AVERAGE
       PSYCHIATRIC TECHNICIAN   AVERAGE[3]

The computer interpretation not only provides much more information
about the individual than does the profile alone but saves the counselor considerable time in the interpretation process. Continued research with the 16PF occupational fitness projections should make them
even more valuable to the career counselor in the future.

The publication of the 16PF generated considerable controversy, especially over Cattell's claim that the instrument measures source
traits of normal personality functioning (Bloxom, 1978). Specifically,
Cattell's use of factor analysis as a method of discovering the casual
traits that lead to comprehensive descriptions of personality has been
challenged (J. A. Walsh, 1978). According to Anastasi (1976) factor
analysis should be used for grouping test items and then matching
these clusters against empirical criteria in validity studies. Cronbach (1970) complains that there is no consistency in classifying and
defining psychological traits. Cattell provides 16 personality factors,
but other theorists have combined or have extended the list of these
personality dimensions. Furthermore, he suggests that personality inventories like the 16PF are not built around a definite theory. It
appears that we can best use the 16PF results for promoting discussion
in career counseling. Extensive reviews of this instrument are provided by Bloxom (1978), Bouchard (1972), and Rorer (1972).

[3]From 16PF by R. B. Cattell, H. W. Eber, and M. M. Tatsuoka, 1967.
Institute for Personality and Ability Testing, Inc. Reproduced by permission of the copyright owner.

Test-retest reliabilities (2-7 day intervals) indicate that most scales of the 16PF are satisfactory. However, some of the scales fall below .70 and should be used with caution. For forms A and B the correlation range for the scales is .45 to .93; scales B, L, M, N, and Q_1 are less than .70. The range for forms C and D is .67 to .86; scales M, N, and Q_2 are less than .72. Bloxom (1978) suggests that form E should not be used until its equivalent form has been developed and the combined forms provide acceptable reliability and validity coefficients.

As illustrated earlier, the 16PF does provide information that can be most useful for career exploration. One should be cautious when using the terms associated with the various scales because they can be confusing and misleading to some individuals. They need to be qualified and explained thoroughly.

Case of a High School Senior Undecided about His Future

Mark, a high school senior, told the counselor that he was completely undecided about what to do after graduation from high school. He had considered going to college but was also thinking of looking for a job. Mark's grades in high school were above average. Mark stated that, because his parents wanted him to go to college as his brothers and sisters had done, he had taken the ACT for college admission. His composite score was well above average with his highest subtest score in natural sciences. His scores on the interest inventory section of the ACT indicated an interest in the sciences.

The counselor asked Mark to clarify his reasons for going to college and for going to work. Mark made it clear that he preferred going to college, but because he was undecided about a major he was considering working until he could make a decision. The counselor informed Mark that many students in his class who planned to attend college were undecided about a major. Besides, as the counselor explained, "most courses you take during your freshman year are required of most majors." The counselor then discussed with Mark the pros and cons of going to college directly after graduation from high school. Eventually, Mark decided that he would feel better about attending college now if he could come to a tentative decision about a major.

The counselor had Mark take a battery of inventories including the 16PF. The 16PF was selected primarily because of its occupational fitness projections. The counselor reasoned that these measures might stimulate Mark to explore several possible majors. Mark's profile closely resembled profiles in the scientific professions as described in the handbook. As the counselor and Mark reviewed his profile, the following exchange took place.

Counselor: Your scores on this personality inventory suggest that you have personality characteristics that are similar to those of individuals in the sciences. Within the scientific group your profile closely resembles that of a biologist.

Mark: Does this mean that I would be an outstanding scientist?

Counselor: No, this does not guarantee that you are going to be an outstanding scientist. It simply indicates that your personality is similar to those of people who work in this field, and there is a good chance that you would feel comfortable in and like this kind of work. However, it does not guarantee that you will be successful.

Mark: Oh, I see. These scores verify that I'm like the people in this field, but they don't mean that I'll be successful unless I'm smart enough or apply myself.

Counselor: Yes, that's exactly right, Mark. You would have to commit yourself to going to college and studying very hard to achieve in one of the scientific professions.

The discussion of personality characteristics as related to occupational environment ignited Mark's interest in career exploration. He decided to investigate several scientific professions in detail. As a result of taking the 16PF, Mark was able to approach the career decision process with an understanding of how to relate himself to working conditions. Projecting his personality characteristics into occupational environments was difficult for Mark but not counterproductive. Armed with information about his individual characteristics, Mark could consider careers in a sophisticated way that was interesting for him.

PERSONAL CAREER DEVELOPMENT PROFILE (PCD Profile)

The PCD Profile, developed by Walter (1977), is a computer interpretation of the 16PF designed specifically for career guidance. The format is narrative in style and nontechnical in nature. The PCD Profile includes the following: problem-solving patterns, patterns for coping with stressful conditions, patterns of interpersonal interaction, and personal career considerations. The 16PF profile is reported along with clinical observations for the qualified professional; these observations can be easily detached from the nontechnical PCD Profile.

The PCD Profile report is comprehensive; up to 50 specific occupations are compared with each individual's 16PF scores. In addition, profile similarities are provided for occupational groups. The report is designed to be easily interpreted by professionals and by most individuals who complete the questionnaire.

Case of an Older Man Changing Careers

Mr. Doe reported to a community college counseling center for pre-enrollment counseling concerning a major and a career choice. He was 34 years old, was married, had two children, and had spent ten years in the Navy as a yeoman. His duties as a yeoman included doing clerical work and handling payroll. Mr. Doe said that he did not reenlist in the Navy because he wanted to spend time with his family. He was now seeking training for a job that would provide his family with a comfortable living. He expressed interest in a variety of business careers such as clerical work, banking, and computer programming. He had saved enough money to see him through a couple years of training.

Mr. Doe graduated from high school with average grades. His extracurricular activities included collecting stamps and building boat models. Mr. Doe's interests were fairly well determined, and the skills he developed in the Navy could be applied to the careers under consideration. The counselor decided that an informal skills identification survey and a personality inventory would be used to stimulate further career exploration. The 16PF and PCD Profile were chosen because of their nontechnical format and the career profiles they yield.

Mr. Doe's profile follows. The counselor asked Mr. Doe to read the profile carefully before discussing it.

Problem-Solving Patterns. Mr. Doe works quite comfortably with problems and situations that involve abstract concepts and relationships. He is usually able to integrate detail into meaningful, logical wholes; nevertheless, he tends to be conservative and values tried-and-true solutions to problems. Mr. Doe's approach to tasks and situations reflects a balance between getting things done and an awareness of the subtle relationships and steps involved in the process of getting them done. He is able to work creatively, to transcend custom, and to generate new ideas, especially in work settings where creativity is an important function.

Patterns for Coping with Stressful Conditions. On the whole, Mr. Doe appears to be well adjusted. He shows little evidence of tension or anxiety under conditions of pressure and stress. He generally tries to approach situations with calm emotional stability. He usually does not desire to let his emotional needs obscure the relevant aspects involved in situations. Generally, when Mr. Doe is faced with conflict or opposition from others, his preferred reaction is to take sufficient time to reexamine the problem or situation and to withhold committing himself until most of the facts are considered.

Patterns of Interpersonal Interaction. On the whole, Mr. Doe's personality orientation is one whereby he focuses his attention primarily on inner thoughts and feelings rather than on people and the world around him. In situations of importance to him, Mr. Doe is generally alert to and shows concerns about his social obligations and the social reactions of others. He may at times need to guard against taking a clever or hardheaded approach in such instances, especially when a more forthright, natural, or spontaneous approach would be most appropriate for achieving understanding. As a leader, Mr. Doe tends to place high value on self-reliance, and therefore he may need to guard against expecting others to perform well and to get things accomplished effectively without provision for needed control, follow-up, and guidelines.

Personal Career Development Considerations. Mr. Doe is likely to enjoy career-oriented activities that entail investigating, observing, and solving problems of a business, cultural, scientific, or social nature; that involve use of ideas, words, and symbols; use of data processing, office practice, verbal, and numerical skills to organize data and tasks according to prescribed plans and well-established procedures and systems; and being near or at the center of group endeavors; and solving problems through discussions with others. Therefore, he indicates rather marked interests for the academic, engineering, medical science, medical service, research, scientific, business system, data processing system, financial clerking, office practice; and educational, health care, religious, and social service career fields.[4]

Each of the profile patterns was discussed, and the counselor asked Mr. Doe to summarize what he learned about himself.

Counselor: Do you feel that your past working experience has helped you in dealing with stressful conditions?

Mr. Doe: Well yes, I believe that had I taken this test sometime earlier, like in my early twenties, it probably would have different results. I think that the experiences I've had have certainly helped me to put things in perspective.

Counselor: You have had to make some important decisions in the past, and you seem to be well satisfied with those decisions. You seem to have decided now that you want to be with your family, and that decision has prompted you to consider a career that keeps you at home. The patterns of interpersonal interaction suggest that you are focusing your thoughts primarily on inner feelings and your own personal situations and have made your decisions based primarily on them.

Mr. Doe: Well yes, I think that I have always felt confident in myself, and I have usually made decisions based on that confidence. In other words, I have felt fairly self-reliant and like to control working situations by doing the work myself.

Counselor: Well, how would these feelings affect your performance in a managerial or leadership position?

Mr. Doe: Yes, I've thought about that. I may have some problems in expecting too much of others; I sort-of experienced that in the Navy. However, my superior in the Navy was able to depend on me, and I feel that I followed through on most assignments fairly well. But not being able to delegate work could be a problem for me as a manager.

The counselor and Mr. Doe continued their discussions concerning interpersonal relationships and problem-solving patterns. Whenever it was plausible the counselor related work environments to personality characteristics. In the final phase of the counseling session, career development was discussed.

Counselor: We have been talking a great deal about how your interpersonal interactions, problem-solving patterns, and ability to handle stressful conditions are linked to different kinds of occupations and work environments. Now, let's take a look at what the profile tells us about personal career development considerations.

Mr. Doe: I see that they have recommended a number of career considerations. However, I think that I can eliminate some of those right off. For example, I don't believe that I am interested in going into an engineering career and having to spend four or five years in college. I am also not interested in medical service or a medical career. I think I lean more toward some sort of business field and something in the way of records and data processing.

---

[4]From *Personal Career Development Profile* by V. Walter, 1977. Institute for Personality and Ability Testing, Inc. Reproduced by permission of the copyright owner.

Counselor: Good! You have been able to eliminate some of the possibilities, and I notice that data processing is one of the options listed. Could you be more specific?

Mr. Doe: I understand that computer programming is a very good
field, and I believe that I may be interested in pursuing this
as a possible career. I am not quite sure what area of computer
work I would like to get into, but I definitely would like to
look into this as a possible career field.

Counselor: Very well. We have some information in our career resource center on this topic, and I can also recommend some people
for you to see. What about other considerations? Perhaps we
should take a look at two or three fields at this time.

Mr. Doe: I agree. I want to take a look at what might be available
in banking, as I've had some past experience in dealing with pay-
rolls and I sort-of enjoyed clerking and office practice as
related to this field. But I'm not sure as to specific jobs and
what sort of potential there may be in the banking industry.

The counselor and Mr. Doe continued to discuss possible career
considerations using the list of careers provided on the computer
printout as a stimulus. Mr. Doe was able to expand this list and thus
consider a number of different options.

TEMPERAMENT AND VALUES INVENTORY (TVI)

The TVI measures two variables: temperament dimensions of personality
as related to career choice and values as related to work rewards
(pleasant work environments). A rational-empirical approach was used
to select and refine the items. Specifically, rational judgments were
used in determining the personality aspects of temperament and the
values to include in the inventory, and the scales were pretested and
subsequently statistically analyzed. The reading level is eighth
grade, and the inventory is not recommended for use below the ninth
grade. The inventory is untimed and computer scored. Two parts of the
inventory require the individual to respond on a Likert-type scale.
The third part is a true-false questionnaire.

INTERPRETING THE TVI

The temperament scales are referred to as personal characteristics
on the score report profile as shown in Figure 8-2. Standard scores
are reported on a bipolar scale ranging from 20 to 80 with a mean of
50 and standard deviation of 10. The advantage of the bipolar scale
is that scores are not as likely to be looked on as outstanding or
poor but simply as describing dimensions of an individual's personality. Differences in scales are regarded as significant if they are
three standard scores or greater.

As shown in Figure 8-3 the reward value scales are reported by standard scores ranging from 20 to 80 with a mean of 50 and a standard
deviation of 10. The manual (Johansson, 1977) reports mean scores for
various occupational groups for additional interpretation.

There are two computer-generated report formats. One is composed
of a profile as shown in Figures 8-2 and 8-3, reporting standard

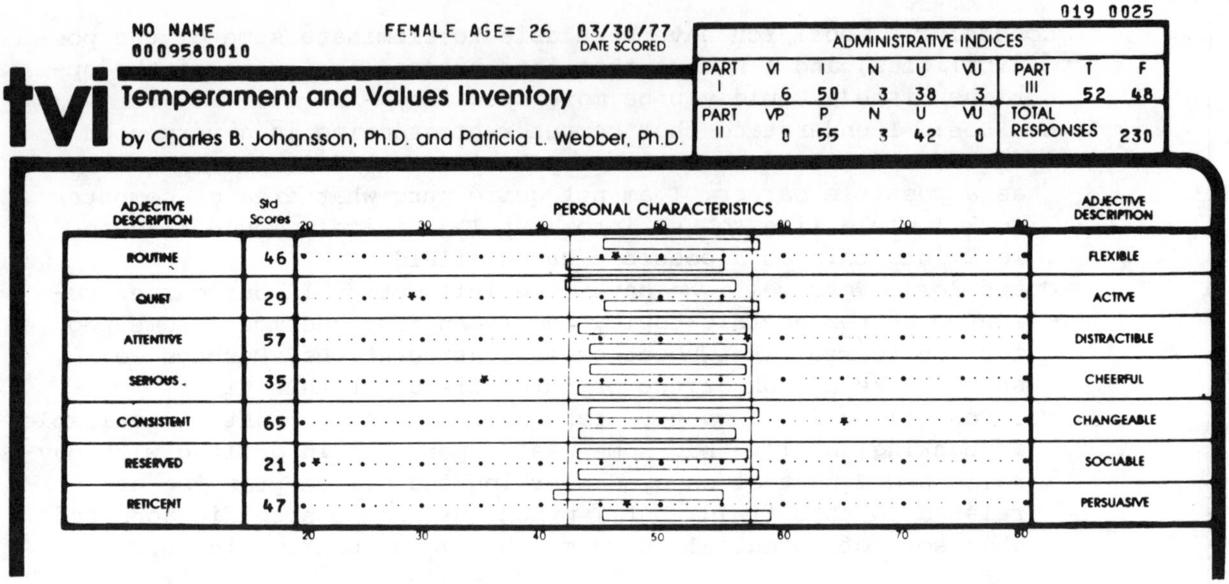

FIGURE 8-2. *TVI personal characteristics profile.* From *Temperament and Values Inventory* by C. B. Johansson and P. L. Webber. Copyright 1977 by NCS/Interpretive Scoring Systems. Reprinted by permission.

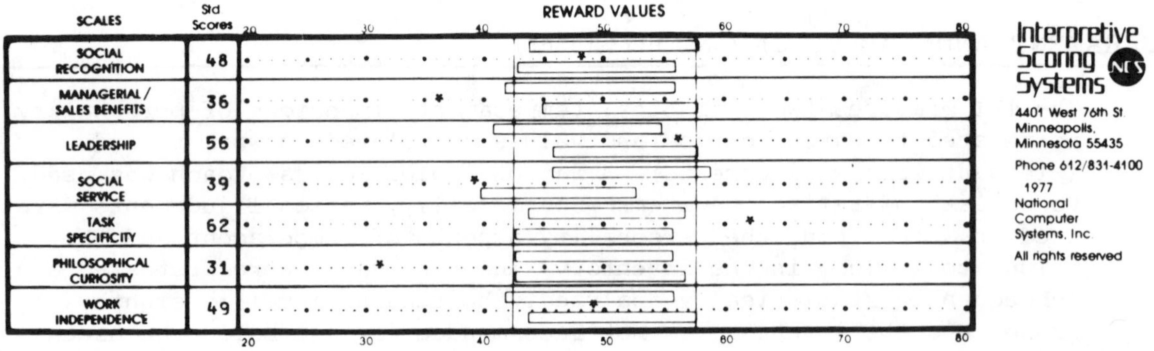

FIGURE 8-3. *TVI reward value profile.* From *Temperament and Values Inventory,* by C. B. Johansson and P. L. Webber. Copyright 1977 by NCS/Interpretive Scoring Systems. Reprinted by permission.

scores with an asterisk. On the back of this report form is a narrative description of each scale. Administrative indices discussed in the manual are also reported.

The other report format is a comprehensive narrative description of the individual. This report begins with a discussion of the usefulness of the results and a brief description of how to interpret the results. The remainder of the report is divided into three parts: personal characteristics, reward values, and response data. A narrative interpretation of the individual's score is reported in detail for the seven personal characteristics scales and the seven reward value scales. An example for quiet-active, one of the personal characteristics scales, follows.

Compared to females and males in a general population your score is in the average range, although slightly more toward the quiet end. Low scores are related to preferences for quiet types of activities, such as reading, building models, watching sports rather than actively participating, or sitting and talking with friends on a free weekend. In contrast, very high scores on this scale indicate more of a liking for being on-the-go, moving around rather than sitting still, and being a participant in active sports rather than a spectator. Sometimes you may feel that you are constantly on-the-go, while at other times you enjoy just sitting and relaxing. Generally, high school students tend to have higher scores on this scale than do adults, but there is a wide range of individual differences for each age group. Compared to just your sex and age group, your score is in the average range.[5]

An example for social recognition, one of the reward value scales, follows.

Compared to females and males in a general population, your score is in the range of scores for people who feel that social recognition is not as important to them as it is to most people. This indicates that even though you may like other people to be seeking your advice, to be friendly to you, or to depend upon, other things may be as important or even more important to you, such as depending upon your own sense of worth. Scores similar to yours tend to be related to interest in scientific activities and skilled trades, where social recognition is not of major importance. In contrast, individuals who have high scores on this scale tend to have interests associated with working in business-enterprising careers, such as sales, public administrator, or school superintendent. Compared to just your sex and age group your score is below the average range of scores.[6]

The TVI thus provides the counselor with information on the individual's work-related temperament and desired work environments—information that can be compared to information on interests and abilities. This information is most useful in the overall career counseling sequence and can be matched with an individual's career aspirations. The counseling information generated by the TVI can be used in career seminars, group career counseling programs, work re-entry counseling, and career education programs.

The TVI is a relatively new instrument and as such should be the subject of further research. The instrument appears to have fairly good face validity in that the items for each section appear to measure what they attempt to measure. In general, more data are needed to establish construct and concurrent validity and reliability. To determine construct validity the TVI was compared with scales on the SCII, the Career Assessment Inventory, and the Self Description Inventory. Although there is evidence of validity, the sample was relatively small for the SCII (123) and Career Assessment Inventory (197). The authors should be commended for the detailed comparisons of each TVI scale with those of other instruments. However, in some instances moderate relationships (correlations of .27 to .32)

[5],[6]From *Temperament and Values Inventory* by C. B. Johansson and P. L. Webber. Copyright 1977 by NCS/Interpretive Scoring Systems. Reprinted by permission.

are not explained, and the reader is left to draw his or her own conclusions. Although the authors present an impressive discussion of concurrent validity, the number of cases from which differentiation among the various groups studied was determined was small. This number should be increased in the future. Test-retest reliabilities (1- and 2-week intervals) range from .82 to .93 for the personal characteristics scales and from .79 to .93 for the reward value scales. Median internal consistency estimates by age group and sex for each scale are in the low .80s. In summary, the TVI is a recently developed instrument, and until more data are collected its validity and reliability should be considered tentative.

Case of a High School Junior Considering Dropping out of School

Sam, a high school junior, had lost interest in school and was considering quitting and going to work. He was referred to the counseling center for assistance. The counselor obtained the following information from Sam's cumulative folder. Sam's father was employed in a local factory, and his mother did odd jobs such as housekeeping and baby sitting. His academic record was below average, but aptitude and ability tests indicated that he was at least of average intelligence and had good mechanical aptitudes.

It was clear that Sam was undecided about his future and had not established career goals. As the conversation progressed, the counselor asked Sam to specify a job choice. Sam stated that he wasn't sure what was required for various jobs but agreed that if he had the opportunity to be trained to do a specific job he would like that much better than just going out and seeking a job.

The counselor then suggested several inventories to help clarify Sam's career goals. One was the TVI, which was chosen to stimulate discussion of work environments as related to personality characteristics and of temperament dimensions as related to career choice. The counselor used the TVI results to encourage Sam to consider an occupational environment as opposed to seeking just any job: "This test is divided into two parts. The first part of the test measures personality characteristics. The second part of the test measures what you consider important in a career or find rewarding in a career. You have high scores on the routine, active, and attentive scales. Specifically, the first score indicates that you prefer rather routine kinds of schedules and set routines in working. The second score shows that you prefer active participation. The third high score suggests that you are not easily distracted when you are doing a task and are able to concentrate even when there is not complete silence."

Sam agreed with the results in general. He especially agreed to preferring routine and vigorous activities. He also reported that he had had to learn to concentrate despite noise in a home with six siblings. Other scores from this part of the test were similarly discussed.

The counselor then said: "Now, let's take a look at the second part of the test. All but two of your scores were near average. Your high score on task specificity suggests that you prefer to work on jobs where the tasks are highly structured and that you like to be able to check out your work in detail rather than hurrying through it. Your high score on work independence suggests that you prefer being your own boss and establishing your own schedule for work."

At this point Sam seemed confused as to what the results meant in relation to a job. The counselor decided to summarize the results in an attempt to link the scores to job duties.

> *Counselor*: Let's remember that you like rather routine type jobs, that you prefer vigorous activities, and that you are not easily distracted. Also, you like to work on tasks where you know exactly what is expected. You like to be able to check your work in detail. You like to set your own schedules and work at your own pace. Now, there are probably a lot of jobs which might fit into this area. Can you think of a job which is routine and requires tasks which are detailed and have to be checked?
>
> *Sam*: Well, I guess it fits pretty well with television repair. Television repair people tackle specific problems, and you've got to check out your work in detail.

The counselor and Sam discussed other possible occupations such as auto mechanic, electrician, small engine repairer. They selected several of the occupations for further exploration. Sam and the counselor also explored the benefits of completing high school and the possibility of entering a vocational training program.

The discussion of the TVI results directed Sam to specific consideration of work tasks and work environments. Considering occupations from this perspective was a realistic approach to searching for a job. Not only was Sam prepared to consider the requirements of a job, but he was able to relate tasks and the work environment to his own values and temperament.

OTHER PERSONALITY INVENTORIES

In addition to the personality inventories discussed in this chapter, the reader may find the inventories listed below useful in career counseling. The evaluation of the normative sample and the description of the scales will help determine their usefulness.

California Test of Personality. There are five levels of this inventory including one for grades 7-10, one for grades 9-college, and one for adults. The inventory is divided into two parts: Part I (six subtests) provides a measure of personal adjustment. Part II (six subtests) is a measure of social adjustment. A combination of the two parts provides a total adjustment score. Scores are expressed as standard scores.

Omnibus Personality Inventory. This instrument is to be used with adolescents and adults. The normative samples for standardization were derived from college students. There are 16 scales—for example, autonomy, altruism, anxiety level, and practical outlook—and one intellectual disposition scale. The manual presents case studies as examples for using this instrument.

Guilford-Zimmerman Temperament Survey. This survey is a measure of the following traits: general activity, restraint, ascendance, sociability, emotional stability, objectivity, friendliness, thought-

fulness, personal relations, and masculinity. Norms were derived from
college samples. Single scores and total profiles may be used to determine personality traits to be considered in career decision-making.

Minnesota Counseling Inventory. This inventory was designed to measure
adjustment of boys and girls in grades 9-12. Scores yield criterion-
related scales as follows: family relationships, social relationships,
emotional stability, conformity, adjustment to reality, mood, and
leadership. Scales are normed separately for boys and girls. The scores
provide indices to important relational and personal characteristics
to be considered in career counseling.

Thorndike's Dimension of Temperament. This instrument has ten scales:
sociable-solitary, ascendant-withdrawing, cheerful-gloomy, placid-
irritable, accepting-critical, tough-minded-tender-minded, reflective-
practical, impulsive-planful, active-lethargic, and responsible-casual.
Percentile norms are based on males and females in grades 11 and 12
and in their freshman year of college.

Myers-Briggs Type Indicator. This instrument is designed to be used
with high school and college students. Scores are converted to percentile equivalents. The inventory is composed of 166 two-choice items
measuring preferences, feelings, and behaviors. The results indicate
tendencies toward extroversion or introversion, sensing or intuition,
thinking or feeling, and judgment or perception.

SUMMARY

The consideration of individual characteristics and traits in career
exploration has been stressed by a number of career theorists. Personality measures provide individuals with the opportunity to examine
their views of themselves. Computer-generated narrative reports may
provide the impetus needed for improving the quality and increasing
the quantity of personality measures used in career counseling. The
computer-generated interpretive reports described in this chapter provide examples of the potential use of personality inventories.

QUESTIONS AND EXERCISES

1. How would you explain the suggestion that personality measures
act as mirrors to help individuals examine their views of themselves?
What are the implications for career counseling?

2. Give an example of a counseling case in which you would recommend using a personality inventory.

3. A faculty member has recommended using a personality inventory
as a predictive instrument for academic success. What would you reply?

4. Explain how you would establish the need for a personality inventory during a counseling interview.

5. What would your strategy be for interpreting personality inventory results that conflict with an individual's career goals?

9
Using Value Inventories

Increasing awareness of the relationship between individual values and career selection and satisfaction has focused attention on the measurement of values in general and of work values specifically. Clarification of values has come to be identified as one of the relevant components of career decision-making (Gelatt, 1962, Katz, 1975). The usefulness of value assessment in career counseling is underscored by Gordon (1975), who suggests that values tend to remain fairly stable and to endure over the life span. Thus, the identification of individual values can help in the career decision process.

Value assessment overlaps the measures of interest and personality. The choice among these types of inventories in career counseling depends upon the purpose for using the results. For example, confusion and conflicts in values concerning religion, work, politics, and friends may best be resolved by discussing the results of a value inventory; the results are directly related to the purpose of testing. A counselor may choose a value inventory because he or she plans an exercise in value clarification. Another counselor may determine that value preferences are more easily related to considerations of career exploration than measured traits from personality and interest inventories. Thus, the choice between a value, personality, or interest inventory should be primarily determined by the needs of the counselee and the objectives of counseling.

Defining values is a complex task. Because value judgments are an integral part of an individual's priorities and world views, most definitions are general in nature. For example, Kluckhorn (1961, p. 18) states that values are "a selective orientation toward experience, implying deep commitment or repudiation, which influences the ordering of choices between possible alternatives and action." Fitzpatrick (1961, p. 93) defines values as "those ideals, norms which guide man's behavior, according to which he judges whether his behavior is right or wrong." Gordon (1975, p. 2) provides another general definition of values: "Values are constructs representing generalized behaviors or states of affairs that are considered by the individual to be important." A most useful explanation of values for career counseling is simply "the importance you attach to stimuli, events, people, and activities" (Zimbardo, 1979, p. 491). In career counseling we are most interested in those values that affect career decisions. Our major goal is to assist individuals in clarifying these values from a self-report.

In this chapter three inventories that inquire into an individual's general values are reviewed. In addition, an inventory of work values is discussed. Examples from both group and individual career counseling programs are presented.

SURVEY OF INTERPERSONAL VALUES (SIV)

The SIV measures six ways in which an individual may want to relate to other people. These interpersonal values are broadly associated with an individual's personal, social, marital, and occupational adjustment. Gordon (1976, p. 1) defines the values measured by this instrument as follows: support—being treated with understanding; conformity—doing what is socially correct; recognition—being looked up to and admired; independence—having the right to do whatever one wants to do; benevolence—doing things for other people; leadership—being in charge of other people.

The inventory can be administered in 15 minutes. It consists of sets of three statements from which the individual must choose the most important and the least important. Three different value dimensions are represented in each triad. For example:

To have a meal at noon.
To get a good night's sleep.
To get plenty of fresh air.[1]

KR-20 reliability estimates range from .71 to .86. Test-retest correlations for an interval of 15 weeks range from .65 to .76. Black (1978) considers these reliabilities adequate, while LaVoie (1978) believes they are not high enough for individual interpretations. Predictive validity is based primarily on studies demonstrating significant differences between groups of workers such as managers and subordinates in a variety of settings. Validity is also demonstrated by correlations between the SIV and other inventories such as the Study of Values and the EPPS. This instrument has been reviewed by Black (1978), LaVoie (1978), Cronbach (1965), and Goodstein (1965).

INTERPRETING THE SIV

The SIV scores are interpreted by percentile equivalents with norms available for both male and female groups. The following groups constituted the normative samples: ninth grade vocational students, high school students, vocational junior college students, college students, and adults. Minority groups are included in all norm groups. Percentile equivalents are grouped into five levels: very high: 94th to 99th percentile; high: 70th to 93rd percentile; average: 32nd to 69th percentile; low: 8th to 31st percentile; very low: 1st to 7th percentile. In addition to percentile equivalents, means and standard deviation by

[1]From *Survey of Interpersonal Values, Revised Examiner's Manual*, by Leonard V. Gordon. Copyright © 1976, 1960, Science Research Associates, Inc. Reprinted by permission of the publisher.

sex are provided for each of the six values for the normative groups, and for additional samples including foreign students.

The SIV is recommended for use in vocational guidance, where values can be related to occupations under consideration, and in personal counseling, where identified values can provide stimulus for discussion.

Despite these recommendations, relatively little information is available concerning the use of SIV results in career counseling. In a separate publication, Gordon (1975) presents profiles for various classes of occupations with recommendations for individual counseling. These profiles are based on seven typological clusters developed by Gordon from factor analysis: bureaucratic managerial (values controlling others in structured and regulated ways), influential indifferent (values controlling and influencing others with little concern for them), independent assertive (values personal freedom), bureaucratic subordinate (values conformity), welfare of others (values helping others), reciprocal support (values having warm, reciprocal relationships with others), and institutional service (values being of service to others).

Using these clusters, Gordon provides a series of profiles for a variety of occupations. For example, managerial and supervisory personnel generally value bureaucratic management and devalue reciprocal support. Retail clerks are generally service oriented and concerned with the welfare of others. Other occupations are reported in a similar fashion. One hopes that additional occupational groups will be described in the SIV manual in the future.

The use of the SIV would be greatly enhanced if the author would provide illustrations of its use in the manual. A detailed explanation of the interpretation of the scales would also increase the utility of this inventory. In addition, a clarification of the meaning and significance of high and low scores is lacking.

The career counselor should be cautious in using the inventory results. As Black (1978) points out, we cannot assume that choice of work accurately reflects what individuals value in relationships. Some individuals ignore the lack of certain values in an occupational environment.

The SIV seems appropriate for use with individuals and groups. It is particularly appropriate for helping individuals toward self-discovery in the career decision process. The results can also be used for improving interpersonal relationships generally and specifically within the work environment.

Case of an Older Woman Searching for a Career for the First Time

Ms. Lunt was considering a career for the first time in her life. She had recently been granted a divorce after a bitter legal battle with her husband. She told the counselor that her divorce presented her with the challenge of reevaluating her total lifestyle. She emphasized that a part of this reevaluation involved clarifying her values and establishing goals. The counselor suggested a values inventory, and the SIV was selected because of its indication of interpersonal values.

The SIV results suggested that Ms. Lunt highly valued support, conformity, and benevolence. The counselor asked her to express the meaning of these values in relation to her recently receiving a divorce and having to rely on herself for support. Ms. Lunt immediately recognized that her strong need for support might be overemphasized at this point in her life. However, Ms. Lunt concluded that this value was probably long standing and should be considered in her career plans.

The counselor suggested that Ms. Lunt consider a work environment that would be congruent with her value system—environments where she would be treated with understanding and kindness, where social conformity would be valued, and where she would be able to help others. Ms. Lunt decided that even though support was her highest measured value, she was more interested in a career that would provide her with the opportunity of helping others. Ms. Lunt then evaluated careers in social service.

The SIV results provided the stimulus for relating Ms. Lunt's interpersonal values to a variety of occupations. Ms. Lunt was able to find several occupations in the social service group that would allow her to help others and to conform to social norms.

SURVEY OF PERSONAL VALUES (SPV)

The SPV was developed as a companion instrument to the SIV to measure another segment of the value domain—ways in which individuals may want to be in their daily lives. Gordon (1967) identifies six values this instrument measures: practical mindedness—values doing things that will pay off; achievement—values striving to accomplish something significant; variety—values doing things that are new and different; decisiveness—values having strong and firm convictions; orderliness—values having well organized work habits; goal orientation—values directing efforts toward clear-cut objectives.

The SPV can be self-administered and is untimed. Administration time is approximately 15 minutes. The individual is forced to choose the most important and least important from sets of three statements, as in the SIV.

INTERPRETING THE SPV

Scores for the SPV, as for the SIV, are reported in percentile equivalents and are interpreted according to the five levels employed in the SIV. Regional high school norms by sex are based on representative examples of urban California students. The author strongly recommends that high schools develop local norms. National separate-sex norms are available for college students. The author suggests that the SPV may be used also with industrial and other adult groups. Apparently, the author feels that local norms would best serve the needs of these other groups.

Reliability studies include a test-retest (7-10 day intervals) of 97 college students and an application of the KR-20 formula to responses of 167 college students. The test-retest reliabilities range from .80 to .92, while the KR-20 reliabilities range from .72 to .92. The author claims validity through the use of factor analysis in that the scales maintained internal consistency through repeated item analysis. Validity was also assessed by comparing correlations of the scales and those of other instruments such as the SIV and the Study of Values. Most of the scales were found to be statistically significant, supporting the author's claim that different sets of values are measured by this instrument. However, these conclusions must be considered tentative as more data and more research are needed. A review by Glass (1972) provides additional information on the development of this instrument.

The criticisms of this instrument for use as a career counseling tool are similar to those for the SIV. Currently lacking is information on the use of the results and the meaning of the scale scores. In the meantime, the SPV items may be used as the basis for discussions concerning personal values and their relationship to careers.

Case of a High School Senior Needing to Link Values to Careers in a Concrete Way

Bruce, a high school senior, had spent considerable time in the counselor's office discussing his future. He was persistent in his efforts to discover the ideal career. Bruce requested and was administered an extensive battery of tests including the SIV. He was stimulated by the results of most of the battery but was especially intrigued with the measures of his interpersonal values. However, he wanted to know more about his values, and specifically he wanted information about values that influenced his everyday living. Both Bruce and the counselor agreed that the SPV might serve this purpose. The SPV yielded very high percentile equivalents in achievement and variety. Bruce read the descriptions of these scales but was unable to link the results with a career.

> *Counselor*: Let's review some factors we have discussed in previous counseling sessions. Your test data indicate an interest and ability in mathematics and the sciences. You also have an outstanding academic record in these two courses. When reviewing occupations, you indicated an interest in becoming a college mathematics teacher. Now let's return to the high scores in achievement and variety on the SPV. I would like for you to project into the future for a few minutes and visualize how these values could influence your career as a mathematician.
>
> *Bruce* (after a brief pause): Oh, I see! I probably want to be the best.
>
> *Counselor*: Go on.
>
> *Bruce*: I'd want a Ph.D. . . . I see what you mean. I could achieve in this field.
>
> *Counselor*: What about the other value—variety?
>
> *Bruce*: Well, if I did do well, I might be able to call the shots. A strong drive for achievement could lead to opportunities for variety.

After a lengthy discussion the counselor suggested that Bruce still needed to be able to link values to career options in specific ways because Bruce continued to make only superficial connections. Bruce was given the following assignment: Research at least two careers in mathematics and two in science in the career resource center. Write a paragraph on how each career might be congruent with your highest measured values. Examples of Bruce's completed assignment follow.

Chemist—I've found that chemists with a master's degree may find work in government agencies and private industry. But better opportunities are available to those who have a Ph.D. There are all kinds of chemists—organic, inorganic, physical, analytical, and biochemists. Chemists are involved in research and development of new products. I would like this kind of work because I would like to accomplish something significant—my achievement value. In regard to my variety value, I would be working on challenging and difficult tasks that would provide me with a variety of experiences.

Mathematician—Mathematicians are employed in government agencies and private industry as teachers, actuaries, computer specialists, and so on. The higher the degree the greater the opportunities for entry and advancement. I believe that I would be most interested in conducting research to develop better techniques and equipment for computers. This career would provide me with a challenging work environment in which accomplishment of goals would be possible. I would have a variety of experiences while accomplishing new and different tasks. Both my achievement and my variety values would be covered with this career.

Both Bruce and the counselor agreed that consideration of a career should involve other data such as aptitudes, interests, and past academic performance. However, they also agreed that the discussion about values gave Bruce insight into additional considerations that are important in career exploration.

STUDY OF VALUES

The Study of Values was developed from Spranger's (1928/1966) six types of personality: theoretical, economic, aesthetic, social, political, and religious. According to Spranger, measuring an individual's values and attitudes is the best means of determining personality. Thus, the authors of this test (Allport, Vernon, & Lindzey, 1970) developed questions to measure the underlying values inherent in Spranger's types of personality. The following explanations of these six types are paraphrased from Allport et al. (1970, pp. 4-5): theoretical—values systematizing knowledge and the search for truth; economic—values practical and applied knowledge; aesthetic—values events on the basis of their artistic nature; social—values caring for and loving people; political—values influence and personal power over others; religious—values unity in the world and values religious experiences as an affirmation of the purpose of life.

This inventory is untimed and can be self-administered and self-scored. In the first part individuals are required to indicate disagreement with, or slight preference for controversial statements or questions. In the second part individuals respond to multiple-choice questions designed to reflect attitudes.

INTERPRETING THE STUDY OF VALUES

Individuals total their scores for each of the six categories and plot them on a profile as shown in Figure 9-1. Below the profile are instructions for interpreting the scores.

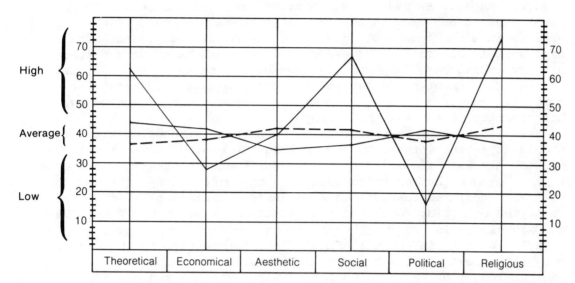

SEX (M or F): _____

PROFILE OF VALUES

FIGURE 9-1. *Study of Values profile.* From *Study of Values* by G. W. Allport, P. E. Vernon, and G. Lindzey, © 1960 by Houghton Mifflin Company. Reprinted by permission of the publisher, The Riverside Publishing Company.

Although the test was developed primarily for college students and adults, high school norms by sex are available. Also included are norms for certain occupations. Means and standard deviations by sex are reported for a number of broad occupational fields such as business, medicine, and religion. The authors caution the career counselor not to become overreliant on the results of this inventory in that the values measured are much broader than occupational interests. Thus, the norms reported may be considered as illustrating differences in values among the occupational groups cited. This inventory seems much more appropriate for stimulating discussions about values in relation to careers than for selection and classification. The items are transparent and are open to faking, particularly when an individual is aware that the results will be used for selection.

Reliability studies include split-half reliabilities ranging from .84 to .95 and test-retest reliabilities (intervals of one and two months) ranging from .77 to .93. External validation was accomplished by examining scores of groups of individuals whose characteristics were fairly well known such as engineering students, nurses, clergy, and teachers. High and low scores for the group studies corresponded with prior expectations.

The manual needs to include more suggestions for illustrations of the use of the results than it now does. Case studies would be helpful for illustrating how to apply the results in a variety of counseling situations. This instrument would also be much more useful for career counseling than it now is if additional data were available on differences in values among occupational groups. See Hogan (1972), Hundleby (1965), and Radcliffe (1965) for in-depth reviews.

Case of a Veteran Seeking a Career

   Carl reported to the counseling center seeking assistance in making
a career choice. He was 26, was married, and had one child. He had
spent over three years in the military and saw action in Viet Nam. He
grew up in a town of about 25,000 and was active in student affairs in
high school. His father was employed in a local bank. He reported that
his family had been supportive during his youth and active in their
church. Carl spent his first year in college taking courses that are
generally required of most students. His grades were outstanding, and
his favorite course was philosophy.

   Carl informed the counselor that he had been struggling with what he
should do in the future. On the one hand he wanted a career that would
provide him with financial security, while on the other hand he wanted
to make a contribution to humanity. As the discussion continued, the
counselor realized that values were an important consideration for
Carl. The counselor suggested that a value inventory might help Carl
clarify his goals. Carl agreed and took the Study of Values.

   Carl's profile is shown in Figure 9-1. Considering these scores, the
counselor viewed Carl as placing a high value on the search for truth
and knowledge, on relating to people with sympathy and unselfishness,
and on actively seeking unity in the world around him. Conversely, he
placed a low value on economic gains and having power over others. The
aesthetic value was average.

   The counselor compared Carl's scores with the mean and standard deviation of college males reported in the manual (Allport et al., 1970,
p. 12). Carl's score was well beyond the first standard deviation on
the social and religious scales.

   Carl admitted that he had always felt a strong identification with
religious activities and the welfare of others. Although he had earlier reported a strong need to provide well for his family, his highest priority was to make a contribution to society. He stated that
this test provided him with the stimulation to assess his true values,
and he was satisfied that the results were accurate—that is, they expressed his values at this time. However, his family's welfare would
remain a primary consideration.

   The counselor talked over these value considerations with Carl a
number of times during Carl's college career. Carl finally decided in
his junior year to enter seminary training.

WORK VALUES INVENTORY (WVI)

The WVI is designed to assess the forms of satisfaction men and women
seek in their work. It is used for academic and career counseling of
high school and college students and for personnel selection and development. The individual is required to rate the importance of each
of 45 work values on a five-point scale. Testing time is approximately
15 minutes.

   Reliability data are based on 99 tenth-graders. Test-retest reliabilities (two-week interval) range from .74 to .83. The manual reports evidence for construct, content, and concurrent validity.

The author reports that data for predictive validity are being collected (Super, 1970).

The WVI measures 15 work values (Super, 1970, pp. 8-10): achievement—values a feeling of accomplishment; altruism—values service to others; aesthetics—values beauty and artistic endeavors; creativity—values inventiveness; intellectual stimulation—values independent thinking; independence—values independent actions; prestige—values status and power; management—values planning and organizing tasks for others to do; economic returns—values ample financial rewards; security—values running little risk of losing a job; surroundings—values a pleasant environment; supervisory relations—values work under a supervisor who is fair and easy to get along with; associates—values working with likeable and desirable people; way of life—values a desirable lifestyle; variety—values doing a variety of tasks.

INTERPRETING THE WVI

Score results are presented in percentile equivalents for each scale. Norms are available for males and females in grades 7-12. Means and standard deviations are available for a limited number of adult male samples derived from older forms of the inventory.

The author suggests that the first step in the interpretation process is to evaluate the raw scores. The two or three values that have the highest rating are to be considered in the counseling process. Next, one should look at the normative data by sex and grade. The manual provides an extensive definition of each value with specific examples of how each value is related to suggested occupations. Interpretations of combinations of scores are provided by factor analytical studies that appear to be tentative and inconclusive. Although no examples of the use of the WVI for counseling are provided in the manual, the definition of each scale provides guidelines for using the results in career counseling. For example, someone who scores high on the altruism scale would probably be interested in jobs such as social worker, counselor, teacher, and religious leader.

This inventory appears to have considerable possibilities as a counseling tool for career exploration. Of serious concern, however, is the lack of data on the long-term stability of the inventory or at least on its stability beyond the two-week intervals used in establishing reliability. The small number of cases used to establish reliability needs to be increased, and, in fact, all data need updating from the 1970 and earlier editions. The use of the instrument is enhanced by the reported means and standard deviations of occupational samples, even though these samples are small. For in-depth reviews of this instrument, see Berdie (1972), Tiedeman (1972), and French (1972).

Using Results in a Group Counseling Program

Sue, Fred, Ruth, and Jim, first-semester freshmen undecided about careers, agreed to discuss their WVI results in a group led by their counselor. This excerpt illustrates how the counselor led the discussion and directed the group in relating work values to broad occupational areas.

After introducing the group members to each other and explaining the purpose of the inventory, the counselor provided members with profiles of their scores. The counselor explained the meaning of percentile equivalents and asked members to locate their three highest scores and their three lowest scores. The counselor then directed members to read the interpretations of their scores as recorded in the manual. After all members had ample time for review, the counselor asked them to discuss their scores.

Jim volunteered: "My surroundings score was the highest, being in the 95th percentile; economic returns was in the 80th percentile; and way of life was in the 75th percentile. My lowest scores were altru-ism, aesthetics, and creativity. It seems that I highly value a pleas-ant environment. The more I think about working, the more this seems to be true. I also like to be comfortable and would like to earn a lot of money. As far as my lowest scores are concerned, I don't value artistic endeavors or being creative or providing service to others."

The counselor recorded Jim's highest and lowest scores on the chalk-board. Next he had the members relate these work values to career op-tions by asking them to record careers congruent with Jim's measured work values. In addition, they were to record occupations in which Jim would not find value congruence. After a brief time, the counselor called for their suggestions.

Sue was the first to speak: "I don't think Jim would want to be a mechanic or to work in a machine shop. He wants a cushy place to work. I'd suggest banker, real estate agent, or some kind of business ca-reer." The other members agreed with Sue's observation and offered further suggestions such as architect, dentist, and optometrist.

The counselor then asked the members to specify how they arrived at their conclusions.

Fred: Well, I think that people who value nice surroundings and economic returns would be happier in business careers or profes-sions that provide opportunities for making a lot of money.

Ruth: I agree, and in Jim's case he does not value art, creativity, and service to others. He would not want to be an art teacher for example. They probably also don't make enough money to take care of Jim's needs. This makes it much clearer that you'd be happier in the occupations we mentioned.

Sue: This is like a puzzle—you try to put all the parts together. Sometimes they fit, and other times they don't.

Counselor: Very good! You have recognized that we have many consid-erations in choosing a career. Work values are one important fac-tor.

A discussion of each group member's scores followed a similar pat-tern. The counselor made certain that each member left the session with a list of career considerations.

OTHER VALUE INVENTORIES

The value inventories listed below should be evaluated for their use in career counseling. These instruments may stimulate discussions of values and their relationship to career decision-making.

Rokeach Values Survey. Both of the two parts of this instrument contain an alphabetical list of 18 values defined by short phrases. Individuals are required to rank-order the two lists. Part 1 consists of "terminal" values: freedom, happiness, national security, true friendship, and so forth. Part 2 contains "instrumental" values: ambition, cheerfulness, courage, obedience, and so forth. This instrument has been used with individuals ranging in age from 11 through adulthood. It is recommended as a general measure of value.

William Lynde and Williams Analysis of Personal Values. The author implies that this instrument is not to be used for selection and placement because there are no significant data on reliability and validity. The instrument is designed primarily to encourage exploration of values in relation to business life and personal life. This instrument should be considered as experimental and used only to foster discussion of values.

Personal Values Inventory. This inventory was designed to measure noncognitive variables related to academic success. Example scales are: direction of aspiration, persistence, need for achievement, and self-control. Counselors might find this instrument useful in stimulating discussions of personal values associated with academic achievement.

Rating Scales of Vocational Values, Vocational Interests, and Vocational Aptitudes. This assessment instrument is designed to integrate values, interests, and aptitudes. Individuals rate 60 activities as to their worthwhileness, interest to them, and aptitude required. This instrument may be used to foster discussion of the activities rated.

Temperament and Values Inventory. See Chapter 8 for full description of this inventory.

SUMMARY

In this chapter the relationship between individual values and career selection and satisfaction has been stressed. Because values tend to remain fairly stable over the life span, general values and work values need to be considered in career counseling. The value assessment instruments discussed in this chapter measure value constructs involved in an individual's relationship with other people, associated with everyday living, inherent in personality types, and associated with the satisfactions men and women seek in their work.

QUESTIONS AND EXERCISES

1. What are the similarities and differences between personality and value inventories? How do these similarities and differences affect their use in career counseling?

2. An individual indicates a high priority for financial independence but also aspires to a relatively low-paying job. What would be your strategy in counseling this person?

3. What are the arguments for and against using a value inventory as a selection instrument for job placement?

4. How would you justify the use of value inventories for individuals who indicate an interest in social service occupations?

5. What are the distinctions between work values and general values? How can both be used in career counseling?

10
Combining Assessment Results

In each of the preceding chapters the discussion of assessment was of necessity limited to one type of inventory or test. I do not want to give the impression, however, that segregating individually measured characteristics and traits is good practice. On the contrary, career counselors should consider the totality of individual needs. Each measured characteristic provides a rich source of information for stimulating discussion about goals and for enhancing self-understanding. The career counselor's aim is to encourage combining this information in the career planning process.

In this chapter two combined assessment programs, the American College Testing (ACT) Career Planning Program and the Career Skills Assessment Program are reviewed and discussed. Examples of the use of these instruments for career counseling are presented. Use of a combination of assessment results is also illustrated by cases that utilize the results of several tests and inventories discussed in preceding chapters.

ACT CAREER PLANNING PROGRAM (CPP)

The CPP consists of several components designed to provide a comprehensive career guidance model for use in high schools and post-secondary institutions. The CPP is also recommended for use as a basic part of career development minicourses and as an organizing theme for displaying and filing occupational information in a career center. In addition, the CPP provides cooperative guidance programs for feeder high schools and postsecondary institutions. Specifically, joint career guidance programs can be offered by the high school and post-secondary institutions through CPP-designed materials and follow-up career days. The CPP ability measures can also be used for placement in mathematics, English, and reading programs.

The CPP assessment instruments consist of a Vocational Interest Profile (VIP), ability measures, experience scales, and a background and plans section. Testing time is two and one-half hours. All scoring is done by computer except for the ability measures, which can be self-scored. Local norms can be generated for the ability measures.

For the VIP, which measures interest in eight occupational areas, estimates of reliability by alpha coefficients for men range from .84 to .93; for women the range is .80 to .90. Test-retest correlations (60-day intervals) range from .62 to .79 for men and from .72 to .88 for women. The correlations indicate that the VIP is sufficiently stable for use in career counseling. The CPP manual presents evidence that the VIP scales successfully discriminate among students enrolled in a variety of educational and training programs.

The six ability measures assess reading skills, numerical skills, language usage, mechanical reasoning, clerical skills, and space relations. Reliability estimates for the ability measures were calculated by KR-20 and test-retest (two-week intervals). The KR-20 reliability estimates range from .77 to .99 with a median of .83. The median test-retest correlations range from .73 to .87. Validity was established by comparing the relationship between test results and course performance in various educational programs. Each ability test appears to be appropriate for assessing specific skills.

The experience scales provide a summary of work-related experience in the eight occupational interest areas on the VIP. The background and plans section includes information on educational and vocational plans, biographical information, information on educational needs, and local items supplied for a specific institutional program or service. Estimates of reliability by alpha coefficients for men range from .74 to .88; for women the range is .65 to .86. Healy (1978) provides additional information for evaluating this instrument.

INTERPRETING THE CPP

The CPP profile reports scores for eight career clusters as shown in Figure 10-1. Sample educational programs that prepare people for careers within each of the clusters are listed. Abilities considered essential for meeting the requirements of jobs within each cluster are also listed. This organization of career clusters is built around Holland's (1973) career typology.

Another part of the profile, shown in Figure 10-2, reports relevant experiences of the individual within each career cluster. These experiences are rated as none, few, some, and many, as compared with a national norm. The eight interest measures and the six ability measures are assigned stanine scores marked on a graph divided into lower quarter, middle half, and upper quarter. An estimated ACT composite score range is also projected; it can be used when higher education is being considered.

The CPP profile report can be self-interpreted. A student handbook offers a concise explanation of scores and a systematic procedure for interpreting the results. Various alternatives and references are given for each major step in career exploration. A counselor can complement the reported information, as many students need assistance in making the most meaningful interpretations of the data reported. For this purpose the CPP *Counselors Guide* (ACT American College Testing Program, 1980) is provided.

CAREER CLUSTERS

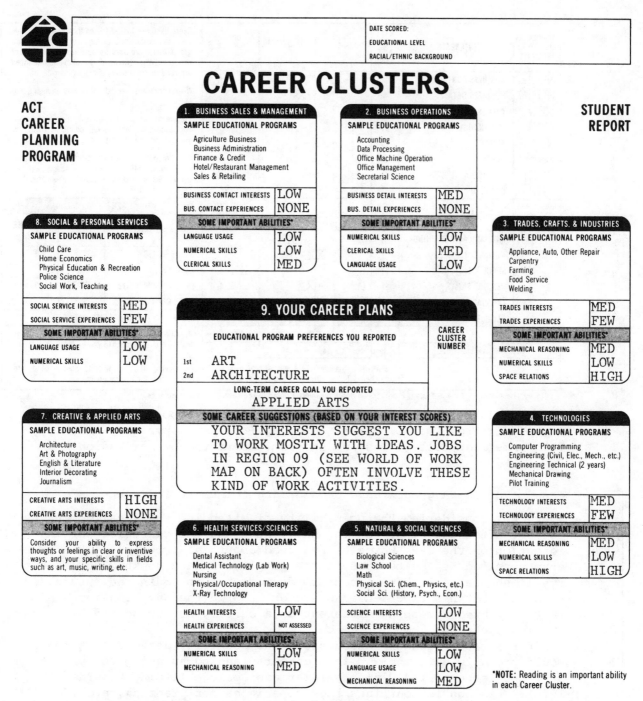

ACT CAREER PLANNING PROGRAM

STUDENT REPORT

DATE SCORED:
EDUCATIONAL LEVEL
RACIAL/ETHNIC BACKGROUND

1. BUSINESS SALES & MANAGEMENT

SAMPLE EDUCATIONAL PROGRAMS

Agriculture Business
Business Administration
Finance & Credit
Hotel/Restaurant Management
Sales & Retailing

BUSINESS CONTACT INTERESTS	LOW
BUS. CONTACT EXPERIENCES	NONE

SOME IMPORTANT ABILITIES*

LANGUAGE USAGE	LOW
NUMERICAL SKILLS	LOW
CLERICAL SKILLS	MED

2. BUSINESS OPERATIONS

SAMPLE EDUCATIONAL PROGRAMS

Accounting
Data Processing
Office Machine Operation
Office Management
Secretarial Science

BUSINESS DETAIL INTERESTS	MED
BUS. DETAIL EXPERIENCES	NONE

SOME IMPORTANT ABILITIES*

NUMERICAL SKILLS	LOW
CLERICAL SKILLS	MED
LANGUAGE USAGE	LOW

8. SOCIAL & PERSONAL SERVICES

SAMPLE EDUCATIONAL PROGRAMS

Child Care
Home Economics
Physical Education & Recreation
Police Science
Social Work, Teaching

SOCIAL SERVICE INTERESTS	MED
SOCIAL SERVICE EXPERIENCES	FEW

SOME IMPORTANT ABILITIES*

LANGUAGE USAGE	LOW
NUMERICAL SKILLS	LOW

3. TRADES, CRAFTS, & INDUSTRIES

SAMPLE EDUCATIONAL PROGRAMS

Appliance, Auto, Other Repair
Carpentry
Farming
Food Service
Welding

TRADES INTERESTS	MED
TRADES EXPERIENCES	FEW

SOME IMPORTANT ABILITIES*

MECHANICAL REASONING	MED
NUMERICAL SKILLS	LOW
SPACE RELATIONS	HIGH

9. YOUR CAREER PLANS

EDUCATIONAL PROGRAM PREFERENCES YOU REPORTED

CAREER CLUSTER NUMBER

1st ART
2nd ARCHITECTURE

LONG-TERM CAREER GOAL YOU REPORTED
APPLIED ARTS

SOME CAREER SUGGESTIONS (BASED ON YOUR INTEREST SCORES)

YOUR INTERESTS SUGGEST YOU LIKE TO WORK MOSTLY WITH IDEAS. JOBS IN REGION 09 (SEE WORLD OF WORK MAP ON BACK) OFTEN INVOLVE THESE KIND OF WORK ACTIVITIES.

7. CREATIVE & APPLIED ARTS

SAMPLE EDUCATIONAL PROGRAMS

Architecture
Art & Photography
English & Literature
Interior Decorating
Journalism

CREATIVE ARTS INTERESTS	HIGH
CREATIVE ARTS EXPERIENCES	NONE

SOME IMPORTANT ABILITIES*

Consider your ability to express thoughts or feelings in clear or inventive ways, and your specific skills in fields such as art, music, writing, etc.

4. TECHNOLOGIES

SAMPLE EDUCATIONAL PROGRAMS

Computer Programming
Engineering (Civil, Elec., Mech., etc.)
Engineering Technical (2 years)
Mechanical Drawing
Pilot Training

TECHNOLOGY INTERESTS	MED
TECHNOLOGY EXPERIENCES	FEW

SOME IMPORTANT ABILITIES*

MECHANICAL REASONING	MED
NUMERICAL SKILLS	LOW
SPACE RELATIONS	HIGH

6. HEALTH SERVICES/SCIENCES

SAMPLE EDUCATIONAL PROGRAMS

Dental Assistant
Medical Technology (Lab Work)
Nursing
Physical/Occupational Therapy
X-Ray Technology

HEALTH INTERESTS	LOW
HEALTH EXPERIENCES	NOT ASSESSED

SOME IMPORTANT ABILITIES*

NUMERICAL SKILLS	LOW
MECHANICAL REASONING	MED

5. NATURAL & SOCIAL SCIENCES

SAMPLE EDUCATIONAL PROGRAMS

Biological Sciences
Law School
Math
Physical Sci. (Chem., Physics, etc.)
Social Sci. (History, Psych., Econ.)

SCIENCE INTERESTS	LOW
SCIENCE EXPERIENCES	NONE

SOME IMPORTANT ABILITIES*

NUMERICAL SKILLS	LOW
LANGUAGE USAGE	LOW
MECHANICAL REASONING	MED

*NOTE: Reading is an important ability in each Career Cluster.

FIGURE 10-1. Career-cluster portion of CPP profile. From *The ACT Career Planning Program.* Copyright 1977 by The American College Testing Program. Reprinted by permission.

EXPERIENCES RELATED TO INTERESTS	INTERESTS	NAT'L STA-NINE (1-9)	LOWER QUARTER	MIDDLE HALF	UPPER QUARTER
			5 10 25	40 60 75	90 95
NONE	BUSINESS CONTACT	3	–XX–		
NONE	BUSINESS DETAIL	4		–XX–|	
FEW	TRADES	6		–XX–	
FEW	TECHNOLOGY	5		–XXL–	
NONE	SCIENCE	3	–XX–		
NOT ASSESSED	HEALTH	2	–XX–		
NONE	CREATIVE ARTS	9			–XX–
FEW	SOCIAL SERVICE	3	–XX–		

ADDITIONAL NORMS STANINES	ABILITIES	NAT'L STA-NINE	LOWER QUARTER	MIDDLE HALF	UPPER QUARTER
			5 10 25	40 60 75	90 95
5	MECHANICAL REASONING	5		–XX–	
4	NUMERICAL SKILLS	3	–XX–		
9	SPACE RELATIONS	8			–XX–|
5	READING SKILLS	4		–XX–	
4	LANGUAGE USAGE	3	–XX–		
5	CLERICAL SKILLS	5		–XX–	

ADDITIONAL NORMS FOR

INSTITUTIONAL CHOICE

5   10   25   40   60   75   90   95
1   2   3   4   5   6   7   8   9

Score Bands—The —XX— on the charts show how your scores compare to those of the nationwide group. *Bands are used because tests are not exact measures.* When two bands do not overlap, chances are good that one score is higher than the other.

N—An N means you did not answer enough questions.

Placement Information—If your English or math composite is 3 or less, ask your counselor about how you can improve these skills.

ACT Composite Range—This estimates what your score would be if you took the ACT Assessment. The average score for students thinking about attending college is 17 to 21.

PLACEMENT INFORMATION

BASIC SKILLS	ASKED HELP?	STANINE ON
STUDY SKILLS	**	
READING SKILLS	**	
ENGLISH COMPOSITE	**	
MATH COMPOSITE	**	

ESTIMATED ACT COMPOSITE RANGE:

PERCENTILE RANK: A percentile rank of 40 means that 40% of students had scores below this point.

STANINES: Stanines are a special type of scale which is divided into 9 equal parts. Stanine bands are numbered 1 (low) through 9 (high), with 5 being the average score for a norm group.

© 1976 by The American College Testing Program. All rights reserved. Printed in the United States of America

FIGURE 10-2. Relevant-experience and abilities portion of CPP profile. From The ACT Career Planning Program. Copyright © 1977 by the American College Testing Program. Reprinted by permission.

Case of an ex-Navy Deck Hand Considering Community College

Abe was considering the possibility of attending the local community college after four years in the Navy. He asked the counselor for information on the CPP, which he had read about in a brochure. This program appealed to Abe because, as he put it, "I want to know more about myself so that I'll have a better idea of what to do in the future." He added that his experience as a deck hand in the Navy convinced him that he wanted something different as a career, but he needed help in finding the right job.

After a rather lengthy discussion, the counselor decided that Abe would probably gain insight into career planning by using the CPP student booklet entitled *Planning* (American College Testing Program, 1976). This booklet outlines the steps in career planning, provides self-awareness exercises, and gives information on job groups and educational programs. The counselor's rationale was that after Abe had completed the tests and planning exercises productive counseling sessions would be possible.

Abe's profiles from the CPP are shown in Figures 10-1 and 10-2. The counselor noted a fairly consistent pattern of scores. For example, the educational program preferences, art and architecture, listed in item 9, were in agreement with the long-term goal of applied arts. The counselor also noted that Abe's highest ability score was in space relations and his highest interest area was creative arts. Space relations, a skill needed to visualize objects in space, is important for applied arts and architecture. However, Abe had no work experiences in this area, probably because he had been working for only a few years.

Abe was not surprised by the results: "I always liked to draw, and I have daydreamed about a job of illustrating for an advertising firm. I guess that I was afraid to admit this to anyone and especially to myself. But I really don't know much about the requirements, training, or pay in commercial art."

Abe felt that he had gained valuable information by using the planning exercises. He explained that he learned that he must evaluate all aspects of his personal characteristics and traits: "The job value exercises in the planning booklet made me think about factors that I never considered before. After working for a while, a person starts thinking about working conditions, and this exercise helped put these considerations in perspective."

Abe was directed to region 9 and 10 of the world-of-work map, shown in Figure 10-3. He recalled listing visual arts and creative arts as

WORLD-OF-WORK MAP

FIGURE 10-3. World-of-work map for CPP. From *The ACT Career Planning Program.* Copyright 1977 by The American College Testing Program. Reprinted by permission.

job groups to explore. He noticed that the results of the interest inventory suggested that his interests were similar to those of individuals who like working with ideas.

As Abe and the counselor reviewed the CPP results, they considered combinations of scores in relation to educational and occupational requirements. If Abe were to decide on commercial art or architecture, a four- or five-year college program would be required. His lower scores in mathematics and reading plus his low high school grades in related subjects indicated possible problems. The counselor called Abe's attention to this possibility and noted that he had asked for help in reading and mathematics on the background and plans section of the profile. The counselor recommended that he seek assistance in upgrading these skills. Abe also indicated a need for financial aid and employment. Because employment would require considerable time, the counselor suggested that Abe learn to plan his schedule well and budget his time wisely.

In this case, the CPP provided Abe with the incentive to explore the results and link them to educational and occupational requirements. The counselor also obtained information for helping Abe meet specific educational requirements and personal needs. For example, the counselor encouraged Abe to investigate potential specific careers within an identified occupational group, to enter special programs for improving basic skills and for learning how to budget time, and to seek financial assistance and employment from the college financial aid office.

CAREER SKILLS ASSESSMENT PROGRAM (CSAP)

In response to the need parents and school officials perceived for preparing students for employment, a career education consortium was formed in the 1970s with the primary purpose of developing the CSAP. This program was field-tested in the consortium member states of Georgia, Maryland, Minnesota, New Jersey, and Ohio with the assistance of the College Entrance Examination Board. Among the purposes of this comprehensive program are to provide guidance for individuals in career planning and decision-making and to allow self-assessment of career skills. Well-designed instructional guides are accompanied by excellent support materials.

Six skill areas considered vital in career planning are assessed: self-evaluation and development skills (ability to interpret information about oneself in relation to occupational, educational, and leisure options), career awareness skills (ability to acquire and evaluate career information), career decision-making skills, employment-seeking skills (ability to locate, apply for, and obtain a job), work effectiveness skills (ability to fulfill job requirements), and personal economic skills (ability to manage personal finances).

Primarily multiple-choice items are used in the six inventories. Some present hypothetical problems for which the individual is required to select the best solution, while others are direct measures of facts and skills.

Reliability estimates for each of the inventories (grades 10, 11, 12) and for the total group range from .85 to .93. Content validity was established by the judgments of content specialists, curriculum developers, and practitioners in each of the fields assessed. The authors have not attempted to establish concurrent validity because they believe that career skills consist of many constructs that necessitate extensive research for their validation.

INTERPRETING THE CSAP

The results of the CSAP are reported by raw score, group stanine, percentile rank, and percentile band. Stanines and percentile ranks and bands are based on the current group taking the test rather than on national equivalents. Development of local norms is encouraged for meaningful comparisons of individual scores. An example of the profile used for reporting scores for career decision-making skills is shown in Figure 10-4.

NAME	TOTAL RAW SCORE	GROUP STANINE	GROUP PERCENTILE RANK	BAND	RAW SCORE BAND
ANDERSON NICK A	12	1	2	1-. 3	XXXXXXX
BARTON SCOTTY D	50	7	83	66 . 90	XXXXXXX
BLANCHARD BAMBI A	50	7	83	66 . 90	XXXXXXX
BOWDEN ANTHONY C	21	2	10	4 . 16	XXXXXXXXX
BRADLEY WILLIAM G	43	5	50	41 . 66	XXXXXXXXX
BRIDGFORD RHONDA F	55	6	95	69 . 99	XXXXX
BROWN SALLY L	19	2	7	3 . 12	XXXXXXXXX
BRYANT FRED D	42	5	47	40 . 64	XXXXXXXXX
BUSKIRK HARVEY G	48	6	74	60 . 86	XXXXXXX
BUTTERWORTH ALAN S	46	6	65	49 . 80	XXXXXXX
CADY BARBARA M	48	6	74	60 . 86	XXXXXXX
CAMPBELL JOE B	13	1	3	1 . 3	XXXXXXX

FIGURE 10-4. *CSAP profile for career decision-making*. Reprinted with permission from *Implementing the Career Skills Assessment Program*. Copyright © 1978 by College Entrance Examination Board, New York.

The CSAP also provides an analysis of the item responses for each of the content areas measured. An example of the profile used for reporting item responses for career decision-making skills is shown in Figure 10-5. On this score report the counselor can locate specific

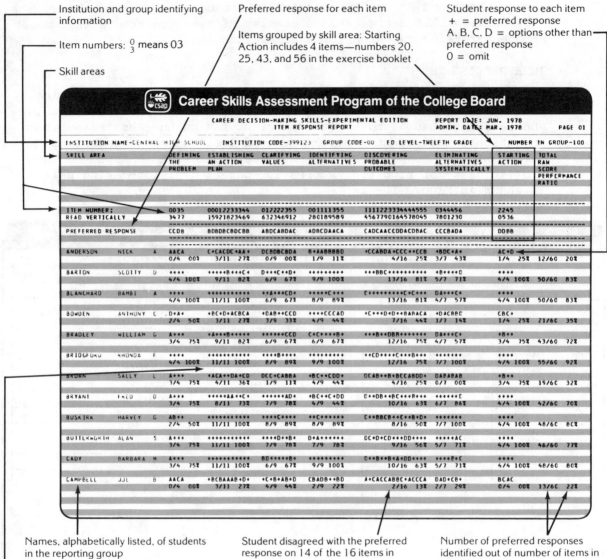

FIGURE 10-5. CSAP profile for reporting item responses. Reprinted with permission from *Implementing the Career Skills Assessment Program.* Copyright © 1978 by College Entrance Examination Board, New York.

skill areas that need improvement; individuals or an entire group can then be given instruction in these areas.

All the skills are thoroughly explained in the many support materials for the program. However, additional information on the validity of the inventories and on exercises for improving the skill areas measured in this program is needed.

Case of a High School Senior Lacking in Self-Awareness

Carol was both confused and infuriated by her poor scores (disagreement with preferred responses) on the CSAP. She felt she was as ready as anyone to make a career decision. "What's all this nonsense about self-evaluation?" she asked herself as she waited outside the counselor's office. "After all, I have been in school almost 12 years, my grades are good, and I'm ready to go to college. Or am I ready to go to college? Maybe I should go to work? Oh well, I'm just like the rest of my classmates; I'll know what to do when I graduate."

The counselor sensed that Carol was upset. He realized that Carol had rarely received what she conceived of as low scores on a test. She had been a model student throughout her school career. With emotional overtones, Carol immediately brought up the issue of low scores. The counselor acknowledged her concerns and suggested that they evaluate her scores by studying the content of the inventories. The counselor explained that the CSAP inventories were different from tests on which one received grades; the CSAP inventories were used primarily as counseling tools to help students in developing skills for career planning and decision-making. This information seemed to have little bearing on Carol's emotional state. The counselor allowed considerable time for Carol to express her feelings of frustration. She eventually returned to the content of the inventories.

The item response profiles were used to identify the specific responses Carol made on the inventories. The counselor and Carol started with the results for self-evaluation and development skills.

Carol: I missed quite a few of the questions dealing with understanding individual differences. I don't know what that means.
Counselor: Okay, let's look at some of the items.

This review revealed that Carol had difficulty recognizing her own emotional states and the emotional reactions of others. Although Carol was threatened by her answers on the items, she recognized the differences between her responses and those considered appropriate. As Carol became increasingly defensive, however, the counselor decided to set up another meeting to give himself time to plot strategy and create a more productive atmosphere.

Carol seemed relaxed at the beginning of the second conference. The counselor hoped that she would be able to accept suggestions for programs that could help her. He began by reviewing the information in the *Guide to Self Evaluation and Development Skills* (College Entrance Examination Board, 1978), provided by the CSAP.

While discussing the section on individual differences, Carol commented that she had difficulty meeting people and felt quite suspicious of others' motives. She also admitted feeling insecure and uncomfortable when around her peers. As the discussion progressed, it became apparent that Carol, a good student, lacked an understanding of herself and the ability to apply knowledge about herself to career opportunities. For example, in the career awareness skills inventory she had difficulty relating values and needs to occupations. She also had difficulty evaluating herself in relation to occupational alternatives as suggested by the results of the career decision-making skills inventory. Finally, she had difficulty in dealing with conflicts in a work situation as suggested by results of the work effectiveness skills inventory.

The combined results of the inventory clearly pointed out the problems Carol would have in career planning. As she recognized her inability to understand individual differences and her lack of self-understanding, she became convinced that action was necessary. The counselor was now in a position to suggest programs and individual exercises that would help Carol in self-concept development. In this case, the results from the various inventories provided both Carol and the counselor with specific information to be used in planning strategies designed to develop skills and enhance self-awareness.

COMBINING SEPARATE TESTS AND INVENTORIES

The preceding sections provide examples of programs specifically designed to provide multidimensional assessment results. Another way to obtain such results is to combine several of the tests and inventories discussed in previous chapters. In the case of Art (below), the results of the DAT, the KOIS, and the WVI were combined to provide information designed to stimulate career exploration. In the case of Harry (below), achievement and aptitude test results were combined with the results of an interest inventory to enhance the self-awareness so vital to career decision-making and educational planning.

Case of a High School Senior Attempting to Decide Whether to Go to College or to Work

During the fall semester of his senior year in high school, Art made an appointment to see the career counselor for help in planning his future. He informed the counselor that he thought about going to college "like everyone else," but he also thought about going to work after graduation. His parents were indifferent about his plans and left these decisions to him. After a rather lengthy conversation concerning Art's likes, dislikes, and options, Art agreed with the counselor that a battery of tests and inventories would help with decision-making. Specifically, Art was to take the DAT to help him understand his abilities and then relate these abilities to his interests as measured by the KOIS and his values as measured by the WVI.

As the counselor reviewed the results of the DAT, shown in Figure 10-6, she questioned whether Art currently possessed the aptitude necessary for college work. She was particularly concerned about the low scores in verbal reasoning and numerical ability, as these two scores provide a fairly reliable index for predicting academic success. She was aware that colleges vary in their requirements and did not want to eliminate this option, but at the same time Art's low scores had to be considered in their discussion. She also noticed that his highest score was in mechanical reasoning.

The results of the KOIS were valid (V score above .45). The highest occupational scores (males) were for engineer, mechanical engineer, industrial, and auto mechanic. His highest college major scores (males) were for engineering, mechanical engineering, civil engineering, and physical education. The counselor wondered whether Art's apparent interest in occupations that require a college degree reflected a current interest Art had in attending college rather than

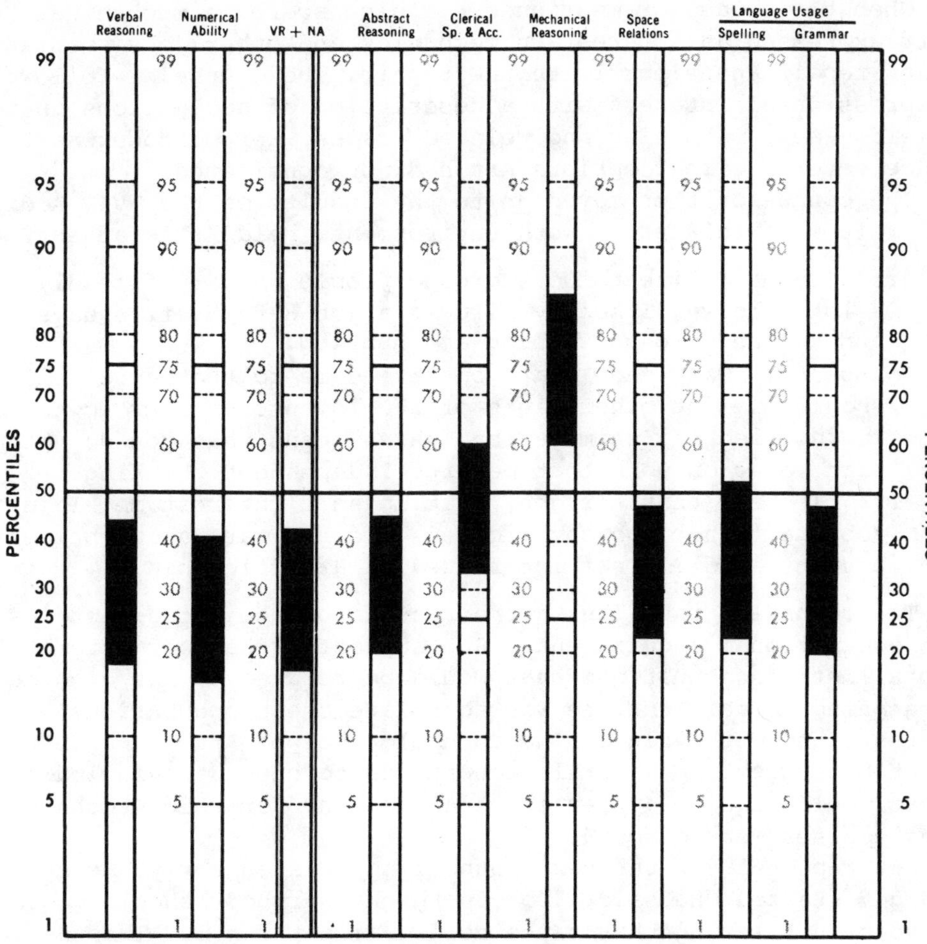

Verbal Reasoning | Numerical Ability | VR + NA | Abstract Reasoning | Clerical Sp. & Acc. | Mechanical Reasoning | Space Relations | Language Usage — Spelling | Grammar

PERCENTILES: 99, 95, 90, 80, 75, 70, 60, 50, 40, 30, 25, 20, 10, 5, 1

FIGURE 10-6. Art's DAT profile. From *Differential Aptitude Test* by G. K. Bennett, H. G. Seashore, and A. G. Wesman, 1974. The Psychological Corporation. Reprinted by permission.

his true interests, especially in light of his low aptitude for college work.

On the WVI, Art's highest scores were in supervisory relations (values a friendly supervisor), associates (values working with desirable people), way of life (values a desirable lifestyle), and surroundings (values a pleasant environment). His lowest scores were in intellectual stimulation (values independent thinking), independence (values independent actions), and aesthetics (values artistic endeavors). These results were of particular interest to the counselor because Art placed a high value on the working environment, but a low value on intellectual stimulation.

Art seemed somewhat embarrassed by the DAT scores but stated that he did not consider himself a good student. The counselor then asked about his interest in attending college. Art replied: "Well, all of my friends are going to college, and I figure that I ought to go too. I got through high school somehow, and I ought to be able to make it in college." These remarks indicated that Art did not know what college would be like. His reason for going to college reflected little knowledge of college requirements and a lackadaisical attitude toward exploring other options available to him.

When the counselor mentioned his high score on mechanical reasoning, Art expressed an interest in mechanics and other jobs such as television repair and electric engine repair. The counselor followed this expression of interest with a description of occupations in technical fields—auto mechanics and related trades. Her purpose was to introduce several career options Art had not considered.

The counselor then moved on to the results of the WVI. A discussion of values as related to work environments held Art's attention.

Art: Yeah, I like to work around people who are friendly and visit a lot. The way I see my life is a job 8-to-5, five days a week, and a chance to go fishing and hunting.

Counselor: Okay, now that you have come to that conclusion, we should examine other parts of the inventory. Your lowest score was in intellectual stimulation, which means that you do not place a high value on work that permits independent thinking.

Art: I guess that's right. That doesn't interest me. I just want a job that's not too complicated. I don't care about being independent, and I'm not interested in artistic things.

The counselor then linked the results of the assessment instruments to occupational requirements. She suggested that Art attempt to develop a list of occupations that would be related to his high mechanical reasoning score. Next, he was to relate these occupations to his interests and work values. The counselor helped Art to begin this assignment by suggesting several occupations to consider, including jobs that would require apprentice training and for which technical training courses were offered.

Art reported for the next counseling session early. He seemed eager to get started. He said: "Do you think everybody should go to college? I've been thinking that maybe college isn't for me. This assignment you gave me helped me to see that I'm actually more interested in jobs that require some education and training but not necessarily a four-year program."

The counselor asked Art to explain how he arrived at this conclusion. Art replied: "When we started talking about my values, I realized that I was thinking about college because 'most everyone else was. That isn't really me; besides my grades and test scores are not very high."

The counselor and Art continued their discussion and reached some tentative conclusions. Art would not give up the idea of college completely, but he would explore other options also. He therefore looked into occupations that require college training as well as into technical occupations and trades.

In this case the combined test results provided the stimulus for considering career options from several perspectives. Measuring aptitudes, interests, and work values provided Art with information he had never considered for career exploration. The discussions of the results helped Art relate his characteristics and traits to occupational and educational information. He was stimulated to explore several different options and gained an understanding of the complexities of the world of work.

Case of a High School Senior with a Poor Attitude Toward School

Being the last one to enter the classroom and the first one to leave typified Harry's attitude toward school. Most teachers wondered why he bothered to stick around for his senior year. Perhaps it was the good time he was apparently having, or maybe it prevented him from having to go to work. The counselor had made numerous attempts for two years to get Harry interested in coming in for counseling, but Harry managed to evade the counselor's office. Thus, the counselor was quite surprised when Harry's name appeared on the appointment list.

Harry further amazed the counselor when he asked for help in planning what to do after high school. He informed the counselor that he began thinking about his future because of the results of a test he had taken. He explained that the entire class had been required to take several tests and that his teacher informed him that he had scored high on the aptitude test. The counselor and Harry set up another meeting in a few days so that the counselor could gather the test data. In the meantime, the counselor suggested that Harry take an interest inventory. The counselor was interested in maintaining Harry's enthusiasm as well as in obtaining a measure of his interests.

The counselor discovered that Harry did indeed do well on the DAT, which had been administered to all seniors. The counselor was surprised to find that his scores were above the 90th percentile for verbal reasoning and numerical ability. Abstract reasoning and mechanical reasoning also were significantly high (above the 75th percentile). The counselor wondered why Harry let all this talent go to waste during his school career.

Achievement test scores reflected Harry's poor academic performance. Most scores were below the 50th percentile (national group) with the exception of mathematics reasoning, which was at the 75th percentile. The counselor concluded that even Harry's high aptitude could not make up for the academic work he had not done.

The SDS provided insights into Harry's modal personal style; enterprising was his dominant personality type. An enterprising person, according to the SDS description, is adventurous, extroverted, and aggressive—a good description of Harry. Although Harry didn't use these characteristics in academic endeavors, he was considered a leader by his peer group. His summary code, ECS (enterprising, conventional, social), suggested that he would prefer sales jobs such as insurance underwriter, real estate salesperson, and grain buyer (Holland, 1979a).

In the next session Harry told the counselor that he was planning to attend college and devote much more of his energy to college courses than he had to high school courses. The counselor took this opportunity to point out the discrepancies between Harry's aptitude test scores, and his grades and achievement test scores. He emphasized that Harry had the potential for making much better grades than he had in the past. Harry was quick to agree that he had goofed off and would have to pay the price now. The counselor suggested that Harry enroll in a summer course sponsored by the community college learning resource center to upgrade his basic skills and improve his study habits.

Harry was undecided about a career because he had given little
thought to his future. The SDS results provided him with several
specific occupations to consider.

Harry: I think I would like sales work of some kind or to have my
   own business. Do you think I should study business?
Counselor: That may be a good possibility. However, I think you
   should take the time to research what is offered in a typical
   school of business at a university. But first let's consider
   what's involved in career decision-making.

The counselor continued by emphasizing the importance of self-
understanding in career planning. He discussed the significance of
modal personal style as identified by the SDS. Harry recognized that
the results of the aptitude and achievement measures also contributed
to his self-understanding; they provided stimulus for further discussion. As a result Harry was challenged by the counselor to devote time
to researching the world of work in relation to his personal characteristics. Harry thanked the counselor for helping him establish some
direction and set up several appointments to discuss and evaluate the
careers he was exploring on the basis of his personal characteristics.

SUMMARY

In this chapter combinations of assessment results were discussed as a
useful way of helping individuals consider their characteristics and
traits in career counseling. This chapter emphasizes that assessment
results should not be used in isolation; we should consider the totality of individual needs. Assessment results taken from different types
of tests and inventories provide useful information in the career
decision process.

QUESTIONS AND EXERCISES

   1. Give at least two examples to illustrate the use of a combination of tests. Include an aptitude test, an interest inventory, and a
value inventory.

   2. How would you determine which instruments to use if you were requested to recommend tests and inventories for a group of 10th graders
interested in career exploration?

   3. Defend the following statement: Multidimensional assessment results are more effective in career counseling than are the results of
only one instrument.

   4. How would you explain to an individual the differences in norms
when using a combination of assessment results some of which are based
on local norms and others on national norms?

   5. Illustrate how assessment results from two different instruments
can support each other and how they can point out conflicts.

11
Using Assessment for the Academically Disadvantaged and Handicapped

Since the early 1970s attention has been focused on rehabilitation services for the physically and mentally handicapped and career counseling programs for the disadvantaged. The major goal of these services and programs is to maximize each individual's potential for employment. Legislation that requires equal access to training and employment for the handicapped and disadvantaged has led to intense scrutinization of assessment methods and procedures. The diverse needs of handicapped and disadvantaged individuals require specially designed assessment instruments to assist them in career planning.

The challenge of meeting their needs is complicated by the fact that both handicapped and disadvantaged people have a wide variety of ethnic and racial backgrounds. It has been claimed that many tests are discriminatory because their norms are based on white, male, middle-class individuals and, therefore, do not account for the unique characteristics of minorities and the special needs of the handicapped. The issue of test discrimination will no doubt affect the future research efforts of numerous individuals in the counseling profession.

In the first part of this chapter examples of tests and inventories specially designed for the academically disadvantaged are reviewed. In the second part specially designed measuring instruments for the handicapped are discussed. Specifically, two achievement tests and one interest inventory for academically disadvantaged and handicapped individuals are reviewed. Also a prevocational information battery that measures skills considered important for employability and one work-sample test for use with the handicapped are reviewed. Sample cases illustrate the use of assessment for these groups. The tests described in this chapter may be supplemented when appropriate with some of the inventories and tests discussed previously.

BASIC OCCUPATIONAL LITERACY TEST (BOLT)

BOLT is an achievement test designed to measure the reading and arithmetic skills of educationally disadvantaged adults. It is published by the U.S. Department of Labor, Manpower Administration, for use by various governmental agencies including state employment agencies. BOLT is used primarily to assess skills for occupational training or occupational entry.

The reading skills part of the test consists of two subtests: reading vocabulary and reading comprehension. Arithmetic skills are assessed by two subtests: arithmetic computation and arithmetic reasoning. The reading passages and arithmetic problems are considered to be of interest to and within the experience of the educationally disadvantaged.

The test has four levels of difficulty: advanced, high intermediate, basic intermediate, and fundamental. The Wide Range Scale is used as a pretest to determine which level should be administered to each individual. Alternate forms are available for each level of difficulty. This instrument has been reviewed by Cronbach (1978) and Tuckman (1978).

Reliability coefficients obtained by KR-20 range from .61 to .82 with a median of .76. Validity data are in the process of being collected. Tuckman (1978) suggests that this test appears to be a good one for predicting job outcomes.

INTERPRETING BOLT

BOLT test results are expressed in standard scores and General Educational Development (GED) levels. Standard score units cannot be compared with GATB standard scores because of the restricted norm sample of educationally disadvantaged adults. However, the standard scores used in BOLT are on the same scale for all levels and therefore can be compared across all four forms. Thus, retest results for an individual can be compared with original test results even though the retest is at a higher level.

The GED functional levels used for interpretation range from 1 to 6. Level 1 is the expected functional level in reasoning, mathematics, and language development for grades 1-3; level 2 for grades 4-6; level 3 for grades 7-8; level 4 for grades 9-12; level 5 for college freshmen and sophomores; level 6 for college juniors and seniors. A detailed explanation of all levels may be found in the DOT.

Using GED levels as a frame of reference, the counselor can determine whether an individual's functional level is appropriate for an occupation under consideration. In some cases the counselor may recommend remedial training to meet job requirements. Thus, the functional levels primarily provide guidelines for educational planning and career exploration. An example of the BOLT score report is shown in Figure 11-1.

Career counselors can locate the nearest agency where this instrument is available. Most state employment agencies or rehabilitation offices should be able to provide it.

Case of an Older Man with Little Education

Mr. Page, at age 52, reported to the rehabilitation counselor needing a job. He had worked for a long time on a large cattle ranch near his home. But the ranch had been sold and was now being developed for housing, leaving Mr. Page without a means of support. He had quit school during his early elementary years and had little job experience other than working cattle and tractor maintenance.

```
PAGE, Charlie    G.
PRINT NAME     Last      First     Middle Initial
Address    General Delivery
           Anytown, U.S.A.
```

Classification

Sex ☒ M ☐ F   ☒ Age 40 to 64

BASIC OCCUPATIONAL LITERACY TEST

Test Date	Test Form	Raw Score	Standard Score	GED Level		Retest Date	Retest Form	Raw Score	Standard Score	GED Level		Wide Range Scale Scores
4/2/80	RV3A	3	69	1								Reading
4/2/80	RC3A	2	71	1								
4/2/80	AC4A	3	70	1								Arithmetic
4/2/80	AR3A	3	63	1								

COMMENTS: *Instructions had to be repeated several times. Charlie worked very slowly and seemed to feel out-of-place. He needed constant encouragement.*

TEST RECORD CARD

NONREADING APTITUDE TEST BATTERY AND BASIC OCCUPATIONAL LITERACY TEST

For sale by the Superintendent of Documents, U.S. Government Printing Office
Washington, D.C. 20402 (in 100's)
Stock No. 029-000-00139-1

U.S. DEPARTMENT OF LABOR
U.S. GOVERNMENT PRINTING OFFICE : 1978 O-267-690

Manpower Administration
MA Form 7-23 (R-9/71)

FIGURE 11-1. BOLT profile. From *Basic Occupational Literacy Test*, 1973. U.S. Government Printing Office.

Because of Mr. Page's limited educational background, the counselor decided to use BOLT to assess his reading and arithmetic levels. The pretest, Wide Range Scale, was administered to determine the level of BOLT to use; the fundamental form of BOLT was selected. The results may be seen in Figure 11.1. They indicated that Mr. Page was functioning at level 1. The counselor reviewed the description of that level in the DOT. As the counselor suspected, Mr. Page would probably be able to carry out only simple instructions and needed a highly structured job with little or no variation in tasks. Most instructions would have to be given to him orally or demonstrated. Mr. Page's educational disadvantage was severe, and the counselor realized that this would place restrictions on his potential for employment.

Mr. Page was a proud and sensitive individual, and the counselor had to approach job considerations with a great deal of diplomacy. He asked Mr. Page to describe some of the skills he had learned on the ranch to determine whether any of them could be applied in local work settings. Because Mr. Page lacked information concerning jobs other than those he had had on the ranch, it was difficult for him to relate the skills he had obtained in his previous work to other occupations. However, Mr. Page admitted his lack of occupational information and told the counselor that he knew that he didn't have much schooling. He said he would be willing to take a job where he would be required to learn something new. Eventually, three job possibilities were agreed on—custodian, tractor mechanic's helper, and assembly line worker in a local factory. The counselor explained each of these jobs

in detail, and a visit to the sites helped Mr. Page decide to apply
for the job as a tractor mechanic's helper.

In this case the test results identified Mr. Page's functional
level. Even though the counselor suspected that Mr. Page's functional
level was low, he wanted an objective measure. The counselor had
learned from experience that many clients had studied on their own and
through experience were able to function at higher levels than that
indicated by their formal education. In many other cases the opposite
was true: individuals functioned below their formal educational levels.
The test also provided a starting point for considering jobs. Both
the counselor and Mr. Page were able to take into account Mr. Page's
current limitations in the job search.

ADULT BASIC LEARNING EXAMINATION (ABLE)

ABLE was designed to measure the general educational level of adults
who have not completed high school. It is used to determine achievement ranging from the primary grade level to the 12th grade level. It
may be used for educational planning or training for job placement.
Three levels have been developed: level I (grades 1-4), level II
(grades 5-8), level III (grades 9-12). Two forms are available for
each level. Levels I and II are not timed. Level III is timed, but the
time limits allow most individuals to complete the test. Split-half
reliabilities are satisfactory; they tend to be in the .80s and .90s
for each subtest. Correlations between ABLE and the Stanford Achievement Test subtests are primarily in the .70s. Additional empirical
evidence of validity is needed.

ABLE measures achievement in vocabulary, reading, spelling, and
arithmetic. The test was not designed to be a diagnostic instrument
in that the results do not reveal specific weaknesses in any of the
areas tested. The test was constructed to cover typical adult problems, tasks, and activities. For example, newspaper articles are used
in the reading section of the test. The authors report that the questions in the test help to establish rapport between the individual
and the counselor because they are common problems encountered by
many adults.

INTERPRETING ABLE

The authors of ABLE strongly suggest that local normative samples be
established whenever possible for meaningful interpretation. This
point is well founded; because of the great diversity in the adult
population, normative samples for adults should be carefully scrutinized before making any significant career decisions based on test
scores. Every effort should be made to find a norm population that
closely matches the individual being tested in ethnic background, experiences, and training.

Table 11-1 provides the descriptive information for the adult samples used to standardize ABLE level III. The five groups shown in the
table are further identified in the ABLE manual for level III. For
example, group III comprised high school equivalency candidates in
Topeka and Wichita, Kansas. Similar information is given for each

TABLE 11-1. Description of Adult Samples for ABLE Level III

Variable	Group III	Group IV	Group V	Group VI	Group VII
N Count	116	173	102	163	221
Sex					
Male	31.9%	51.4%	87.3%	7.4%	90.5%
Female	68.1	48.6	12.7	92.6	9.5
Age					
50 and over	3.4%	3.5%	——	0.6%	0.5%
40-49	18.2	15.0	2.9%	17.8	3.6
30-39	45.6	21.4	7.9	34.4	23.5
20-29	25.0	29.5	50.0	39.2	60.6
below 20	7.8	30.6	39.2	8.0	11.8
Median Age	34	27	22	30	26
Race					
White	96.6%	89.6%	98.0%	27.6%	99.1%
Black	1.7	9.8	2.0	69.3	——
Other	1.7	.6	——	3.1	.9
Employed	63.8%	57.2%	47.1%	0.0%	0.0%
Last Grade Completed					
12 or over	.9%	2.3%	86.3%	4.3%	.5%
11	22.4	13.9	1.0	17.8	1.8
10	31.9	28.3	4.9	26.4	12.2
9	20.7	22.6	2.9	25.7	32.1
8	19.8	12.1	3.9	16.6	44.8
7	4.3	12.1	——	4.3	5.4
6	——	5.2	1.0	3.1	1.8
5	——	1.2	——	——	——
4 or below	——	2.3	——	1.8	1.4
Median Grade Completed	10	9	12	9	8
Median Stanford Achievement Test: High School Standard Scores					
Reading	40.0	42.0	47.0	39.1	39.0
Spelling	39.3	45.0	44.7	46.7	40.4
Numerical Computation	41.0	43.3	48.1	36.8	47.0

Reproduced from the Adult Basic Learning Examination by permission. Copyright © 1970 by Harcourt Brace Jovanovich, Inc. All rights reserved.

group. The descriptive information given on sex, age, race, and educational background should allow the counselor to determine whether the local adult population matches closely enough to provide meaningful interpretations of the test results.

An important characteristic of the ABLE test results is that they correspond to Stanford Achievement Test results—that is, scores from ABLE can be converted to Stanford Achievement Test score equivalents. Comparing Stanford results with ABLE results provides the counselor with the vast amount of information on school achievement available from research conducted with the Stanford test.

ABLE is well constructed and meets its primary goal of measuring levels of achievement of adult groups. Reviews of ABLE are provided by Hieronymus (1972), Fry (1972), and Hall (1972).

Case of a School Dropout Seeking Work

Gus had a poor educational background. During his school years the truant officer was constantly after him. Gus disliked school so much that he ran away from home and got a job for several years as able seaman in the Merchant Marine.

The counselor tried to make Gus feel comfortable when he reported for his first session. It was apparent that Gus felt out of place. Gus needed placement in a local job because he had the responsibility of taking care of his aging parents and maintaining their home. However, the counselor was concerned about Gus's educational background and decided that some measure of his academic abilities was necessary. Her plan was to administer the ABLE to determine whether Gus had the educational background required for employment in a local firm. Because ABLE provides measures of spelling, reading, and numerical competence, the counselor had discovered that a total battery score provided a fairly reliable estimate of an individual's ability to perform in local industry. Fortunately, the counselor had collected data from and developed local norms based on individuals placed in this firm.

When Gus was approached about the possibility of taking an achievement test, he was intimidated. The counselor explained that the test was designed to cover typical adult problems, tasks, and activities and was not like a test that a student would take in high school. She also added that the scores would help her determine whether he was capable of working at a local firm. Gus's anxiety was somewhat lowered by this explanation; he was particularly interested in placement in the local firm, for he had heard that working conditions were fairly good and that the pay was reasonable. Working there, he reasoned, would provide him with an outside income to maintain a home.

The results of ABLE indicated that Gus's chances of success in the local firm were fairly good; he scored in the fifth stanine within the local norms developed by the counselor.

Counselor: Your scores are in the average range compared with others from our community who have taken this test during the last eight years. This indicates to me that you have a fairly good chance of being successful in the local firm we have discussed. However, if you want to move up in the firm, you will need further training in the basics such as reading and arithmetic.

Gus: It has been a mighty long time since I have taken a test like this. I don't know what to say except that I was able to do a little studying on my own when I wasn't doing my chores, and I would like very much to improve my reading, spelling, and arithmetic skills.

The counselor explained to Gus that even though the test was a fairly good indication of his ability to compete in the local firm, he
would have to adjust to a working environment that was different from
the one he was accustomed to. She explained that he now would be working with people whose values might be quite different from his. The
counselor offered to help Gus adjust to the new working environment
and to provide him with suggestions for upgrading his educational
skills.

In this case, results from ABLE not only were used as a link to
local employment, but also provided a basis for discussing adjustment
to a new working environment. In addition, the test results provided
an opening for the counselor to discuss the importance of upgrading
basic educational skills for occupational mobility.

WIDE RANGE INTEREST-OPINION TEST (WRIOT)

The WRIOT is a pictorial interest inventory developed for measuring
interests and attitudes of the academically disadvantaged and the
severely disabled. The 450 pictures are presented in groups of three
(150 combinations); the individual chooses the most liked and the
least liked. The activities portrayed in the pictures come from a wide
range of unskilled, technical, professional, and managerial occupations. The WRIOT is untimed and may be administered to groups or individually. The authors report that the time for individual administration is approximately 40 minutes and for group administration 50-60
minutes. Scoring is done either by hand or by computer.

Split-half reliability coefficients by the Cureton formula (Guilford, 1954) for each scale in the 1979 edition range from .83 to .95
for males and from .82 to .95 for females. Validity was established
by correlations between the WRIOT and the Geist Picture Interest Inventory. Most correlations are high and within satisfactory ranges.
However, additional validity studies are needed for women, mental
retardates, and ethnic minority groups.

INTERPRETING THE WRIOT

The results are organized into 18 interest clusters and eight attitude clusters. These are shown in the computer format in Figure
11-2. The manual provides a definition of each interest cluster with
information on correlations with other clusters by sex, job title,
and lists of positive and negative items as related to the cluster.
The eight attitude clusters are similarly defined. Norms for all
scales are available by sex and age (from age 5 on up). Means and
standard deviations by sex and age are also provided for each interest and attitude cluster.

The results are reported by standard score (mean = 50, S.D. = 10)
for each cluster and attitude scale. The profile reports scores by
five categories ranging from very low (20-31) to very high (69-80).
Scores of 50 or more are considered positive interests and attitudes;
below 50, negative. The authors suggest that the individual consider
the entire profile of scores (both negative and positive measures)
in career exploration.

JASTAK ASSESSMENT SYSTEMS

PROFILE FOR WRIOT
WIDE RANGE INTEREST — OPINION TEST
JOSEPH F. JASTAK, Ph.D. — SARAH JASTAK, Ph.D.

NAME Arturo   AGE 17   SEX M   DATE 9/18/81   EXAMINER Mr. Jones

RAW	T	CLUSTER	VERY LOW 20-31	LOW 32-37	BELOW AVG. 38-43	AVERAGE 50 44-49	51-56	ABOVE AVG. 57-62	HIGH 63-68	VERY HIGH 69-80	DESCRIPTION (Scores and Graph explained on back)
	35	A ART		――――――							is skilled in arts and crafts
	25	B LITERATURE	―――――								reads, writes, communicates by word
	38	C MUSIC			――――						plays, composes, and enjoys music
	37	D DRAMA		―――――――――							goes to stage plays; acts out own feelings
	39	E SALES			―――						gets people to buy things and ideas
	35	F MANAGEMENT		―――――							directs the work of others
	30	G OFFICE WORK	――――――――――――――――――								types, files, does paper work
	40	H PERSONAL SERVICE			―――――――――――						caters to individual needs and comforts
	38	I PROTECTIVE SERVICE			―――――						safeguards people, property, country
	43	J SOCIAL SERVICE			―――――――――						works in education, health, employment
	30	K SOCIAL SCIENCE	―――――――――								studies the actions of people and groups
	32	L BIOLOGICAL SCIENCE	――――								studies the bodies of living things
	30	M PHYSICAL SCIENCE	――――――――――――――――								studies the motion of bodies in space-time
	39	N NUMBER			――――						works with numbers; knows algebra; computes
	67	O MECHANICS						+++++			designs, builds, and maintains machines
	65	P MACHINE OPERATION						+++++			operates machines, processes materials
	64	Q OUTDOOR						+++++			works on farm, in forest, in garden, at sea
	43	R ATHLETICS		―――――――――――――							takes part in group or individual sports
	35	S SEDENTARI-NESS		―――							sits mainly in one place on the job
	43	T RISK			―――――――						takes on dangerous and risky jobs
	52	U AMBITION				++++++					wants to improve self, income, status
	38	V CHOSEN SKILL LEVEL			――――――――――――						works at shown level of difficulty
	55	W SEX STEREOTYPE					+++++++				prefers work formerly done by persons of own sex
	32	X AGREEMENT	――――――――――――――――								likes/dislikes pictures most people like/dislike
	40	Y NEGATIVE BIAS		―――――――							motivated by dislikes
	57	Z POSITIVE BIAS						+++++++			motivated by likes

Copyright 1978 By Jastak Associates, Inc.   1526 Gilpin Avenue   Wilmington, DE 19806

FIGURE 11-2. WRIOT profile. From Wide Range Interest-Opinion Test by J. F. Jastak and S. Jastak. Copyright 1978 by Jastak Associates, Inc. Reprinted by permission.

The manual for the WRIOT has been well prepared in that each scale is clearly defined. Additional information on using the test with mental retardates and individuals who have reading problems is needed because this instrument was designed especially for nonreaders. The difficulty in hand scoring the test most likely will make it mandatory for most users to have it computer scored. This instrument has been reviewed by Zytowski (1978).

Case of a High School Student Lacking Basic Education Skills

Shortly after Arturo's arrival at Central High, his teacher referred him to the counselor's office for the purpose of placement in a proper educational program. The teacher reported that Arturo had a low reading level and could not compete with the students in her class. She had talked briefly to Arturo about his background but did not have the time to investigate the reasons for his lack of educational achievement. The counselor discovered that because Arturo's family had moved around a great deal in the last ten years he had missed a significant amount of schooling.

When the counselor mentioned tests, Arturo said that he had taken a series of tests at the school he had previously attended. The counselor called the school and asked for the test results. The achievement test indicated that Arturo was performing very much below grade level in all areas. He was particularly low in language skills, having a third grade reading level. The counselor discovered that Arturo's mother could speak only Spanish and his father knew little English. Arturo stated that he forgot the English he learned at school after spending a summer at home. Arturo explained that he had some interest in academic subjects but was more interested in finding a job because his family needed an additional source of income. However, Arturo was unable to specify a vocational choice.

The counselor selected the WRIOT as an instrument that might provide some stimulus for discussion of future occupations. Because this inventory measures interests by having the individual respond to activities portrayed in pictures, Arturo's poor reading ability did not handicap him.

Arturo's profile is shown in Figure 11-2. As expected, Arturo had little interest in academic subjects but did show a high interest in mechanics, machine operations, and outdoor activities. The counselor was pleased to see that Arturo scored on the positive side of the ambition scale, which supported his claim of wanting to improve his vocational skills and income. Arturo agreed with the high score on the sex stereotype scale in that he basically preferred work traditionally done by men. The results also indicated that Arturo was highly motivated by his likes as opposed to being motivated by his dislikes.

Arturo responded positively to the results and indicated that he felt that they were a fairly good measure of his interests. He added that he much preferred to work with his hands as opposed to reading or writing. The counselor turned to the mechanics scale description and reviewed some of the key positive items, as shown in Figure 11-3. He noticed that the positively keyed items include upholstering, assembling, repairing, servicing, and construction work. The job titles for this scale include automobile mechanic, cabinet maker, carpenter, concrete layer, construction worker, draftsman, electrician, gas

Mechanics
O – **Mechanics**

Cluster Items
The following items are consistently liked by persons wishing to engage in **Manual Building** and **Repair** activities and are therefore positively correlated with this cluster.

Female	Key Positive Items	Male
2 A. upholster chair		2 A. upholster chair
6 C. put up steel girders		6 C. put up steel girders
20 C. repair telepnone lines		20 C. repair telephone lines
41 B. repair TV sets		31 B. assemble machines
43 A. repair record players		41 B. repair TV sets
47 B. make cabinets		43 A. repair record players
48 B. cut out dress patterns		47 B. make cabinets
65 A. construct field fences		50 C. repair steeples
73 C. do masonry work		61 B. service cars
78 C. repair office machines		71 C. install traffic lights
82 C. build roofs		73 C. do masonry work
95 C. build bridges		78 C. repair office machines
106 C. do carpentry work		82 C. build roofs
110 C. pour concrete floors		95 C. build bridges
141 A. make candy		106 C. do carpentry work
		110 C. pour concrete floors
		139 B. install electric fixtures
		140 C. lay bricks

Female	Secondary Positive Items	Male
5 B. do plumbing work		5 B. do plumbing work
17 B. bake pastry		10 C. polish floors
32 C. repair appliances		29 B. work as ship steward-stewardess
37 C. skin dive		46 B. set type for print
61 B. service cars		48 B. cut out dress patterns
70 A. work on airplanes		49 C. sell hardware
71 C. install traffic lights		57 C. paint house
75 B. run steamroller		66 A. drive dump truck
84 B. wrap packages		67 C. spray trees
87 C. operate a bulldozer		74 B. run a mixing machine
91 C. trim hedges		84 B. wrap packages
101 C. check soil temperature		87 C. operate a bulldozer
128 A. saw lumber		91 B. operate cranes
142 C. repair shoes by machine		112 B. examine leaf etchings
149 A. do welding		122 A. operate street cleaner
		141 B. run duplicating machine
		142 C. repair shoes by machine
		145 C. operate power hammer

The following items are consistently disliked by persons wishing to engage in **Manual Building** and **Repair**. Their negative choices are positively correlated with this cluster.

Female	Key Negative Items	Male
2 C. sell appliances		5 C. broadcast the news
20 B. explain sales graph		20 B. explain sales graph
32 A. massage person's back		22 B. sell real estage
50 A. chauffeur		33 A. conduct orchestra
58 B. pitch baseballs		42 B. carry trays in restaurant
75 C. serve as congressperson		49 A. sell fire, burglary insurance
86 B. drill recruits		70 B. file archives, records
87 B. act as army general		71 A. work as bartender
88 C. work as receptionist		83 B. guide tours
89 B. attend executive meetings		85 B. collect coins
95 B. advise on bank loans		87 B. act as army general
114 C. prepare newspaper ads		107 C. speak at club
127 C. argue before jury		134 B. sell theater tickets
142 A. run city as mayor		141 C. sing in opera
149 B. sell stocks and bonds		142 A. run city as mayor
		149 B. sell stocks and bonds

Definition
Choices in this cluster express preferences for the designing, building, assembling, erecting, maintaining, and repairing of three-dimensional structures.

Significant Correlations with other clusters:
Females: Positive: art (A), machine operation (P), outdoor (Q)

Negative: literature (B), sales (E), management (F), office work (G), protective service (I), social service (J), social science (K), number (N)

Males: Positive: art (A), physical science (M), machine operation (P), risk (T)

Negative: literature (B), music (C), drama (D), sales (E), management (F), personal service (H), social service (J), social science (K), number (N)

Job Titles
Titles may recur in clusters positively correlated with this one.

airplane mechanic
automobile designer
automobile mechanic
automotive engineer
beekeeper
boiler inspector
boiler mechanic
bookbinder
bridge builder
building inspector
cabinet maker
camera repairperson
carpenter
civil engineer
combustion engineer
concrete layer
construction foreperson
construction inspector
construction worker
dental technician
die designer
die maker
draftsman, draftswoman
electrical engineer
electrician
electricians helper
factory foreperson
farm foreperson
fence builder
gas station attendant
gift wrapper

gunsmith
hardware salesperson
heating repairperson
house painter
industrial engineer
leaf examiner
machine assembler
manufacturing foreperson
masonry worker
mechanic
mechanical engineer
medical lab technician
office machine repairperson
pattern cutter
phonograph repairperson
plumber
radio operator
radio technician
recording engineer
refrigeration engineer
roofer
ship steward, stewardess
steel worker
telephone repairperson
television repairperson
toolroom manager
traffic light installer
typesetter
x-ray technician

FIGURE 11-3.   Description of mechanics scale on the WRIOT. From Wide Range Interest-Opinion Test *by J. F. Jastak and S. Jastak. Copyright 1978 by Jastak Associates, Inc. Reprinted by permission.*

station attendant, television repairer, roofer, and machine assembler. The counselor pointed out to Arturo that he also had a high level of interest in machine operations and was interested primarily in outdoor work. Arturo stated that he liked working with machines and working outdoors, but he had never given a great deal of thought to specific jobs. The counselor presented some of the occupations from the list as a point of reference for discussion. Arturo obviously needed additional information about requirements, environments, and skills needed for certain jobs, but the counselor felt that this was a good beginning for career exploration. Specific occupations selected for further investigation by Arturo included electrician's helper, auto mechanic, sheet metal worker, machine operator.

The counselor pointed out that certain academic skills would be required in these jobs and that it would therefore be necessary for Arturo to apply himself in the academic area as well as in specific training programs. The counselor suggested that Arturo visit the vocational-technical training division of the school to learn about the jobs he had elected to explore.

The results of this interest test provided the opportunity for the counselor to help Arturo identify and clarify his interests through activities portrayed in pictures. His motivation for career exploration was also significantly increased by the discussion of the test results. In addition, the results were easily linked to occupational groups and to specific occupations. Finally, the counselor was able to emphasize academic requirements in addition to specific occupational requirements.

SOCIAL AND PREVOCATIONAL INFORMATION BATTERY (SPIB)

The SPIB was developed to measure five long-range goals that are considered to be relevant for educationally and mentally retarded (EMR) students in junior and senior high school. These goals are identified with specific objectives as follows: employability (job search skills and job-related behavior), economic self-sufficiency (banking, budgeting, and purchasing), family living (home management and physical health care), personal habits (hygiene and grooming), and communication (responding appropriately to safety, emergency, and general information signs). The entire test consists of 277 items, which are mostly true-false and are administered verbally.

Reliability estimates obtained by KR-20 for each subtest ranged from .65 to .82 with a median of .75. Test-retest reliabilities over two-week intervals are approximately the same. Meyers (1978) considers the validity acceptable because these scales provide more adequate information for placement and identification of needs than could generally be expected from subjective ratings and appraisals.

INTERPRETING THE SPIB

Three norm-referenced groups are available for interpreting the results of the SPIB: junior high school students, senior high school students, and combinations of junior and senior high school students.

The authors suggest a task-analysis method of evaluating specific competences in each domain measured by the SPIB. For this evaluation method, each content area is divided into subcontent areas. For example, for job-related behavior, the subcontent areas are: knowledge of role and duties of a supervisor, knowledge of appropriate communications, knowledge of what constitutes job completion, and recognition and knowledge of appropriate relations with fellow employees. Each subcontent area also provides the basis for developing instructional activities and for measuring the outcomes of the instructional activities.

SPIB results give the career counselor some indication of the readiness of the handicapped individual to enter the job market. In addition, the information obtained from this battery can be used to establish counseling programs that assist individuals in making an adequate adjustment to the work environment.

A Group Program Based on SPIB Results

The teacher of EMR students made an appointment in early October to see the counselor. She informed the counselor that several of her students would be ready for placement at the end of the school year. However, the SPIB administered at the beginning of the fall term indicated that some students did not have job-related behaviors and job search skills. The teacher requested help from the counselor in developing modules that would simulate work environments in order to teach the students about supervisor-worker relationships, the importance of communication on the job, and factors affecting job performance. Additional modules would be developed to teach students how to prepare resumes, how to conduct themselves in interviews, and how to increase their knowledge of sources of occupational information. The following outline is for the module designed to promote an understanding of supervisor-worker relationships:

Module I: To promote understanding of supervisor-worker relationships.
  Objective: To understand the role of the supervisor.
  Strategy: Worker-supervisor simulation.
  Participants: Two students.
  Materials: Eighteen pencils, six rubber bands.
  Activity: 1. Worker is given orders by supervisor to secure six pencils together with rubber bands.
        2. Supervisor inspects work. Makes suggestions and gives constructive criticism. Changes orders to secure five pencils together.
        3. Classmates, as observers, identify supervisor as boss and identify the supervisor's activities as praising, criticizing, suggesting, instructing, inspecting, and assigning duties.

In this case, the SPIB results identified the need for an educational program and provided the specific data for forming instructional units. A posttest provided data for evaluating the effectiveness of the program and for determining the need for additional programs.

MICRO-TOWER

The Micro-Tower system of vocational evaluation was developed by ICD Rehabilitation and Research Center of New York City. The original instrument, Tower, is an acronym for Testing, Orientation, and Work Evaluation in Rehabilitation. Tower consists of 94 individually administered work samples. Micro-Tower consists of 13 work samples that can be administered to a group over a three-to-five-day period. The Micro-Tower work samples are performance tests that measure aptitudes for a number of unskilled and skilled occupations. These aptitudes are grouped into five broad areas, each measured by specific tests: motor—electronic connector assembly, bottle capping and packing, lamp assembly; clerical perception—zip coding, record checking, filing, mail sorting; spatial—blueprint reading, graphics illustration; numerical—making change, payroll computation; verbal—want ads comprehension, message taking.[1]

The reading level required is third to fourth grade. The work samples can be administered to an individual who is sitting down but do require the use of at least one hand. The individual is required to understand spoken English.

A unique feature of the Micro-Tower system is the involvement of the clients in group discussions designed to explore interests, values, lifestyles, and so forth. A separate manual outlines specific procedures and variations for the discussion groups. One of the major objectives of the discussion groups is to improve the clients' motivation for job placement. Discussion groups are also used before the test in an effort to make the testing situation as nonthreatening as possible.

INTERPRETING MICRO-TOWER

Several kinds of normative data are available including data for a general rehabilitation population, Spanish-speaking individuals, left-handed individuals, the physically disabled, the psychiatrically disturbed, the brain damaged, individuals with cerebral palsy, students in special education, the socially disadvantaged, former drug abusers, former alcoholics, adult offenders, males and females. The variety of norms available for interpretation increases the usefulness of this instrument.

Interpretive materials for the Micro-Tower system are elaborate and thorough. The results are reported on a graph that ranges from weak to strong for the general aptitudes and specific work samples. Additional information for the counselor includes: a report of behavioral observations during testing, a summary of the client's interests and performance; a client data sheet; a summary report, which includes a narrative of the test results; a recommendation summary sheet, which covers areas such as special training; a list of referral recommendations; and a list of vocational recommendations.

The Micro-Tower system grew out of a need for a work evaluation instrument that could be administered to a group in a relatively short period of time. The evaluation system may also be used as a screening

[1]Adapted from Micro-Tower, ICD Rehabilitation and Research Center, New York. Copyright 1977. Reprinted by permission.

device to determine which clients would benefit from an extensive evaluation of specific aptitudes. A manual converts Micro-Tower scores into estimates of the DOT aptitude levels. Several other work-sample tests such as Micro-Tower have been developed, sometimes on a local basis, to meet the specific needs of the handicapped.

Both Micro-Tower and SPIB point out the need for specially developed norms or criterion-referenced objectives based on specific population samples. A growing number of the tests and inventories on the market today have developed normative data from disadvantaged and handicapped population samples. One hopes that additional assessment instruments will be developed in the future to meet the needs of these special groups.

Case of a Brain-Damaged Individual Seeking Employment

The rehabilitation counselor was pleased to see Rex after his long stay in the hospital after a car accident. Rex had substantial head injuries and brain damage. The counselor was particularly concerned about Rex's motor coordination. Rex had been a construction foreman before his accident and was now ready to seek employment again. He had stated earlier that he desired a change of jobs and had agreed that several local industries might provide opportunities for him.

Previous testing revealed that Rex had average intelligence and had maintained his previous academic achievement levels. The counselor arranged for Rex to take the Micro-Tower tests of motor coordination: electronic connector assembly (to assess finger dexterity); bottle capping and packing (to assess manual dexterity), and lamp assembly (to assess manual assembly skills). The counselor felt that these tests were most essential for determining whether Rex was able to handle the tasks required in the local industries under consideration. The results of the test were to be judged as satisfactory (based on level of performance for productive workers in the industries) or un-satisfactory.

On the electronic connectors test (placing metal pins into discs) Rex's performance was satisfactory compared with that of workers in the local industries. The scorer observed that Rex's performance was somewhat affected by his lack of speed but he was able to complete most of the tasks. On the bottle capping and packing test, Rex's performance was also judged satisfactory. The scorer observed that his manual dexterity was good and that Rex was able to learn these tasks quickly. On the lamp assembly test, which requires the use of a screw driver, wire stripper, and long-nose pliers in assembling a lamp, Rex's average performance was judged as satisfactory for meeting local job requirements. The counselor felt that this work sample was crucial because it closely resembled the kinds of tasks required in a number of local industries.

Rex seemed pleased with his performance: "I was really under pressure before I took those tests. I just didn't know if I could handle it. Now I feel more confident that I can take on another job."

The counselor informed Rex that his physician felt that he would continue to show improvement in tasks requiring fine visual-motor co-ordination. In the meantime, the counselor suggested that they consider how his physical condition would affect his personal relationships in a new working environment and the conflicts that might arise when he returned to work with a handicap.

In this case the test results provided vital information for evaluating the motor coordination of a handicapped individual. The results also provided specific information concerning Rex's ability to handle certain tools and to perform tasks that could be related to similar tasks in several local firms. This case illustrates how tests such as Micro-Tower can be used to assist the handicapped in evaluating their level of performance and linking their performance with occupational requirements.

OTHER INSTRUMENTS

The diverse needs of the handicapped and educationally disadvantaged necessitate specially designed assessment instruments. Those listed below are examples of the kinds of instruments that may serve some of the purposes of assessment for the handicapped and disadvantaged.

Tests of General Ability. These tests are appropriate for students from culturally deprived backgrounds as measures of general intelligence and basic learning ability. All items are pictorial, and the examiner's manual has been translated into Spanish. One part of the test measures an individual's ability to recognize relationships and to understand meanings of pictures and basic concepts. The second part of the test measures reasoning ability.

Chicago Non-Verbal Examination. This intelligence test is designed specifically for individuals with reading difficulties or those who have been reared in foreign-language environments. The test is administered either verbally or in pantomime. Standardization samples include 70% native and 30% foreign-born students.

Tests of Adult Basic Education. The four levels of this test are designed to identify the need for instruction in basic skills. The subtests are: reading vocabulary, reading comprehension, arithmetic reasoning, and arithmetic fundamentals.

California Occupational Preference Survey. This test has been translated into Spanish and is designed primarily to assist individuals in defining broad areas of interest.

Geist Picture Interest Inventory. A special edition of this interest inventory for Spanish-speaking and bilingual males uses pictures of occupational activities. The general interest areas are persuasive, clerical, mechanical, musical, scientific, outdoors, literary, computational, artistic, social service, and dramatic. This inventory may be used with many other male groups besides Spanish-speaking and bilingual males.

J.E.V.S. Worksample System. J.E.V.S. is a work-sample system similar to the Micro-Tower system discussed in this chapter. It is designed primarily for the vocational assessment of rehabilitation clients. The battery helps the counselor evaluate an individual's skills, behaviors, and interests.

Vocational Evaluation System. This is a work-sample test for vocational assessment of adults. It assesses more than 20 work activities including bench assembly, drafting, woodworking, welding, medical service, and soil testing.

SUMMARY

Legislation that requires equal access to training and employment for the handicapped and disadvantaged has encouraged the development of specially designed assessment instruments. These instruments must meet the needs of individuals from many ethnic and racial backgrounds. In this chapter the counselor has been encouraged to carefully evaluate the reference groups from which assessment data have been derived. Norm groups should match the individuals being tested in cultural background and other characteristics.

QUESTIONS AND EXERCISES

1. Why is it important to have specially developed norm data for the handicapped and disadvantaged?

2. Explain how you would use aptitude test results for the handicapped when special norms for the handicapped are not available.

3. An individual states that he has been turned down for jobs because of his low educational achievement. He claims that he can read, spell, and do some arithmetic. He is now confused about what kind of job he wants. While considering other counseling needs, what kind of assessment instruments would you use?

4. Should pictorial interest inventories for nonreaders include activities that depict high-level jobs requiring college degrees? Explain your answer.

5. Explain how you could most effectively interpret test data to a handicapped individual who is applying for a job in a local industry. Under what conditions would the results be most meaningful?

12
Using Nonstandardized Self-Assessment Inventories

In recent years career counseling programs have incorporated self-assessment techniques to identify individual characteristics and traits. Self-assessment inventories include a variety of self-scored questionnaires, checklists, rating and ranking formats that evaluate specific characteristics for use in career counseling. For example, Bolles (1978) uses self-assessment of developed skills as a vital step in career decision-making. Fogel (1974) employs self-assessment techniques in a group guidance program designed to increase certainty about career goals. Self-estimates of ability as they are related to Holland's (1973) six modal personal styles and matching work environments are an integral part of the SDS. Harrington and O'Shea (1976) recommend the use of self-estimates of ability in their system of career decision-making. Lathrop (1977) emphasizes self-estimates of skills and abilities as an important step in finding an ideal job. McKinlay (1971) has developed a questionnaire for identifying skills and interests; results are used to obtain appropriate career information from a computerized system. Zunker (1981) suggests methods of self-assessment of skills for adults.

Super's (1953) emphasis on self-concept has encouraged the development of programs for increasing self-awareness (Healy, 1974). For example, life planning workshops (Thomas, 1972) incorporate self-assessment exercises for increasing self-awareness in order to stimulate career exploration. Tyler (1961) developed a vocational card sort as a technique for increasing self-awareness. Dinkmeyer and Caldwell (1970) recommend the use of an autobiography for developing self-awareness. Other career development programs that assess self-awareness include those by Osborn (1977), Ballard (1976), Dauw (1977), Figler (1975), and Kirn and Kirn (1975).

A number of research projects suggest that self-estimates of ability are valid in that individuals tend to function in ways that are consistent with their self-perceptions (Baird, 1969). In a study of National Merit Scholars, the best predictors of college achievement were high school grades and self-estimates of scholastic ability (Holland & Astin, 1962). Baird (1969) found that the best predictors of grade point average among college freshmen were self-ratings of scholastic ability. A study of high school students by Payne (1962) revealed a high degree of predictive validity for achievement based on self-concepts. Other research studies of secondary students by

Binder, Jones, and Strowig (1970), Wylie (1963), and Bowen (1968) also produced evidence that self-estimates of ability are efficient predictors of achievement.

Despite this evidence of the validity of self-assessment in general, the self-assessment methods discussed in this chapter do not meet the criteria for standardized instruments. They are designed primarily to stimulate discussion of career options and to supplement or raise questions about information obtained in other ways. Because the validity and reliability of the instruments reviewed here have not been established, the results must be used with caution. The counselor interested in measuring personal characteristics related to the entire spectrum of jobs should use a standardized interest or ability inventory.

Several methods of self-assessment are discussed in this chapter. By discussing these instruments I do not intend to imply that self-assessment techniques should replace standardized tests and inventories. Career decision-making is a process in which all aspects of individuality should receive consideration. When career counseling programs incorporate all relevant information, including self-estimates, the chances of career decision-making being dominated by any one source are decreased.

QUEST QUESTIONNAIRE

QUEST is an integral part of the Career Information System (CIS) developed at the University of Oregon (McKinlay, 1974). CIS is a computerized and needle sort system of providing career information. (See Zunker, 1981, for a description of computerized systems for career guidance.) The needle sort system allows an individual to sort through a deck of cards with a needle while responding to a questionnaire. When he or she is finished, the remaining cards are the preferred occupations worth further consideration. The purpose of QUEST is to aid individuals in identifying which of the 240 occupations contained in the CIS files are related to their interests, values, and abilities. Each of the questions in QUEST has been thoroughly reviewed so that it correlates with a CIS occupation. If an individual's responses are consistent with factors judged to be critical in particular occupations, those occupations are listed for consideration. Likewise, occupations are rejected if the individual's responses are inconsistent with critical factors.

QUEST consists of 21 questions divided into six sections. The first section deals with the nature of work—that is, whether an individual prefers work that is continuous or precise or that involves using facts, working with others, persuading others, making decisions, or being creative. In the second section the individual assesses abilities: eye/hand coordination, working with fingers, checking accuracy, using words, using numbers, catching on to things, seeing detail, and being physically active. In the third section the individual indicates how much education or training is needed for entry into his or her chosen career. In the fourth section the individual estimates the earnings considered appropriate for various careers. In the last two sections the individual indicates preferences for work environments: city, size, region, and work setting.

Although QUEST is not considered to be a standardized test, it was evaluated for validity and readability. After extensive field testing, counselors and clients rated it as easy or very easy to use. Expert reviewers, including Leona Tyler and Norman Sunberg, consider QUEST to be technically sound and observe that "validity in the usual sense of the term is perhaps the wrong word to use; rather one should test the questionnaire for utility" (McKinlay, 1971, p. 24).

The computer or the needle card sort deck links the results of QUEST to occupations. As an example, the occupations list from the computerized system for the student Angie follows.

THERE ARE 14 OCCUPATIONS THAT CORRESPOND TO THE ANSWERS YOU GAVE.
'QUEST' LIST FOR ANGIE
CLERICAL OCCUPATIONS (1400):
1415 SHORTHAND REPORTERS
  BOOKKEEPING, ACCOUNTING & COMPUTER OCCUPATIONS (1600):
1684 PROGRAMMERS & SYSTEMS ANALYSTS
  LABORATORY OCCUPATIONS (2600):
2644 OPTICIANS
2656 LABORATORY TESTERS
  MECHANICS OCCUPATIONS (3100):
3184 JEWELERS
3186 INSTRUMENT REPAIRERS
  TIMBER PRODUCTS OCCUPATIONS (4500):
4574 PULP AND PAPER WORKERS
  GRAPHIC ARTS OCCUPATIONS (4700):
4766 PRINTING PRODUCTION OCCUPATIONS
  TRANSPORTATION OCCUPATIONS (6100):
6156 YARDING AND LOADING OCCUPATIONS
6172 RAILROAD ENGINEERS
6188 PILOTS AND FLIGHT ENGINEERS
  HEALTH SERVICE OCCUPATIONS (8100):
8117 PHYSICIANS' ASSISTANTS
8127 PHYSICAL THERAPISTS
8174 DENTAL HYGIENISTS[1]

The major value of QUEST is that it encourages individuals to explore occupational alternatives based on personal preferences.

One limitation of QUEST is that individuals may interpret key terms —such as *continuous, precise, using facts, persuading, change,* and *creative*—in different ways. Although these terms are defined to some extent by the questions in which they are used, they will inevitably be misinterpreted in relation to work activities and work environments. Misinterpretations can to some extent be avoided because individuals have the opportunity to review responses (see below). Therefore, users of QUEST should encourage a review of responses in order to obtain accurate results.

Another limitation of QUEST is that it encourages discussion of job labels rather than of personal characteristics. The strategy recommended in this book is that all personal characteristics and traits be considered in career decisions. Therefore, when using QUEST, the counselor should encourage the consideration of values, interests, and other personal characteristics in relation to the results.

[1]From *Developing a Career Information System* by B. McKinlay. Copyright 1974 by University of Oregon. Reprinted by permission.

A unique feature of QUEST is that individuals are encouraged to review responses to questions in relation to the lists of occupations.
For example, an individual can be shown why some occupational areas
were deleted as a result of his or her responses. Joe was interested
in counseling as an occupation, but counseling did not appear on his
list. He found that his response to question 5, "no, I would not,"
eliminated this occupation.

5. Persuading. On some jobs you try to influence other people's
    actions or ideas. Would you want to do this type of work?
        Yes, I would
        No, I would not
        No preference or I'm not sure[2]

Joe explained that he considered persuasion as being related to sell-
ing and sales jobs rather than to the helping occupations. He changed
his response after carefully rereading the question.

LIFESTYLE ORIENTATION SURVEY (LOS)

The LOS (Zunker, 1977) is a counseling tool designed to assist individuals in determining their lifestyle orientations: preferences for
career style, family style, leisure style, place of residence, and
work environment. The results of the survey may be used in a variety
of counseling programs, but the survey is designed primarily to facilitate discussion in groups or individually with a counselor about
important career/life decisions.

Students determine individual lifestyle dimensions by choosing those
preferred from a list of 80; they also answer several questions concerning desired geographic location; writing an essay is optional. In
the first part of the survey, students read a list of phrases and respond to them, as illustrated below.

Directions: This is not a test but an inventory to help you in
thinking in terms of a lifestyle after graduation from college. The
first part contains a list of statements concerning such matters as
job style, leisure style, membership style, home study, and family
styles. You are to read through the list very carefully and place a
circle around the number of those which you consider to be important
to you both now and in the future. It is important that you think in
terms of your own desires, needs, and interests. More specifically,
you are to do the following:
1. Read the list very carefully and then circle the numbers of
the statements you consider to be important in your lifestyle and put
an X on the numbers of the statements you consider to be unimportant
in your lifestyle.
    Ex. ___ ⑩ Actively engage in Civil Affairs.
        ___ ✗ A job from 8-5, five days a week.
2. After completing the list, using the following two-point scale,
assign a value to each statement that you have circled by writing
the appropriate number in front of each of them.

[2]From *Developing a Career Information System* by B. McKinlay. Copyright 1974 by University of Oregon. Reprinted by permission.

> 1. Of moderate importance
> 2. Of greatest importance
> Ex. <u>2</u> ⑩ Actively engage in Civil Affairs.
> <u>1</u> ㉞ Hobbies at home.
> 3. Continue on to Part II and read the directions for this part.

After completing the first section of the survey, the individual chooses a region of residence, a state of preference or a foreign country, and community preference from lists provided.[3] Items marked "of greatest importance" provide relevant information for discussion. For example, a preference for living in different parts of the country or for "a job that is easy going with little or no pressure" is clarified and considered in the decision-making process.

When significant discrepancies are found between lifestyle needs, such as financial expectations, and the realities of potential careers, the individual is required to establish priorities for lifestyle needs. Through discussion individual priorities can be clarified, and realistic alternatives and options can be developed.

For example, Mike's completed LOS indicated a strong orientation toward financial compensation. During group discussion he examined the potential financial rewards of careers he was considering. He learned that some of the careers would probably not provide the salary he expected. In explaining to the group why he had selected those careers for consideration, he became aware that lifestyle needs other than financial rewards—for example, having time for his family and obtaining satisfaction from his job—were important to him. Through further discussion he was able to establish priorities for his needs.

Susan, too, found that she had some lifestyle needs that conflicted with career goals. LOS results indicated a strong orientation toward raising a family, toward having time for leisure activities, and toward having a job with little pressure. However, she was considering careers that involved much pressure, long hours, and considerable dedication. During the discussion she identified these striking differences and decided to give further thought to career requirements before deciding which of her needs were most important. The approach of the counselor was not to disparage any of the identified needs but to promote an understanding of potential conflicts and further clarification of lifestyle orientations and career requirements.

These examples illustrate how consideration of lifestyle factors can assist in setting career goals. Lifestyle orientation is a factor that can be ignored in career planning because students may have difficulty in projecting their needs into the future. The LOS stimulates clarification of individual lifestyle orientation and thereby enhances the individual's capacities for effective planning.

CAREER SELF ASSESSMENT (CSA)

Snodgrass (1980) developed the CSA for analyzing career plans. Specifically, the inventory introduces the basic elements of career

---

[3] In each case the individual can indicate undecided or no preference.

planning and aids individuals in determining their progress in this area. The inventory was built around Super's (1953) theory of self-concept; individuals are encouraged to evaluate their interests, values, abilities, personalities, and other specific characteristics. For example, individuals indicate their reasons for selecting a college major or career by responding to questions such as the following:

2) If you stated your major in number 1, above, can you state why you selected that major? If you have not made a choice, move to question number 6.
   a) It sounded interesting.
   b) I didn't know what else to choose.
   c) It will prepare me for a job.
   d) It will prepare me for a career I have thoroughly researched and planned; it is required.
   e) I felt that I was supposed to choose a major as soon as possible.
   f) Other _____

3) How certain are you that you have selected a major most appropriate for you?
   a) very certain
   b) certain
   c) somewhat certain
   d) not very certain
   e) not certain at all

4) How satisfied are you with your major selection?
   a) very satisfied
   b) satisfied
   c) somewhat satisfied
   d) not very satisfied
   e) not satisfied at all
   f) too early to tell

5) Did you know what the field was about before you selected your major? Yes ___   No ___

In other questions the individual is challenged to state why a career has been selected. Examples of questions follow:

10) List below the three primary factors that were considered before making your [career] choice.

11) From what resources did you learn about this field (e.g., career brochures, pamphlets, books, people working in the field)?

12) How much do you feel you know about this field?
   a) very much
   b) I have general information about it.
   c) not very much
   d) very little[4]

---

[4]From *Career Self Assessment* by G. Snodgrass. Southwest Texas State University, unpublished document, 1980. Reprinted by permission.

The inventory also requires the individual to indicate assistance needed in career planning. The individual is then directed to either group or individual counseling programs or to the career resource center.

The CSA is a well-designed instrument for introducing the basic elements of career planning. Informal evaluation of it has been positive. The instrument should promote stimulating discussions about the relationship between college majors and careers. Ideally, individuals should also learn how to make rational decisions about college majors and careers.

Case of a University Freshman Who Needs to Establish Career Objectives

Erik, a university freshman, was involved in a course project that required him to complete the CSA and then discuss it with a counselor in the career resource center. During the discussion, Erik told the counselor that he had to choose a major and, even though he didn't know much about it, business seemed as practical as anything else. Erik told the counselor further that he had not given much thought to his career goals; he had just assumed he would go into business. He then indicated that he realized he had chosen his career without much forethought and perhaps he should give some consideration to other options.

Reviewing the CSA further, the counselor noted that Erik had had some difficulty completing the section that required him to list personal characteristics such as interests, skills, values, and personality traits. Erik told the counselor that he found it difficult to describe himself in those terms but that he realized it would be helpful to know more about himself in order to choose a suitable career. The counselor and Erik agreed that self-awareness would be a good starting point for career planning. Erik then made an appointment to continue career counseling the following week. This example illustrates the use of the CSA in helping students establish objectives.[5]

QUICK JOB HUNTING MAP

Bolles (1978) has devised a self-assessment method for identifying functional and transferable skills. The Quick Job Hunting Map is divided into six categories according to Holland's (1973) classification system: realistic, investigative, artistic, social, enterprising, and conventional. A portion of section A, realistic, is shown in Figure 12-1.

The individual is required to provide detailed information about experiences in life that relate to skills. The boxes that represent skills used get colored in. Next, the individual identifies specific skills, such as horticultural skills, and records additional

[5]Adapted from *Career Self Assessment* by G. Snodgrass. Southwest Texas State University, unpublished document, 1980, p. 3. Reprinted by permission.

A^2 Athletic/ Outdoor/ Traveling Skills I can do because I have proven:		Sample	1	2	3	4	5	6	7	Additional Explanation
	Motor/Physical coordination & agility; *Eye-Hand-Foot coordination;* Walking/Climbing/Running									
	Skilled at general sports: Skilled in small competitive games; Skilled at ___ (a particular game)									
	Swimming: Skiing/Recreation; Playing. Hiking/Backpacking/Camping/Mountaineering; Outdoor survival skills; Creative, planning, organizing outdoor activities; Traveling									
	Drawing samples from the earth; Keen oceanic interests; Navigating									
	Horticultural skills; Cultivating growing things; Skillful at planting/nurturing plants; Landscaping and groundskeeping	■								
	Farming; Ranching; Working with animals									
	Other skills which you think belong in this family, but are not listed above:									

FIGURE 12-1. *Portion of the Quick Job Hunting Map.* From *What Color Is Your Parachute?* by R. N. Bolles. Copyright © 1980 by Ten Speed Press. Reprinted by permission.

experiences related to that skill. Skills are ranked according to self estimates of proficiency.

Upon completion of skills identification, the individual is directed to consider geographical location, co-workers, and working conditions. Additional help in the job search is given in the form of specific suggestions for job site visits and for finding additional information. The Quick Job Hunting Map is a thorough method of identifying a variety of skills. However, the time necessary to complete the map may limit use in some career counseling programs.

GUIDE TO CAREER PLANNING AND DEVELOPMENT

A career development manual was designed by Hanson (1976) in association with the Lawrence Livermore Laboratory in California. The manual is divided into three sections. The first section contains exercises and suggestions for self-evaluation of personal values and goals. Interests are identified by using the SCII. The second section contains self-assessment techniques for identifying satisfying and dissatisfying events in one's life and analyzing abilities used during these events. The third section contains self-assessment techniques for defining the ideal job and relating personal qualities to job requirements. The purpose of the manual is to have individuals focus on career objectives. All data from the self-assessments are placed on a profile, which is used in career exploration.

An example of the personal values section is shown on the next page. Individuals are instructed to rank order the phrases according to their own values. The top six values are used with other data when considering career objectives.

Recognition	to be acknowledged	1.	_____
Duty	to dedicate myself to what I call responsibility	2.	_____
Expertness	to become an authority	3.	_____
Independence	to have freedom of thought and content	4.	_____
Pleasure	to enjoy life; to be happy and content	5.	_____
Power	to have control over others	6.	_____
Leadership	to become influential and to lead other people	7.	_____
Affection	to obtain and to share companion-ship and affection	8.	_____
Parenthood	to raise a fine family; to have heirs	9.	_____
Acceptance	to be received with approval	10.	_____
Financial success	to earn a great deal of money	11.	_____
Health	to enjoy physical well-being	12.	_____
Service	to contribute to the satisfac-tion of others	13.	_____
Self-realization	to optimize personal development	14.	_____
Security	to have a secure and stable position	15.	_____
Prestige	to become well known and to have status	16.	_____
Stability	to have the ability or strength to withstand change	17.	_____
Professional accomplishment	to attain work goals	18.	_____
Intimacy	to be close to others	19.	_____ [6]

Overall, this guide is well prepared and concise, and it clearly ties together the steps used in career planning. However, the list of values should be explained and their relationship to work environments and job satisfactions clarified.

COMMUNITY COLLEGE GROUP COUNSELING PROGRAM

Fogel (1974) emphasizes self-assessment techniques in a career devel-opment program for community college students. The program is based on Super's (1953) belief that interests, values, and other individual

[6]From *Guide to Career Planning and Development* by M. C. Hanson. Copyright 1976 by Lawrence Livermore Laboratory. Reprinted by per-mission.

traits are important aspects of vocational development. Thus, a major goal of the program is the development of self-awareness to improve the participants' ability to choose a career. Self-assessments of interests, strengths (skills), personality, and values are an integral part of the program.

An example of the interest assessment component of this program follows:

> Check the areas that represent your real interests.
> When I really have my free choice I prefer to:
> ___ Work with things (fix my car, make a dress, etc.)
> ___ Work with business (think of a money-making scheme, be involved in business and selling, etc.)
> ___ Do something systematic and predictable (make something similar to what I have made before, keep my work in order, etc.)
> ___ Do something to help others (do volunteer work, be a camp counselor)
> ___ Do something where I'll get recognition from others (speak in public, act as an officer or leader, etc.)
> ___ Do something outdoors (hike, garden, work with a harvest crew, etc.)
> ___ Work with people and communicate ideas (play in a musical group, join a discussion, etc.)
> ___ Do something scientific (work on a collection, read about some part of science, etc.)
> ___ Do something creative (plan a project I've never done before, write a story or paint, etc.)
> ___ Work with machines or processes (take and develop photos, operate an electric drill, sewing machine, etc.)
> ___ Do something where I get tangible results (make jewelry or a fish pond, etc.)
> ___ You name it; what other interests would you like to express in your work?
>
> _____
> _____
>
> Which three interests do you consider to be most important to use in your work? (1) _____ (2) _____
> (3) _____
> Are you sure these are your interests? ___ How can you find out if you're not sure? _____
> Would others agree that the three interests you listed are right for you? _____ [7]

Two problems are apparent. First, only one item is used to assess interest in a whole category, such as an interest in things, an interest in business, an interest in helping others. This limitation makes one question the reliability of the instrument. Authors of standardized instruments find that it is necessary to have several items to adequately measure a personal trait or characteristic. Second, the rationale used to select interest categories is not clear. It would

---

[7]From *Development of a Replicable Group Vocational Counseling Procedure for Use with Community College Students* by A. J. Fogel, 1974. Unpublished doctoral dissertation, University of California, Los Angeles. Reprinted by permission.

perhaps have been wiser to select items that could be classified under systems such as Holland's, the DOT, or Kuder's. However, the instrument should stimulate discussion of interests as they are related to the activities listed.

SUMMARY

In this chapter several nonstandardized self-assessment methods were discussed. Evidence indicates that self-estimates of ability are valid. Many self-assessment questionnaires and checklists have been developed to evaluate specific characteristics that are of interest in career counseling. The use of self-assessment is encouraged in order to lessen the chances that career decision-making will be dominated by any one source. Nonstandardized self-assessment devices have limitations but are useful for stimulating discussion and for supplying supplementary information for career exploration.

QUESTIONS AND EXERCISES

1. What are the major advantages of using self-assessment measures in career counseling?

2. What strategy would you use to introduce measures of interests and values after using QUEST?

3. Develop a strategy for interpreting the results of an instrument for assessing lifestyle orientations. Explain how you would use information on dimensions of lifestyle with other data.

4. What are the advantages and disadvantages of an instrument like the Quick Job Hunting Map?

5. Build a self-assessment instrument for measuring values of high school seniors. Explain how you would incorporate this instrument into a career counseling program.

Appendix
List of Tests, Authors, and Publishers

Instrument	Author	Publisher and Address
Academic Promise Test	G. K. Bennett, M. G. Bennett, D. M. Clendenen, J. E. Doppett, J. H. Ricks, H. G. Seashore, and A. G. Wesman	Psychological Corporation 757 Third Avenue New York, N.Y. 10017
Adult Basic Learning Examination (ABLE)	B. Karlsen, R. Madden, and B. Gardner	Harcourt Brace Jovanovich, Inc. Psychological Corporation 757 Third Avenue New York, N.Y. 10017
American College Testing (ACT) Career Planning Program (CPP)	Staff	American College Testing Program P.O. Box 168 Iowa City, Iowa 52240
American College Testing (ACT)	Staff	American College Testing Program P.O. Box 168 Iowa City, Iowa 52240
Armed Services Vocational Aptitude Battery (ASVAB)	Staff	U.S. Department of Defense Washington, D.C. 20301
Basic Occupational Literacy Test (BOLT)	Staff	U.S. Department of Labor Manpower Administration Washington, D.C. 20210
Basic Skills Assessment Program	Staff	Educational Testing Service Princeton, N.J. 08540

Brainard Occupational Preference Inventory	P. P. Brainard and R. T. Brainard	Psychological Corporation 757 Third Avenue New York, N.Y. 10017
California Achievement Test (CAT)	E. W. Tiegs and W. W. Clark	CTB/McGraw-Hill Book Co. Del Monte Research Park Monterey, Calif. 93940
California Occupational Preference Survey	R. R. Knapp, B. Grant, and G. D. Demos	Educational and Industrial Testing Service P.O. Box 7234 San Diego, Calif. 92017
California Test of Personality	L. P. Thorpe, W. W. Clark, and E. W. Tiegs	Publishers Test Service 2500 Garden Road Monterey, Calif. 93940
Career Assessment Inventory	C. B. Johansson	NCS/Interpretive Scoring Systems P.O. Box 1416 Minneapolis, Minn. 55440
Career Development Inventory (CDI)	D. E. Super, A. S. Thompson, R. H. Lindeman, J. O. Jordaan, and R. A. Myers	Consulting Psychologists Press 577 College Avenue Palo Alto, Calif. 94306
Career Maturity Inventory (CMI)	J. O. Crites	CTB/McGraw-Hill Book Co. Del Monte Research Park Monterey, Calif. 93940
Career Skills Assessment Program (CSAP)	Staff	College Entrance Examination Board 888 Seventh Avenue New York, N.Y. 10019
Chicago Non-Verbal Examination	A. W. Brown	Psychological Corporation 757 Third Avenue New York, N.Y. 10017
Cognitive Vocational Maturity Test (CVMT)	B. S. Westbrook and J. W. Parry-Hill	Department of Psychology North Carolina State University Raleigh, N.C. 27607

College Entrance Examination Board Scholastic Aptitude Test	Staff	Educational Testing Service Princeton, N.J. 08540
Comprehensive Test of Basic Skills	Staff	CTB/McGraw-Hill Book Co. Del Monte Research Park Monterey, Calif. 93940
Cooperative English Test	Staff (Educational Testing Service)	Addison-Wesley Testing Service Reading, Mass. 01864
Cooperative Mathematics Test	Staff (Educational Testing Service)	Addison-Wesley Testing Service Reading, Mass. 01864
Cooperative Science Test	Staff (Educational Testing Service)	Addison-Wesley Testing Service Reading, Mass. 01864
Cooperative Social Studies Test	Staff (Educational Testing Service)	Addison-Wesley Testing Service Reading, Mass. 01864
Diagnostic Reading Scales	G. D. Spache	CTB/McGraw-Hill Book Co. Del Monte Research Park Monterey, Calif. 93940
Differential Aptitude Test (DAT)	G. K. Bennett, H. G. Seashore, and A. G. Wesman	Psychological Corporation 757 Third Avenue New York, N.Y. 10017
Edwards Personal Preference Schedule (EPPS)	A. L. Edwards	Psychological Corporation 757 Third Avenue New York, N.Y. 10017
Flanagan Aptitude Classification Test	J. C. Flanagan	Science Research Associates, Inc. 259 East Erie Street Chicago, Ill. 60624
Geist Picture Interest Inventory	H. Geist	Western Psychological Services 12031 Wilshire Boulevard Los Angeles, Calif. 90025
General Aptitude Test Battery (GATB)	Staff	U.S. Government Printing Office Washington, D.C. 20402

Guilford-Zimmerman Aptitude Survey	J. P. Guilford and W. S. Zimmerman	Sheridan Psychological Services P.O. Box 6101 Orange, Calif. 92667
Guilford-Zimmerman Temperament Survey	J. P. Guilford and W. S. Zimmerman	Sheridan Psychological Services P.O. Box 6101 Orange, Calif. 92667
Harrington/O'Shea Systems for Career Decision-Making (CDM)	T. F. Harrington and A. J. O'Shea	Career Planning Associates P.O. Box 273 Needham, Mass. 02192
Iowa Test of Basic Skills	A. N. Hieronymus, E. F. Linquist, and H. D. Hoover	Riverside Publishing Co. 1919 South Highland Avenue Lombard, Ill. 60148
J.E.V.S. Worksample System	Staff	Vocational Research Institute Jewish Employment and Vocational Service 1624 Locust Street Philadelphia, Pa. 19103
Kuder Occupational Interest Survey (KOIS)	F. Kuder	Science Research Associates, Inc. 259 East Erie Street Chicago, Ill. 60624
Mastery: Survival Skills Test (SST)	Staff	Science Research Associates, Inc. 259 East Erie Street Chicago, Ill. 60624
Metropolitan Achievement Test High School Battery	W. N. Dorost, W. H. Evans, J. D. Leake, H. A. Bowman, C. Cosgrove, and J. G. Read	Harcourt Brace Jovanovich 757 Third Avenue New York, N.Y. 10017
Micro-Tower	Staff	ICD Rehabilitation and Research Center 340 East 24th Street New York, N.Y. 10010
Minnesota Counseling Inventory	R. F. Berdie and W. L. Layton	Psychological Corporation 757 Third Avenue New York, N.Y. 10017

Minnesota Vocational Interest Inventory	K. E. Clark D. P. Campbell	Psychological Corporation 757 Third Avenue New York, N.Y. 10017
Myers-Briggs Type Indicator	J. B. Myers	Consulting Psychologists Press 577 College Avenue Palo Alto, Calif. 94306
New Mexico Career Education Test Series (NMCETS)	C. C. Healy and S. P. Klein	Monitor Book Co. 195 South Beverly Drive Beverly Hills, Calif. 90212
Non-Sexist Vocational Card Sort (NSVCS)	C. R. Dewey	C. R. Dewey Route 4, Box 217 Gainesville, Fla. 32601
Ohio Vocational Interest Survey	A. G. D'Costa, D. W. Winefordner, J. G. Odgers, and P. B. Koons, Jr.	Harcourt Brace Jovanovich 757 Third Avenue New York, N.Y. 10017
Omnibus Personality Inventory	P. A. Heist, T. R. McConnell, H. D. Webster, and G. D. Yonge	Psychological Corporation 757 Third Avenue New York, N.Y. 10017
Personal Values Inventory	G. E. Schlesser, J. A. Finder, and R. Lynch	Colgate University Testing Service Hamilton, N.Y. 13346
Primary Mental Abilities Test	L. L. Thurstone and T. G. Thurstone	Science Research Associates, Inc. 259 East Erie Street Chicago, Ill. 60624
Rating Scales of Vocational Values, Vocational Interests, and Vocational Aptitudes	G. D. Demos and B. Grant	Educational and Industrial Testing Service P.O. Box 7234 San Diego, Calif. 92107
Rokeach Values Survey	M. Rokeach	Halgen Tests 837 Persimmon Sunnyvale, Calif. 94087
Self Description Inventory	C. B. Johansson	NCS/Interpretive Scoring Systems P.O. Box 1416 Minneapolis, Minn. 55440
Self-Directed Search (SDS)	J. L. Holland	Consulting Psychologists Press 577 College Avenue Palo Alto, Calif. 94306

Sixteen Personality Factor Questionnaire (16PF)	R. B. Cattell, H. W. Eber, and M. M. Tatsuoka	Institute for Personality and Ability Testing 1602 Coronado Drive Champaign, Ill. 61820
Social and Pre-Vocational Information Battery (SPIB)	L. K. Irwin, A. Halpern, and W. M. Reynolds	CTB/McGraw-Hill Book Co. Del Monte Research Park Monterey, Calif. 93940
Stanford Achievement Test	R. Madden, E. F. Gardner, H. C. Rudman, B. Karlsen, and J. C. Merwin	Harcourt Brace Jovanovich 757 Third Avenue New York, N.Y. 10017
Stanford Diagnostic Arithmetic Test	L. S. Beatty, R. Madden, and E. F. Gardner	Psychological Corporation 757 Third Avenue New York, N.Y. 10017
Strong-Campbell Interest Inventory (SCII)	E. K. Strong and D. P. Campbell	Stanford University Press Stanford, Calif. 94305
Study of Values	G. W. Allport, P. E. Vernon, and G. Lindzey	Houghton Mifflin 2 Park Street Boston, Mass. 02107
Survey of Interpersonal Values (SIV)	L. V. Gordon	Science Research Associates, Inc. 259 East Erie Street Chicago, Ill. 60624
Survey of Personal Values (SPV)	L. V. Gordon	Science Research Associates, Inc. 259 East Erie Street Chicago, Ill. 60624
Temperament and Values Inventory (TVI)	C. B. Johansson and P. L. Webber	NCS/Interpretive Scoring Systems P.O. Box 1416 Minneapolis, Minn. 55440
Tests of Adult Basic Education	E. W. Tiegs and W. W. Clark	CTB/McGraw-Hill Book Co. Del Monte Research Park Monterey, Calif. 93940
Tests of General Ability	H. T. Manuel	Guidance Testing Associates 6516 Shirley Avenue Austin, Tex. 78752

Thorndike's Dimension of Temperament	R. L. Thorndike	Psychological Corporation 757 Third Avenue New York, N.Y. 10017
Vocational Evaluation System	Staff	Singer Education Division Career Systems 80 Commerce Drive Rochester, N.Y. 14623
Wide Range Achievement Test (WRAT)	J. F. Jastak and S. Jastak	Jastak Associates, Inc. 1526 Gilpin Avenue Wilmington, Del. 19806
Wide Range Interest-Opinion Test	J. F. Jastak and S. Jastak	Jastak Associates, Inc. 1526 Gilpin Avenue Wilmington, Del. 19806
Wide Range Scales	Staff	U.S. Department of Labor Manpower Administration Washington, D.C. 20210
William Lynde and Williams Analysis of Personal Values	R. W. Henderson	William, Lynde and Williams 153 East Erie Street Painesville, Ohio 44077
Work Values Inventory (WVI)	D. E. Super	Riverside Publishing Co. 1919 South Highland Avenue Lombard, Ill. 60148
Writers Skills Test	Staff	Educational Testing Service Princeton, N.J. 08540

Bibliography

Adams, G. S. Review of the Stanford Achievement Test. In O. K. Buros
(Ed.), *The seventh mental measurement yearbook* (Vol. 1). Highland
Park, N.J.: Gryphon Press, 1972.

Allen, M. J., & Yen, W. M. *Introduction to measurement theory.*
Monterey, Calif.: Brooks/Cole, 1979.

Allport, G. W., Vernon, P. E., & Lindzey, G. *Manual for the Study of
Values.* Boston: Houghton Mifflin, 1970.

American College Testing Program. *Career planning program.* Iowa City,
Iowa: Author, 1974.

American College Testing Program. *Planning.* Iowa City, Iowa: Author,
1976.

American College Testing Program. *Counselor's guide.* Iowa City, Iowa:
Author, 1980.

American Psychological Association. *Standards for educational and
psychological tests.* Washington, D.C.: Author, 1974.

Anastasi, A. *Psychological testing* (4th ed.). New York: Macmillan,
1976.

Arbeiter, S., Aslanian, C. B., Schmerbeck, F. A., & Brickell, H. M.
40 million Americans in career transition: The need for information.
New York: College Entrance Examination Board, 1978.

Baird, L. L. The prediction of accomplishment in college: An exploration of the process of achievement. *Journal of Counseling Psychology*, 1969, *16*, 246-254.

Ballard, J. *How to be doing what you'd like to be doing—and get paid
for it (Why not?).* Amherst, Mass.: Mandala, 1976.

Bannatyne, A. Review of the Differential Aptitude Test. In O. K.
Buros (Ed.), *The eighth mental measurement yearbook* (Vol. 1). Highland Park, N.J.: Gryphon Press, 1978.

Bennett, G. K., Seashore, H. G., & Wesman, A. G. *Differential Aptitude
Test - Career Planning Program.* New York: Psychological Corporation,
1974.

Bennett, G. K., Seashore, H. G., & Wesman, A. G. *Handbook for Differential Aptitude Test (Forms S and T).* New York: Psychological Corporation, 1974.

Berdie, R. F. Review of the Work Values Inventory. In O. K. Buros
(Ed.), *The seventh mental measurement yearbook* (Vol. 2). Highland
Park, N.J.: Gryphon Press, 1972.

Binder, D. M., Jones, J. C., & Strowig, R. W. Non-intellective self-report variables as predictors of scholastic achievement. *Journal of Educational Research*, 1970, *63*, 364-366.

Bingham, W. C. Review of the Career Development Inventory. In O. K. Buros (Ed.), *The eighth mental measurement yearbook* (Vol. 2). Highland Park, N.J.: Gryphon Press, 1978.

Birk, J. M. Reducing sex bias: Factors affecting the client's view of the use of career interest inventories. In E. E. Diamond (Ed.), *Issues of sex bias and sex fairness in career interest measurement*. Washington, D.C.: National Institute of Education, 1975.

Bixler, R. H., & Bixler, V. H. Test interpretation in vocational counseling. *Educational and Psychological Measurement*, 1946, *6*, 145-146.

Black, J. D. Review of the Survey of Interpersonal Values. In O. K. Buros (Ed.), *The eighth mental measurement yearbook* (Vol. 1). Highland Park, N.J.: Gryphon Press, 1978.

Bloxom, B. M. Review of the Sixteen Personality Factor Questionnaire. In O. K. Buros (Ed.), *The eighth mental measurement yearbook* (Vol. 1). Highland Park, N.J.: Gryphon Press, 1978.

Bodden, J. L. Review of the New Mexico Career Education Test Series. In O. K. Buros (Ed.), *The eighth mental measurement yearbook* (Vol. 2). Highland Park, N.J.: Gryphon Press, 1978.

Bolles, R. N. *A practical manual for job-hunters and career changers: What color is your parachute*? Berkeley, Calif.: Ten Speed Press, 1978.

Bolton, B. F. Review of the Sixteen Personality Factor Questionnaire. In O. K. Buros (Ed.), *The eighth mental measurement yearbook* (Vol. 1). Highland Park, N.J.: Gryphon Press, 1978.

Bordin, E. S. *Psychological counseling* (2nd ed.). New York: Appleton-Century-Crofts, 1968.

Borgen, F. H. Review of the Career Development Inventory. In O. K. Buros (Ed.), *The eighth mental measurement yearbook* (Vol. 2). Highland Park, N.J.: Gryphon Press, 1978.

Bouchard, T. J. Review of the Sixteen Personality Factor Questionnaire. In O. K. Buros (Ed.), *The seventh mental measurement yearbook* (Vol. 1). Highland Park, N.J.: Gryphon Press, 1972.

Bouchard, T. J. Review of the Differential Aptitude Test. In O. K. Buros (Ed.), *The eighth mental measurement yearbook* (Vol. 1). Highland Park, N.J.: Gryphon Press, 1978.

Bowen, C. W. *The use of self-estimates of ability and measures of ability in the prediction of academic performance*. Unpublished doctoral dissertation, Oklahoma State University, 1968.

Bradley, R. W. Person-referenced test interpretation: A learning process. *Measurement and Evaluation in Guidance*, 1977, *10*, 84-89.

Brown, F. G. Review of the Kuder Occupational Interest Survey. In O. K. Buros (Ed.), *The seventh mental measurement yearbook* (Vol. 2). Highland Park, N.J.: Gryphon Press, 1972.

Brown, F. G. Review of the Self-Directed Search. In O. K. Buros (Ed.), *The eighth mental measurement yearbook* (Vol. 2). Highland Park, N.J.: Gryphon Press, 1978.

Bryan, M. M. Review of the California Achievement Test. In O. K. Buros (Ed.), *The eighth mental measurement yearbook* (Vol. 1). Highland Park, N.J.: Gryphon Press, 1978.

Buros, O. K. *Tests in print.* Highland Park, N.J.: Gryphon Press, 1972.

Buros, O. K. (Ed.), *The eighth mental measurement yearbook* (2 vols.). Highland Park, N.J.: Gryphon Press, 1978.

Campbell, D. P. *Manual for the Strong-Campbell Interest Inventory.* Stanford, Calif.: Stanford University Press, 1974.

Cattell, R. B. Theory of fluid and crystallized intelligence: A critical experiment. *Journal of Educational Psychology*, 1963, *54*, 1-22.

Cattell, R. B., Eber, H. W., & Tatsuoka, M. M. *Handbook for the Sixteen Personality Factor Questionnaire (16PF).* Champaign, Ill.: Institute for Personality and Ability Testing, 1970.

Cole, N. S., & Hansen, G. R. Impact of interest inventories on career choice. In E. E. Diamond (Ed.), *Issues of sex bias and sex fairness in career interest measurement.* Washington, D.C.: National Institute of Education, 1975.

College Entrance Examination Board. *Guide to self evaluation and development skills.* New York: Author, 1978.

Cooper, J. F. Comparative impact of the SCII and the Vocational Card Sort on career salience and career exploration of women. *Journal of Counseling Psychology*, 1976, *23*, 348-352.

Crites, J. O. Career counseling: A review of major approaches. In H. J. Peters & J. C. Hansen (Eds.), *Vocational guidance and career development.* New York: Macmillan, 1977.

Crites, J. O. Review of the Self-Directed Search. In O. K. Buros (Ed.), *The eighth mental measurement yearbook* (Vol. 2). Highland Park, N.J.: Gryphon Press, 1978. (a)

Crites, J. O. Review of the Strong-Campbell Interest Inventory. In O. K. Buros (Ed.), *The eighth mental measurement yearbook* (Vol. 2). Highland Park, N.J.: Gryphon Press, 1978. (b)

Cronbach, L. J. Review of the Survey of Interpersonal Values. In O. K. Buros (Ed.), *The sixth mental measurement yearbook.* Highland Park, N.J.: Gryphon Press, 1965.

Cronbach, L. J. *Essentials of psychological testing.* New York: Harper & Row, 1970.

Cronbach, L. J. Review of Basic Occupational Literacy Test. In O. K. Buros (Ed.), *The eighth mental measurement yearbook* (Vol. 1). Highland Park, N.J.: Gryphon Press, 1978.

Cronbach, L. J. The Armed Services Vocational Aptitude Battery—A test battery in transition. *Personnel and Guidance Journal*, 1979, *57*, 232-237.

Cutts, C. C. Review of the Self-Directed Search. In O. K. Buros (Ed.), *The eighth mental measurement yearbook* (Vol. 2). Highland Park, N.J.: Gryphon Press, 1978.

Dauw, D. C. *Up your career.* Prospect Heights, Ill.: Waveland Press, 1977.

Dewey, C. R. Exploring interests: A non-sexist method. *Personnel and Guidance Journal*, 1974, *52*, 311-315.

Diamond, E. E. Overview. In E. E. Diamond (Ed.), *Issues of sex bias and sex fairness in career interest measurement.* Washington, D.C.: National Institute of Education, 1975.

Dinkmeyer, D., & Caldwell, E. *Developmental counseling and guidance: A comprehensive approach.* New York: McGraw-Hill, 1970.

Dolliver, R. H. An adaptation of the Tyler Vocational Card Sort. *Personnel and Guidance Journal*, 1967, *45*, 916-920.

Dolliver, R. H. Review of the Kuder Occupational Interest Survey. In O. K. Buros (Ed.), *The seventh mental measurement yearbook* (Vol. 2). Highland Park, N.J.: Gryphon Press, 1972.

Dolliver, R. H. Review of the Strong-Campbell Interest Inventory. In O. K. Buros (Ed.), *The eighth mental measurement yearbook* (Vol. 2). Highland Park, N.J.: Gryphon Press, 1978.

Dolliver, R. H., & Hansen, R. N. Review of the Self-Directed Search. In O. K. Buros (Ed.), *The eighth mental measurement yearbook* (Vol. 2). Highland Park, N.J.: Gryphon Press, 1978.

Dolliver, R. H., Irvin, J. A., & Bigley, S. S. Twelve-year follow-up of the Strong Vocational Interest Blank. *Journal of Counseling Psychology*, 1978, *19*, 212-217.

Edwards, A. L. Edwards personal preference schedule manual. New York, N.Y.: The Psychological Corporation, 1959.

Elbel, R. L. Review of the Stanford Achievement Test. In O. K. Buros (Ed.), *The eighth mental measurement yearbook* (Vol. 1). Highland Park, N.J.: Gryphon Press, 1978.

Figler, H. E. *Path: A career workbook for liberal arts students.* Cranston, R.I.: Carroll Press, 1975.

Fitzpatrick, J. P. Individualism in America. In D. N. Barrett (Ed.), *Values in America*. Notre Dame, Ind.: University of Notre Dame Press, 1961.

Fogel, A. J. *Development of a replicable group vocational counseling procedure for use with community college students.* Unpublished doctoral dissertation, University of California, Los Angeles, 1974.

French, J. W. Review of the Work Values Inventory. In O. K. Buros (Ed.), *The seventh mental measurement yearbook* (Vol. 2). Highland Park, N.J.: Gryphon Press, 1972.

Fry, E. B. Review of Adult Basic Learning Examination. In O. K. Buros (Ed.), *The seventh mental measurement yearbook* (Vol. 1). Highland Park, N.J.: Gryphon Press, 1972.

Fryer, D. *Measurement of interests*. New York: Holt, Rinehart & Winston, 1931.

Garcia, V., Zunker, V. G., & Nolan, J. *Analysis of a pre-vocational training program.* Unpublished manuscript, Southwest Texas State University, 1980.

Gelatt, H. B. Decision-making: A conceptual frame of reference for counseling. *Journal of Counseling Psychology*, 1962, *9*, 240-245.

Ghiselli, E. *The validity of occupational aptitude tests*. New York: Wiley, 1966.

Ginzberg, E., Ginsburg, S. W., Axelrad, S., & Herma, J. L. *Occupational choice: An approach to a general theory*. New York: Columbia University Press, 1951.

Glass, G. V. Review of the Survey of Interpersonal Values. In O. K. Buros (Ed.), *The seventh mental measurement yearbook* (Vol. 1). Highland Park, N.J.: Gryphon Press, 1972.

Goldman, L. *Using tests in counseling* (2nd ed.). New York: Appleton-Century-Crofts, 1972.

Goodstein, L. D. Review of the Survey of Interpersonal Values. In O. K. Buros (Ed.), *The sixth mental measurement yearbook*. Highland Park, N.J.: Gryphon Press, 1965.

Gordon, L. V. Survey of Personal Values Examiner's Manual. Chicago: Science Research Associates, 1967.

Gordon, L. V. *The measurement of interpersonal values*. Chicago: Science Research Associates, 1975.

Gordon, L. V. *Survey of Interpersonal Values*. Chicago: Science Research Associates, 1976.

Gribbons, W. D., & Lohnes, P. R. *Emerging careers*. New York: Teachers College Press, 1968.

Guilford, J. P. *Psychometric methods* (Rev. ed.). New York: McGraw-Hill, 1954.

Hall, J. W. Review of Adult Basic Learning Examination. In O. K. Buros (Ed.), *The seventh mental measurement yearbook* (Vol. 1). Highland Park, N.J.: Gryphon Press, 1972.

Hanna, G. S. Review of the Differential Aptitude Test. In O. K. Buros (Ed.), *The eighth mental measurement yearbook* (Vol. 1). Highland Park, N.J.: Gryphon Press, 1978.

Hanson, M. C. *Guide to Career Planning and Development*. Livermore, Calif.: Lawrence Livermore Laboratory, 1976.

Harmon, L. W. Technical aspects: Problems of scale development, norms, item difficulties by sex, and the rate of change in occupational group characteristics—I. In E. E. Diamond (Ed.), *Issues of sex bias and sex fairness in career interest measurement*. Washington, D.C.: National Institute of Education, 1975.

Harrington, T. F., & O'Shea, A. J. *The Harrington/O'Shea System for Career Decision-Making manual*. Needham, Mass.: Career Planning Associates, 1976.

Havighurst, R. J. *Human development and education*. New York: Longman, 1953.

Healy, C. C. *Career counseling in the community college*. Springfield, Ill.: Charles C Thomas, 1974.

Healy, C. C. Review of the American College Testing Career Planning Program. In O. K. Buros (Ed.), *The eighth mental measurement yearbook* (Vol. 2). Highland Park, N.J.: Gryphon Press, 1978.

Heilbrun, A. B. Review of the Edwards Personal Preference Schedule. In O. K. Buros (Ed.), *The seventh mental measurement yearbook* (Vol. 1). Highland Park, N.J.: Gryphon Press, 1972.

Hemphill, J. K. Review of the Survey of Interpersonal Values. In O. K. Buros (Ed.), *The sixth mental measurement yearbook*. Highland Park, N.J.: Gryphon Press, 1965.

Hieronymus, A. N. Review of Adult Basic Learning Examination. In O. K. Buros (Ed.), *The seventh mental measurement yearbook* (Vol. 1). Highland Park, N.J.: Gryphon Press, 1972.

Hogan, R. Review of the Study of Values. In O. K. Buros (Ed.), *The seventh mental measurement yearbook* (Vol. 1). Highland Park, N.J.: Gryphon Press, 1972.

Holland, J. L. *Making vocational choices: A theory of careers*. Englewood Cliffs, N.J.: Prentice-Hall, 1973.

Holland, J. L. The use and evaluation of interest inventories and simulations. In E. E. Diamond (Ed.), *Issues of sex bias and sex fairness in career interest measurement*. Washington, D.C.: National Institute of Education, 1975.

Holland, J. L. *The occupations finder*. Palo Alto, Calif.: Consulting Psychologists Press, 1979. (a)

Holland, J. L. *The Self-Directed Search: Professional manual.* Palo Alto, Calif.: Consulting Psychologists Press, 1979. (b)

Holland, J. L., & Astin, A. W. The prediction of academic, artistic, scientific, and social achievement. *Journal of Educational Psychology*, 1962, *53*, 132-143.

Hoyt, K. B. *Career education: What it is and how to do it.* Salt Lake City: Olympus, 1972.

Hundleby, J. D. Review of the Study of Values. In O. K. Buros (Ed.), *The sixth mental measurement yearbook.* Highland Park, N.J.: Gryphon Press, 1965.

Johansson, C. B. Technical aspects: Problems of scale development, norms, item differences by sex, and the rate of change in occupational group characteristics—II. In E. E. Diamond (Ed.), *Issues of sex bias and sex fairness in career interest measurement.* Washington, D.C.: National Institute of Education, 1975.

Johansson, C. B. *Manual for the Temperament and Values Inventory.* Minneapolis: Interpretive Scoring Systems, 1977.

Johnson, R. W. Review of the Strong-Campbell Interest Inventory. In O. K. Buros (Ed.), *The eighth mental measurement yearbook* (Vol. 2). Highland Park, N.J.: Gryphon Press, 1978.

Katz, M. R. *SIGI: A computer-based system of interactive guidance and information.* Princeton, N.J.: Educational Testing Service, 1975.

Katz, M. R. Review of the Career Maturity Inventory. In O. K. Buros (Ed.), *The eighth mental measurement yearbook* (Vol. 2). Highland Park, N.J.: Gryphon Press, 1978.

Kirn, A. G., & Kirn, M. O. *Life work planning.* New York: McGraw-Hill, 1975.

Kluckhorn, C. The study of values. In D. N. Barrett (Ed.), *Values in America.* Notre Dame, Ind.: University of Notre Dame Press, 1961.

Krumboltz, J. D., Mitchell, A., & Gelatt, H. G. Applications of social learning theory of career selection. *Focus on Guidance*, 1975, *8*, 1-16.

Krumboltz, J. D., & Sorenson, D. L. *Career decision making.* Madison, Wis.: Counseling Films, 1974.

Kuder, G. F. A rationale for evaluating interests. *Educational and Psychological Measurement*, 1963, *23*, 3-10.

Kuder, G. F. *Kuder Occupational Interest Survey: General manual.* Chicago: Science Research Associates, 1979.

Lathrop, R. *Who's hiring who.* Berkeley, Calif.: Ten Speed Press, 1977.

LaVoie, A. L. Review of the Survey of Interpersonal Values. In O. K. Buros (Ed.), *The eighth mental measurement yearbook* (Vol. 1). Highland Park, N.J.: Gryphon Press, 1978.

Lehmann, I. J. Review of the Stanford Achievement Test. In O. K. Buros (Ed.), *The eighth mental measurement yearbook* (Vol. 1). Highland Park, N.J.: Gryphon Press, 1978.

Linn, R. L. Review of the Differential Aptitude Test. In O. K. Buros (Ed.), *The eighth mental measurement yearbook* (Vol. 1). Highland Park, N.J.: Gryphon Press, 1978.

Lunneborg, P. W. Review of the Strong-Campbell Interest Inventory. In O. K. Buros (Ed.), *The eighth mental measurement yearbook* (Vol. 2). Highland Park, N.J.: Gryphon Press, 1978.

Mastie, M. M. Review of the Differential Aptitude Test. In O. K. Buros (Ed.), *The eighth mental measurement yearbook* (Vol. 1). Highland Park, N.J.: Gryphon Press, 1978.

McKee, M. G. Review of the Edwards Personal Preference Schedule. In O. K. Buros (Ed.), *The seventh mental measurement yearbook* (Vol. 1). Highland Park, N.J.: Gryphon Press, 1972.

McKinlay, B. *Validity and readability of the occupational information access system "QUEST" Questionnaire*. Eugene, Ore.: Career Information System, 1971.

McKinlay, B. *Developing a career information system*. Eugene, Ore.: Career Information System, 1974.

Merwin, J. C. Review of the Wide Range Achievement Test. In O. K. Buros (Ed.), *The seventh mental measurement yearbook* (Vol. 1). Highland Park, N.J.: Gryphon Press, 1972.

Meyers, C. E. Review of the Social and Prevocational Information Battery. In O. K. Buros (Ed.), *The eighth mental measurement yearbook* (Vol. 2). Highland Park, N.J.: Gryphon Press, 1978.

Murray, H. A. *Exploration in personality*. New York: Oxford University Press, 1938.

Osborn, R. H. *Developing new horizons for women*. New York: McGraw-Hill, 1977.

Parsons, F. *Choosing a vocation*. Boston: Houghton Mifflin, 1909.

Passow, A. H., & Schiff, J. H. Review of Stanford Achievement Test. In O. K. Buros (Ed.), *The eighth mental measurement yearbook* (Vol. 1). Highland Park, N.J.: Gryphon Press, 1978.

Payne, D. A. The concurrent and predictive validity of an objective measure of academic self-concept. *Educational and Psychological Measurement*, 1962, *22*, 773-780.

Pietrofesa, J. J., & Splete, H. *Career development: theory and research*. New York: Greene and Stratton, 1975.

Prediger, D. J. The role of assessment in career guidance. In E. L. Herr (Ed.), *Vocational guidance and human development*. Boston: Houghton Mifflin, 1974.

Prediger, D. J. Review of the New Mexico Education Test Series. In O. K. Buros (Ed.), *The eighth mental measurement yearbook* (Vol. 2). Highland Park, N.J.: Gryphon Press, 1978.

Prediger, D. J., & Johnson, R. W. *Alternatives to sex-restrictive vocational interest assessment* (Research Rep. 79). Iowa City, Iowa: American College Testing Program, 1979.

Prediger, D. J. The marriage between tests and career counseling: An intimate report. *The Vocational Quarterly*, 1980, *28*, 297-305.

Radcliffe, J. A. Review of the Study of Values. In O. K. Buros (Ed.), *The sixth mental measurement yearbook*. Highland Park, N.J.: Gryphon Press, 1965.

Ricks, J. H. Review of the Career Development Inventory. In O. K. Buros (Ed.), *The eighth mental measurement yearbook* (Vol. 2). Highland Park, N.J.: Gryphon Press, 1978.

Roe, A. *The psychology of occupations*. New York: Wiley, 1956.

Rorer, L. G. Review of the Sixteen Personality Factor Questionnaire. In O. K. Buros (Ed.), *The seventh mental measurement yearbook* (Vol. 1). Highland Park, N.J.: Gryphon Press, 1972.

Sarason, S. B., Sarason, E. K., & Cowden, P. Aging and the nature of work. In H. J. Peters & J. C. Hansen (Eds.), *Vocational guidance and career development*. New York: Macmillan, 1977.

Seligman, R. Review of the Self-Directed Search. In O. K. Buros (Ed.), *The eighth mental measurement yearbook* (Vol. 2). Highland Park, N.J.: Gryphon Press, 1978.

Siegel, L. Review of the Survey of Interpersonal Values. In O. K. Buros (Ed.), *The sixth mental measurement yearbook*. Highland Park, N.J.: Gryphon Press, 1965.

Snodgrass, G. *Career Self Assessment*. Unpublished manuscript, Southwest Texas State University, 1980.

Sorenson, G. Review of the Career Maturity Inventory. In O. K. Buros (Ed.), *The eighth mental measurement yearbook* (Vol. 2). Highland Park, N.J.: Gryphon Press, 1978.

Spranger, E. *Types of men* (5th ed.) (Vol. 3). (P.J.W. Pigors, Trans.) New York: Stechert-Hafner, 1966. (Originally published, 1928).

Stahmann, R. F. Review of the Kuder Occupational Interest Survey. In O. K. Buros (Ed.), *The seventh mental measurement yearbook* (Vol. 2). Highland Park, N.J.: Gryphon Press, 1972.

Steinhaurer, J. C. Review of the Strong-Campbell Interest Inventory. In O. K. Buros (Ed.), *The eighth mental measurement yearbook* (Vol. 2). Highland Park, N.J.: Gryphon Press, 1978.

Strong, E. K., Jr. *Vocational interests of men and women*. Stanford, Calif.: Stanford University Press, 1943.

Super, D. E. Testing and using test results in counseling. *Occupations,* 1950, *29*, 95-97.

Super, D. E. A theory of vocational development. *American Psychologist,* 1953, *8*, 185-190.

Super, D. E. *Work Values Inventory: Manual*. Boston: Houghton Mifflin, 1970.

Super, D. E. *Measuring vocational maturity for counseling and evaluation*. Washington, D.C.: National Vocational Guidance Association, 1974.

Super, D. E., & Crites, J. O. *Appraising vocational fitness by means of psychological tests* (Rev. ed.). New York: Harper & Row, 1962.

Super, D. E., Starishesky, R., Matlin, N., & Jordaan, J. P. *Career development: Self concept theory*. New York: College Entrance Examination Board, 1963.

Thomas, L. E. Life planning workshops in community colleges and four-year universities. In D. Aigaki (Chair), *Career development*. Symposium presented at the meeting of the American Psychological Association, Honolulu, September 1972.

Thompson, A. P. Client misconceptions in vocational counseling. *Personnel and Guidance Journal*, 1976, *55*, 30-33.

Thorndike, R. L. Review of the Wide Range Achievement Test. In O. K. Buros (Ed.), *The seventh mental measurement yearbook* (Vol. 1). Highland Park, N.J.: Gryphon Press, 1972.

Thorndike, R. L., & Hagen, E. *10,000 careers*. New York: Wiley, 1959.

Tiedeman, D. V. Review of the Work Values Inventory. In O. K. Buros (Ed.), *The seventh mental measurement yearbook* (Vol. 2). Highland Park, N.J.: Gryphon Press, 1972.

Tiedeman, D. V., & O'Hara, R. P. *Career development: Choice and adjustment*. New York: College Entrance Examination Board, 1963.

Tuckman, B. W. Review of Basic Occupational Literacy Test. In O. K. Buros (Ed.), *The eighth mental measurement yearbook* (Vol. 1). Highland Park, N.J.: Gryphon Press, 1978.

Tyler, L. E. Research explorations in the realm of choice. *Journal of Counseling Psychology*, 1961, *8*, 195-201.

Tyler, L. E. *The work of the counselor*. Englewood Cliffs, N.J.: Prentice-Hall, 1969.

U.S. Department of Defense. *Armed Services Vocational Aptitude Battery counselor's guide*. Ft. Sheridan, Ill.: Military Enlistment Processing Command, 1979.

U.S. Department of Labor. *General Aptitude Test Battery manual, section III*. Washington, D.C.: Government Printing Office, 1970.

U.S. Department of Labor. *Dictionary of occupational titles*. Washington, D.C.: Government Printing Office, 1977.

U.S. Department of Labor. *U.S. newsletter*. Washington, D.C.: Government Printing Office, 1978.

U.S. Department of Labor. *Occupational outlook handbook*. Washington, D.C.: Government Printing Office, 1978-1979.

U.S. Department of Labor. *Guide for occupational exploration*. Washington, D.C.: Government Printing Office, 1979. (a)

U.S. Department of Labor. *Occupational aptitude pattern structure*. Washington, D.C.: Government Printing Office, 1979. (b)

Viernstein, M. C. The extension of Holland's occupational classification to all occupations in the *Dictionary of Occupational Titles*. *Journal of Vocational Behavior*, 1972, *2*, 107-121.

Walsh, J. A. Review of the Sixteen Personality Factor Questionnaire. In O. K. Buros (Ed.), *The eighth mental measurement yearbook* (Vol. 1). Highland Park, N.J.: Gryphon Press, 1978.

Walsh, W. B. Review of the Kuder Occupational Interest Survey. In O. K. Buros (Ed.), *The seventh mental measurement yearbook* (Vol. 2). Highland Park, N.J.: Gryphon Press, 1972.

Walter, V. *Personal Career Development Profile*. Champaign, Ill.: Institute for Personality and Ability Testing, 1977.

Weiss, D. J. Review of the General Aptitude Test Battery. In O. K. Buros (Ed.), *The seventh mental measurement yearbook* (Vol. 2). Highland Park, N.J.: Gryphon Press, 1972.

Weiss, D. J. Review of the Armed Services Vocational Aptitude Battery. In O. K. Buros (Ed.), *The eighth mental measurement yearbook* (Vol. 1). Highland Park, N.J.: Gryphon Press, 1978.

Westbrook, B. W. Review of the New Mexico Education Test Series. In O. K. Buros (Ed.), *The eighth mental measurement yearbook* (Vol. 2). Highland Park, N.J.: Gryphon Press, 1978.

Westbrook, B. W., Cutts, C. C., Madison, S. S., & Arcia, M. A. The validity of the Crites model of career maturity. *Journal of Vocational Behavior*, 1980, *16*, 249-281.

Westbrook, B. W., & Mastie, M. M. Three measures of vocational maturity: A beginning to know about. *Measurement and Evaluation in Guidance*, 1973, *6*, 8-16.

Westbrook, B. W., & Parry-Hill, J. W., Jr. *The construction and validation of a measure of vocational maturity* (ERIC document 101 145). Raleigh: Center for Occupational Education, North Carolina State University, 1973.

Williamson, E. G. *How to counsel students: A manual of techniques for clinical counselors*. New York: McGraw-Hill, 1939.

Williamson, E. G. *Counseling adolescents*. New York: McGraw-Hill, 1949.

Willis, C. G. Review of the Harrington/O'Shea Systems for Career Decision-Making. In O. K. Buros (Ed.), *The eighth mental measurement yearbook* (Vol. 2). Highland Park, N.J.: Gryphon Press, 1978.

Womer, F. B. Review of the California Achievement Test. In O. K. Buros (Ed.), *The eighth mental measurement yearbook* (Vol. 1). Highland Park, N.J.: Gryphon Press, 1978.

Wylie, R. C. Children's estimates of school work ability. *Journal of Personality*, 1963, *31*, 203-224.

Zimbardo, P. G. *Psychology and life*. Glenview, Ill.: Scott Foresman & Co., 1979.

Zunker, V. G. *Lifestyle Orientation Survey*. Unpublished manuscript, Southwest Texas State University, 1977.

Zunker, V. G. *Career counseling: Applied concepts of life planning*. Monterey, Calif.: Brooks/Cole, 1981.

Zytowski, D. G. Review of the Career Maturity Inventory. In O. K. Buros (Ed.), *The eighth mental measurement yearbook* (Vol. 2). Highland Park, N.J.: Gryphon Press, 1978. (a)

Zytowski, D. G. Review of Wide Range Interest-Opinion Test. In O. K. Buros (Ed.), *The eighth mental measurement yearbook* (Vol. 2). Highland Park, N.J.: Gryphon Press, 1978. (b)

Name Index

Subject Index